# SPEAKING OF BEARS

# Praise for *Speaking of Bears*

"*Speaking of Bears* is a fascinating, rare, and eminently readable behind the scenes look at the complex world of bear management. It is
filled with the stories behind the stories, all told by the people who
lived them. After reading this book, even the casual bear aficionado
will understand why it often takes more than sound science to solve
human-wildlife conflict; it also takes curiosity, intelligence, perserver-
ance, and passion."

—Linda Masterson, author, *Living With Bears Handbook*,
updated 2nd edition

"*Speaking of Bears* is not only an essential history of bears in the
Sierra, but an invaluable roadmap on how to balance wildlife and
parks in the years to come."

—Phil Schiliro, Former Special Advisor and Director of Legislative Affairs
to President Barack Obama

"Rachel Mazur has made a substantial contribution to the behavioral
science research with this insightful work, but perhaps more importantly, she brings these stories to life."

—Sean O'Keefe, Fellow of the National Academy of Public Administration, Former Administrator of NASA, Secretary of the Navy, and Deputy
Assistant to President George H. W. Bush

"Until recently, black bears wanting people's food or edible garbage in
Yosemite, Sequoia, and Kings Canyon National Parks broke into cars,
ripped into tents, threatened people, and more. Mazur tells the story of
how the parks finally became close to 'bear proof' by building her
book around quotes from the people who were on the front lines of
bear management. What results is a lively, fascinating tale."

—Stephen Herrero, PhD, professor emeritus at the University of Calgary
and author of *Bear Attacks: Their Causes and Avoidance*

# SPEAKING OF BEARS

*The Bear Crisis and a Tale of Rewilding from Yosemite, Sequoia, and Other National Parks*

**Rachel Mazur**

**FALCONGUIDES**

Guilford, Connecticut
Helena, Montana

**FALCONGUIDES®**

An imprint of Rowman & Littlefield
Falcon, FalconGuides, and Outfit Your Mind are registered trademarks of
Rowman & Littlefield.

Distributed by NATIONAL BOOK NETWORK

Copyright © 2015 by Rachel Mazur

Maps by Melissa Baker © Rowman & Littlefield

British Library Cataloguing in Publication Information Available

Library of Congress Cataloging-in-Publication Data Available

ISBN 978-1-4930-0822-3 (paperback)
ISBN 978-1-4930-1498-9 (e-book)

∞ ™ The paper used in this publication meets the minimum requirements of
American National Standard for Information Sciences Permanence of Paper for
Printed Library Materials, ANSI/NISO Z39.48-1992.

For my father, who inspires me with his curiosity.

# CONTENTS

# PREFACE

It was well after seven o'clock on a summer night in 2001 when Harold Werner, a longtime wildlife ecologist at Sequoia and Kings Canyon National Parks, Michelle [Monroc], and I arrived on site, but we had our capture equipment ready. As soon as Harold got a clear view of the unsuspecting black bear through the ponderosa pine trees outside Lodgepole Campground, he loaded the Telazol-filled dart, took aim, and squeezed the trigger. Even from a long distance at dusk, Harold darted the bear, also known as K95, perfectly in the rump.

Michelle and I then had the job of following K95, not so closely that he would run, but near enough not to lose him. At the time, I worked for Harold as the parks' wildlife biologist, and Michelle worked for me as the lead bear technician. So off we went, over downed trees and boulders, and straight into the river where the bear decided to sit down, rest his head, and go into a deep, drug-induced sleep. Harold caught up quickly and held the bear's head out of the water with the barrel of his dart gun. Meanwhile, Michelle and I scrambled up the hill to the employee recreation hall for help and blankets. It was late, and the only people there were three slightly inebriated off-duty maintenance workers who agreeably stumbled after us to help. Together, we pulled the four hundred-pound bear out of the river, wrapped him in a silver space blanket covered with a wool blanket for extra warmth, and put Michelle on top to keep him from slipping into hypothermia.

Evening became night before the drug wore off enough for K95 to stand and shake off the wool blanket. He wobbled, turned, and walked directly back to the campground, only now with new ear tags, a radio collar, and the silver blanket stuck to him like a superhero's cape as he moved out of sight. Sadly, there were no real heroes in this particular tale because K95 had to be destroyed on his next capture. His habits of bluff charging employees and breaking into latched dumpsters would no longer be tolerated when they escalated into bluff-charging visitors and breaking into occupied trailers.

That was the tail end of a decades-long period when nights like this were business-as-usual for those living in the Sierra Nevada. Being immersed in that constant drama with bears, on top of being in charge of making it better—at least in Sequoia and Kings Canyon National Parks—I often wondered how the situation became so bad and what had been tried over the years to fix it. Although a small part of that history can be found in annual reports, research summaries, and published articles, the bulk of it has never been documented. I therefore sought to learn the history by asking some of the longer-term employees, but found no one knew much beyond their own experience. Frustrated by the lack of information about the past, I went back to working with my mind solidly in the present. Then in 2009, I left my park job and moved to Reno to work for the U.S. Forest Service. During a family vacation to New York, I visited Ellis Island and and saw how to use oral histories to collectively research the past. Armed with new energy and the hope the people I sought were still alive and accessible, I started to interview them and record their memories. At the end of each interview, the interviewee would direct me to others who were involved with bears, and I found that while each person knew a different piece of the history, collectively, they knew the whole story.

Pat Quinn, a former trail crew member, recalled successfully reviving a bear with CPR after it was accidentally overdosed with Sucostrin. Dave Graber, the recently retired chief scientist for the Pacific West Region of the NPS and former bear researcher, described the trials and tribulations of installing the first food-storage lockers in Yosemite. Long-term wilderness ranger George Durkee explained how he and Mead Hargis figured out how to counterbalance rather than tie-off a backcountry food hang. Barrie Gilbert, an expert in bear behavior who was once badly mauled while studying grizzlies, explained the unexpected way he first conceived the idea to build a bear-resistant food canister. Former Yosemite biologist Kate McCurdy recalled making daily morning rounds to release bears stuck in dumpsters until her neighbor had an "aha" moment and thought of the simple solution that finally bear-proofed the dumpsters. As I listened to these people talk about past mistakes, failures, and successes, I realized how much could be learned from their stories, and *Speaking of Bears* was born.

Rachel Mazur
Mountain Top, Pennsylvania

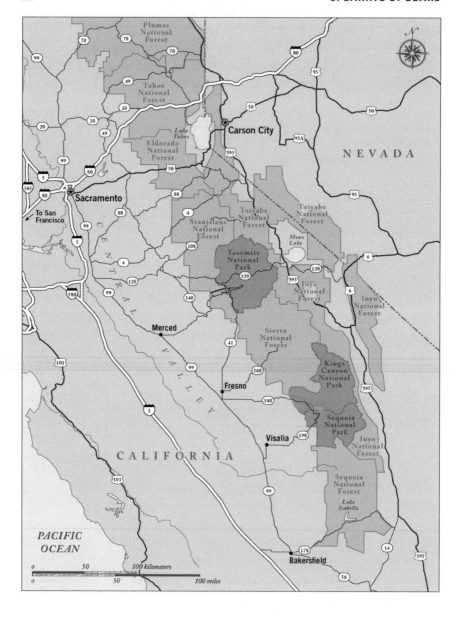

# INTRODUCTION

## ABOUT THE BOOK

*Speaking of Bears* is not your usual collection of bear stories. Rather, it is the tale, told through the voices of more than one hundred individuals, of how Yosemite, Sequoia, and Kings Canyon National Parks, all in California's Sierra Nevada, created a human-bear problem so bad there were eventually more than two thousand incidents in a single year. It is also the tale of the pivotal moments when park employees used trial-and-error, invented devices, conducted research, collaborated with other parks, and found funding to get the crisis back under control. Because of the extensive use of quotes from the people involved, the book also provides a glimpse into the inner workings of the national parks and of the employees who work tirelessly and passionately within them.

Although these Sierran parks had some of the worst bear problems in the country, hosted a lot of the research, and invented the bulk of the technological solutions, they were not the only ones. For that reason, intertwining stories from several other parks including Yellowstone, the Great Smoky Mountains, Denali, and Banff-Canada are included. National parks and other areas across the United States have struggled with, and continue to struggle with, conflicts between humans and a variety of wildlife species ranging from bears to alligators to raccoons. The same is true across the globe. There are conflicts between humans and baboons in South Africa, elephants in Indonesia, and jackals in Israel. Many of these species have a great deal in common with bears, including curiosity, persistence, cleverness, and a desire to obtain human food.

As a result, while this story is set in the Sierra and is focused on bears, its implications are far-reaching, both geographically and across a myriad of species. This book is written for bear lovers, national park buffs, historians, wildlife managers, biologists, policy makers, and anyone who wants to know the who, what, where, when, and why of what once was and could be again if we aren't careful. For anyone seeking solutions to human-wildlife conflicts throughout the world, the lessons learned are invaluable and widely applicable.

The book opens with an introduction to the parks, a history of grizzlies in California, and a primer on black bear biology and then launches into the story. For the first half of the 1900s, I relied primarily on written documents, but for the remainder of the history, I relied primarily on interviews. For that reason, the use of quotes increases throughout the book. In the end, the stories came from formal interviews with more than one hundred people and informal conversations with many others. The interviews are not exhaustive but include key people involved in the main events. Although some people did things that would be considered unethical by today's standards, most spoke openly about the past. Several have since died, and I am grateful to have met them and have the unique opportunity to share their stories.

Had someone else written this book, I may have been one of those interviewed. I worked for the NPS in various capacities from 1989 through 2008, and then moved to Reno to work for the U.S. Forest Service (USFS). From 2000 through 2008, I ran the bear management program at Sequoia and Kings Canyon National Parks and worked closely with the biologists at Yosemite. I also studied black bear ecology in the Sierran parks for my PhD dissertation at UC Davis. But I wrote this book from the perspective of an observer and not a participant, as a citizen and not an employee. Any reference I make to my own government work, with the exception of the story in the preface and a few parenthetical notes in the text, is through reference to existing reports or publications rather than personal memory. I conducted all interviews, compiled information, and wrote the book on my own time and on my personal computer.

## ABOUT THE PARKS

Yosemite, Sequoia, and Kings Canyon National Parks are all located in the Sierra Nevada mountain range in eastern California that John Muir famously called the "Range of Light." All three boast stunning geology, enormous sequoia trees, free-flowing rivers, and extensive backcountry. Yosemite is famous for Half Dome, El Capitan, and Bridalveil Falls. Visitors travel to Sequoia to see the General Sherman Tree, the largest tree in the world, and climb Mount Whitney, the highest peak in the continental United States. In Kings Canyon, a winding mountain road descends into the deepest canyon in the continental United States. These are the features that bring millions of visitors to the parks each year, though from the bears' perspective, what matters are the extensive networks of meadows, the oaks, and the conifers.

Yosemite, established as a national park in 1890, with Yosemite Valley and the Mariposa Grove added in 1906, encompasses 747,956 acres, nearly the size of the state of Rhode Island. It ranges from 2,127 to 13,114 feet in elevation. There are thirteen developed campgrounds, seven lodging options in the front country, five lodging options in the backcountry (i.e., the High Sierra camps), 1,133 total buildings, and 214 miles of paved road. The majority of the development is in Yosemite Valley, with smaller developments in Wawona and Tuolumne Meadows. Due to its high level of visitation and high population of employees, the valley has been said to resemble a small town, even providing grocery stores and a sixteen-person jail. These developments, which annually attract millions of visitors, lie mostly within the park's prime bear habitat, encompassing much of the lower elevation oak belt and several large meadows.

General Grant National Park was established in 1890 and then expanded and renamed Kings Canyon in 1940. As Kings Canyon, it now covers 461,901 acres that range from 2,100 to 14,248 feet in elevation. The park has seven developed campgrounds, two areas with lodging, 336 total buildings, and 41 miles of paved road. Only one main road enters the park: CA Highway 180. It enters from the west to provide access to a developed area called Grant Grove and then turns south toward Sequoia National Park. On the way, the road crosses into USFS land and provides access to its associated campgrounds and restaurants, and then crosses back into Sequoia National Park. There is also a branch of the road that turns northeast from Grant Grove to take visitors on a stunning drive descending through a river canyon and ending at the other developed area in Kings Canyon, called Cedar Grove. This road is only open during summer. Most of Kings Canyon is inaccessible by road.

Sequoia, also established in 1890, encompasses 404,063 acres, ranging from 1,350 to 14,497 feet in elevation. It contains 514 buildings and 77 miles of paved road. The road from Kings Canyon continues through Sequoia, allowing visitors access to the main developments in the park. They are Dorst Campground, Wuksachi Lodge, Lodgepole Campground and development, and the Giant Forest museum. These developments are much smaller in scale than those in Yosemite Valley and lie above the oak belt but are surrounded by several meadow complexes and sugar pine trees that are heavily used by bears. For most of the twentieth century, the Giant Forest was also home to a large development including cabins, a restaurant, and employee housing that was ground zero for bear issues. Although park management wanted to remove this development from the park's prime natural attraction decades earlier, it was finally removed in the late 1990s because its dilapidated plumbing could not be replaced without damaging sequoia roots. A more modest development at Wuksachi replaced it in 1998. South of the Giant Forest, the road begins a steep decline with a series of switchbacks into the oak belt, which is mostly undeveloped due to its topography until it reaches the foothills, where there are campgrounds, a visitor center, and park headquarters. Sequoia is the only one of the three parks to have extensive lower-elevation habitat. This includes a layer of marble and other metamorphics with more than two hundred known caves, although few are used by bears for winter dens. There is also a seasonally open 25-mile-long winding dirt road up to Mineral King where there are several private cabins and two small campgrounds.

Yosemite is east of San Francisco; Kings Canyon lies southeast and adjacent to the Sierra National Forest, which lies southeast and adjacent to Yosemite. Sequoia lies southeast of, and mostly adjacent to, Kings Canyon. USFS system lands surround all three parks. Yosemite receives about four million visitors a year including a lot of day-use visitors. Gateway communities include Mariposa and Oakhurst. Together, Sequoia and Kings Canyon receive approximately 1.6 million visitors a year. Kings Canyon has a few tiny gateway communities on the way to Fresno, and just outside Sequoia lies Three Rivers, an unincorporated community of just more than two thousand people on the way to Visalia. Most visitors access the parks from the west, but some come from the east, particularly those entering Yosemite over Tioga Pass. Yosemite is managed independently, but Sequoia and Kings Canyon are managed jointly. In this book, when an event applies to both Sequoia and Kings Canyon, the abbreviation Sequoia-Kings is used.

## NOTE TO READERS

The first time I quote someone, I include his or her affiliation, but after that, I use just his or her name to maintain the flow of the writing. For reference, a full list of the people I interviewed is included within the acknowledgments. Although most park employees are technically rangers, each ranger's work is increasingly specialized, therefore their specializations are included in their titles such as "protection rangers" (i.e., law enforcement and search-and-rescue) and "ranger-naturalists" (i.e., interpretation, education, and outreach). Some terminology in the book is inconsistent. There are several reasons for that, including speaking styles (colloquial versus scientific terminology), political designations ("backcountry" versus "wilderness"), and technological advances (i.e., before bear spray was specifically designed, we used pepper spray). Over time, names and terminology also change. In 1934, "wild life" became "wildlife." In 1925, Sequoia started to refer to "wild animals" instead of "game." In the 1990s, "backcountry rangers" became "wilderness rangers." In 2012, the Yosemite Association and the Yosemite Fund merged to become the Yosemite Conservancy. In 2013, the California Department of Fish and Game became the California Department of Fish and Wildlife. I therefore ask you not to get stuck on semantics and instead just enjoy the story.

## DISCLAIMER

The views and opinions of the author or any Federal employee interviewed for this book do not state or reflect those of the United States government. Any reference within the book to any specific commercial products, process, or service by trade name, trademark manufacturer, or otherwise, does not constitute or imply its endorsement, recommendation, or favoring by the United States government.

# I

# The Basics

# I

# THE DEMISE OF THE GRIZZLY BEAR
# IN CALIFORNIA

Today, only black bears occur in California, but that wasn't always the case. Less than one hundred years ago, grizzly bears also lived throughout the state. Their range once included all three of these national parks, Yosemite, Sequoia, and Kings Canyon, where they would graze in the high mountain meadows during summers and eat acorns in the foothills during fall.

James Capen "Grizzly" Adams, a mountain man famous for training grizzly bears, captured two of his grizzlies right near Yosemite. In 1854, he took "Ben Franklin" as a cub from his mother's den at the headwaters of the Merced River (now within Yosemite), and caught "Samson" the same year between the waters of the South Fork of the Tuolumne and the Merced rivers (near Yosemite). The bears eventually weighed in at roughly fifteen hundred pounds each. Grizzly Adams tamed these bears by beating them into submission and supported himself by displaying them to the public at impromptu shows and, eventually, at his own museum. Ben Franklin became so loyal, he once saved Adams from an attacking mother grizzly, although both Ben Franklin and Grizzly Adams were horribly injured. When Ben Franklin died on January 18, 1858, he was so famous the *San Francisco Evening Bulletin* memorialized the bear with his own obituary. As for Adams, he struggled along for two more years, continuing to perform while sustaining more injuries, including one that left his brain tissue exposed. In 1860, during the last weeks of his life, he moved east to join P. T. Barnum's circus and then sold his menagerie to Barnum on his deathbed.

The public's interest in seeing captive grizzlies like these did not translate into a tolerance for grizzlies or a desire to protect them in the wild. The recent history of grizzlies in California is about exploitation and cruel, relentless pursuit. When settlers arrived, they shot and poisoned grizzlies to protect their livestock. Hunters killed thousands of the bears. In many cases, grizzlies weren't killed quickly, but rather tortured to death. Grizzlies were commonly matched against bulls in fights to the death, with a win only meaning another day in the ring. When bulls weren't available, other opponents were used, even rats. In 1850, there were an estimated ten thousand grizzly bears in California. By 1925, they were gone.

What is unique about the extirpation of the grizzly in California is that it wasn't systematic, as has been true of other predators. There were never government bounties offered or a conscious effort to kill them off, but instead, it was the relentless killing of individuals that led to their demise. They were killed off so quickly that no one thought to save any evidence, and today, there are hardly even any skulls or hides in existence, and not a single complete specimen with full data and measurements remains. Although most of the calculated torture of grizzlies occurred along the coast, the killing of grizzlies occurred throughout the state, generally to prevent or end conflict. In and around the parks, grizzlies conflicted with sheepherders in the high mountain meadows, and grizzlies conflicted with stage drivers down lower, such as on the road between Wawona and the Yosemite Valley. And as was the case outside the parks, there was zero tolerance for grizzlies. Those that were encountered were killed.

The last known grizzlies from Yosemite were shot at Buck Camp in 1887 and at Crescent Lake, east of Wawona, in 1895. The last known grizzly killed from Sequoia is up for debate. It is generally credited to Jesse Agnew, who, in August 1922, shot a grizzly near his cattle ranch after having lost several calves. It was at about 7,500 feet in elevation at Horse Corral Meadow, right outside of Sequoia National Park. A tooth pried from the skull was sent to C. H. Merriam, the chief of what was then the U.S. Biological Survey, who positively identified it as a grizzly. Unfortunately, as with so many others, the full skin and skull were never sent and are now lost to science. This grizzly was likely the same bear seen the year before at the Giant Forest bear pit, where on August 7, eleven visitors reported observing a bear with a distinct muscle hump that was almost twice as big as the other bears.

There are additional, later accounts of grizzlies in and around Sequoia. In April 1924, a park employee, James Small, and his road repair crew reported several sightings of a large bear near Moro Rock within the park. In October 1924, Alfred Hengst, a local cattleman, reported coming into close contact with a huge bear near the headwaters of Cliff Creek. Since this bear was blamed for recent sheep and cattle depredations, professional hunters with dogs were hired to kill it. The hunters were unsuccessful, though a bear killed many of their dogs. In 1925 and 1926, posses of locals again tried to kill the bear, but again without success.

Then in 1926 there is a record of Jacob Rice killing a grizzly bear in Three Rivers, just south of Sequoia National Park, after it made nightly raids on his apple orchards. Wally Rice, Jacob Rice's grandson, recalls the event:

> Grandpa Rice took after four bears on the North Fork Ranch and shot one of them. There is an article in the *Visalia Times Delta* that tells about it. He didn't realize it was a grizzly bear. He had this fruit stand, and he was out there selling nice fruits and here comes a guy who wants to buy that bear pelt. So Grandpa sold it to him. A ranger came through and saw pictures and says, "Hey, that is a grizzly bear." Well, Grandpa did get the skull back and took it to Berkeley to have it identified and prove it was a grizzly. And as far as we know, that was the last grizzly killed in California. Grandpa never liked that because he was a bear guy.

While there are no museum specimens or official records for the bears Jesse Agnew killed in 1922 or Jacob Rice killed in 1926, they are likely the last two grizzlies killed in California. The last California grizzly to become a museum specimen was the Santa Ana grizzly killed in 1908 and preserved in the National Museum of Natural History (USNM 156594). There is occasional talk of restoring grizzlies to California. In June 2014, the Center for Biological Diversity submitted a petition to the U.S. Fish and Wildlife Service to expand its 1993 grizzly bear recovery plan to include the grizzlies' entire historic range—including the Sierra Nevada of California. However, the political reality is that people are afraid of grizzlies, and the ecological reality is that the habitat has been converted to agriculture and cities, including Fresno and Merced. Ironically, the grizzly remains a major symbol of California, even residing on the state flag.

Black bears, on the other hand, still range throughout the state, with the California Department of Fish and Wildlife estimating the current population to be between thirty thousand and forty thousand. The focus of this story is therefore on the history of conflict between humans and black bears, starting just before the parks were created and continuing to the present. Conflicts between humans and black bears are different than those between humans and grizzly bears. Rather than being about maulings or death, they tend to be about nuisances such as bears begging by roadsides, stealing food from picnic tables, or breaking into cars. For humans, these conflicts are sometimes amusing, but more often result in ruined vacations and thousands of dollars in property damage. Injuries to humans do occur, but more often from proximity than from aggression. For bears, the result of these conflicts is often death—a death not usually caused by the scavenged food itself, as it does provide needed calories, but from the humans who get tired of the nuisances or who fear potential injury and decide to kill the bears.

# 2

# A PRIMER ON BLACK BEAR BIOLOGY

**W**hy do conflicts between humans and black bears occur? To understand the nature and causes of the conflict, one must first understand black bear biology and behavior.

The bear family, Ursidae, originated in Europe about 20 million years ago. Presently, there are eight species of bears: the polar bear, brown bear (including the grizzly bear), American black bear, Asian black bear ("moon bear"), sun bear ("honey bear"), spectacled bear ("Andean bear"), sloth bear, and giant panda; neither koalas nor red pandas are bears. Only polar, brown, and American black bears (hereafter, black bear) occur in North America. Although the black bear's range has shrunk from its former distribution throughout forested North America and northern Mexico, they are still found in all Canadian provinces except Prince Edward Island, in forty-one U.S. states, and in limited numbers in eight states in northern Mexico. The U.S. black bear population is currently expanding its range and is now estimated at between 850,000 and 950,000 according to the International Union for the Conservation of Nature. Black bears are not at risk of extinction with the exception of one subspecies, the Louisiana black bear, *Ursus americanus luteolus*, which is listed as federally threatened under the U.S. Endangered Species Act (ESA). Sadly, most other species of bears are in steep decline due to overhunting, habitat loss, gall bladder poaching, and human-bear conflict. For polar bears, climate change is the biggest stressor, so much so that, like the Louisiana black bear, they too are listed as federally threatened under the U.S. ESA.

Black bears have a round, heavy body with large ears and a short furry tail. When they stand on all four feet, their head hangs low and they are tallest at the rump. They have plantigrade feet, meaning they are flat-footed, and they walk heel to toe like a human. With five toes on each foot, their tracks even resemble human footprints. Being plantigrade, they also stand and balance easily. A female adult is often referred to as a sow and a male adult as a boar, although those are technically agricultural terms. The young ones are called cubs. In their second year of life, the cubs are called yearlings. The female average weight is roughly 150 pounds, and the male average weight is roughly 250 pounds. Adults are mainly solitary except during breeding or when a female is caring for her cubs. Black bears have overlapping home ranges, rather than discretely defended territories, which they mark with hair rubs, bite and claw marks, deeply worn tracks, and scent.

Their fur is thick and long and may be blond, cinnamon, brown, or black. In Alaska, there are slate gray bears that are called "blue" or "glacier" bears. On small isolated islands off the western coast of British Columbia, there are white bears called "spirit" or "Kermode" bears. These bears are not albino; they have brown eyes and noses. In the eastern United States, most black bears are black. In California, only 10 percent of black bears are black. Some bears have a blaze of white fur on their chests that can change from year to year. One sow can have cubs of different colors in the same litter. Bears molt once every summer. The molt starts at the eyes and lower limbs and then continues up the limbs, down the face and flank, and ends along the spine. It is fairly easy to observe because the new guard hairs of the top coat are shorter and darker than the older, sun-bleached hairs.

In some regions of northwestern United States and western Canada, grizzlies and black bears both occur. It is sometimes difficult to tell them apart since their coloration and size can overlap, but there are some key differences. Grizzly bears have a distinct shoulder hump, a concave facial profile, and short round ears. When viewed in profile, their head is about as high as their rump. Their long front claws are slightly curved. As adults, they don't use their claws to climb like black bears, but climb limb-to-limb like humans. Adult black bears have little or no shoulder hump, a straight facial profile, and tall pointed ears. When seen in profile, their head is lower than their rump. Their front claws are shorter and strongly curved. They are expert tree climbers, even as newly emerged cubs. Male bears even have a muscle that pulls their penis up against their body when they are climbing so it doesn't scrape against the tree.

The differences between grizzly and black bears make sense when one compares their life history strategies. Grizzly bears evolved on the plains and generally live in open areas where they dig for food and rely on strength and aggression for safety, including readily defending their cubs. Black bears reside in forested areas where they forage for food and rely on retreat for safety, including protection of their cubs. These life history strategies explain why it is so much more dangerous to get between a grizzly sow and her cubs than a black bear sow and her cubs and why climbing high in a tree is only advised to escape from adult grizzlies.

Like all bears, black bears are classified in the taxonomic order Carnivora along with dogs, cats, weasels, and raccoons. A carnivore is a meat-eater and tends to have a morphology that lends itself to hunting, killing, and eating prey. Predators need speed to hunt down their prey, and many sprint quickly on their toes using long, tapered leg muscles. To kill and consume their prey, many carnivores have flesh-cutting cheek teeth and long, sharp claws. Bears eat meat, but are actually designed to be omnivores. They have sharp canines and incisors and sharp claws that allow them to cut into meat, but they also have broad molars for grinding plant food. They appear pigeon-toed, but move efficiently and quietly with a flowing gait. They can run up to 35 miles per hour for short distances, including up and down hills, and swim efficiently, but their thick muscles are for strength more than speed. They can flip rocks weighing hundreds of pounds and use their massive jaw muscles to bite through live branches and the bones of adult deer. They can manipulate objects with their paws, tongue, and prehensile lips. The only strictly carnivorous member of the bear family is the polar bear, and that is not due to their morphology, but rather their food options.

When bears do kill prey, they bite straight down on the neck or across the back of the spine. Since they avoid eating hair, bears often rip into their prey from the underside to eat the heart and liver first, and then skin the carcass before consuming the flesh. Animals killed by bears often have more broken bones than are found in animals killed by other predators. Mountain lions generally kill prey by jumping on it, biting the neck and twisting the spine and snapping it or biting the trachea. Dogs generally kill by attacking their prey's hindquarters and starting to feast before the animal is even dead.

Other traits that allow bears not only to be omnivorous, but opportunistic, include their excellent memories, their ability to reason and problem solve, and their curiosity. Their intelligence has been compared to that of a three-year-old human and is said to be greater than the average German shepherd. Bears also have excellent senses, especially their sense of smell. The area of nasal mucous membranes in a bear's head is so large that it has one hundred times more sensory receptor cells than a human's that are used to detect airborne odor particles. A bear's sense of smell is often said to be seven times greater than that of a bloodhound (although I've never been able to locate an original citation on that statistic). They use it to find food, avoid danger, locate mates, and identify cubs. Bears, like many wildlife species, also have a Jacobson's organ on the roof of the mouth that, in addition to pheromones, detects heavy moisture-borne odor particles. Bears also have good hearing and eyesight, although they are somewhat nearsighted. Their night vision is enhanced, as is true for many vertebrates, by an extra reflective layer called the tapetum lucidum on the back of the eyeball that allows light to be reflected twice.

With these traits, black bears are able to have seasonally opportunistic diets, starting when they emerge from their dens in the spring. Males begin to emerge in April, when food is scarce, followed by solo females and juveniles, and finally, sows with new spring cubs. Almost immediately upon emergence, their low body temperature increases, but it takes a few weeks for their metabolic processes, which have slowed during hibernation, to return to normal, so at first they are lethargic and continue to lose weight. In May, they eat more and begin to regain their strength and weight. They will have to regain the 15 to 30 percent of their weight that they lost the previous winter; 40 percent for sows with newborn cubs. At this time, they focus on the plant material found in mountain meadows. They stick to the tender parts, including roots, grasses, leaves, and flower buds because, like us, they can't digest the parts of the plants that are high in cellulose. In late spring, they turn their focus to insects. They knock over anthills and rip into nests and decaying logs to find ants, yellow jacket larvae, and spiders.

In early June, spring cubs start eating solid foods and yearlings disperse, freeing the sow to go into estrus and mate once again. This is a perilous time for yearling bears, especially the males, as they disperse over greater distances. Based on observations of sows aggressively chasing their yearlings off at this time, it may be that yearlings don't choose to be on their own, but are forced to leave. Sows that kept their cubs with them at all times now chase them off, tree them, and even hit them. From a human perspective, it is harsh and relentless and may give managers some indication of how persistent hazing—the use of deterrents to get a bear to stop an undesirable behavior—must be to have any effect. Once the offspring do disperse, siblings often stick together for the remainder of the summer and sometimes den together the following winter.

Until this point in early summer, adult males have focused on eating, but as their testosterone levels increase, they turn their attention to mating. They abandon food and roam widely to find fertile females, which in the Sierra are generally those four years or older that are not raising spring cubs. Upon finding females, they follow them closely, sniffing them often, impatiently waiting for them to come into estrus. Until the female is ready, she ignores the male's advances and continues to eat. At this time, it is easy to distinguish males from females when you see them together. Females are standing in the middle of meadows eating and males are standing right behind them, waiting. When the female finally ovulates, she allows him to mount her and the two may rest and play together for a few days, but then she will run him off. The female will then go back to feeding, and the male will search for other females. There is no further relationship between the two, and he will have no role in raising the cubs. A female may mate with several males and, because she releases multiple eggs, more than one male may fertilize her. After mating, any fertilized eggs begin to divide into a tiny ball of cells called a blastocyst, but then rather than implanting in the uterus, the grain-sized blastocyst floats freely for almost six months, during which time any further development is suspended. The same occurs in mustelids, including weasels, martens, and wolverines.

In midsummer, bears move away from the meadows to feed on berries. In the Sierra, this includes elderberries, bitter cherry, coffee berries, and manzanita. They eat the fruit and discard the pits, stems, and seeds. They also prey on newborn fawns, a scene that may be observed throughout the parks, even in crowded picnic areas and campgrounds. Through spring and summer, bears eat about five thousand calories per day. Since they have few predators to fear other than humans, an occasional mountain lion, or a male bear, they can spend much of their day searching for food. A bear will get up in the morning and start its search, nap in the heat of the day, and then tirelessly search its home range for food again until night.

In the fall, the focus on food intensifies, as bears now must consume up to twenty thousand calories a day and gain up to thirty pounds a week to prepare for hibernation. This fervent eating is called "hyperphagia." Even spring cubs are focused on stuffing themselves, as they are generally weaned by late August. Bears are still eating berries, but now also feed on crops of nuts and acorns that are full of fat and calories.

Finally, in late fall, the feeding frenzy slows and bears seek out dens within their home range. Pregnant females do this as early as mid-October, whereas adult males may wait until December. If there is abundant food all winter, bears may skip denning altogether, with the exception of pregnant sows because they give birth in the den. Bears generally seek out a new den every year, but may reuse their own or other bears' dens. In the Sierra, dens are often in the base of a white fir tree on a gentle slope. Dens may also be in giant sequoias, rock piles, a depression in the ground, or under a porch. The opening of a den only needs to be wide enough to accommodate a bear's head; females don't have wide hips because their cubs are born tiny. The most important features of any den are that they are not prone to flooding and that they hold the bear's body heat. The bear's heat is also protected by its fur, which is new and thick in the fall, therefore doubling its insulative value. The fur is thin on the bear's legs, nose, and underside, and it sleeps curled to minimize heat loss from these areas. If a female has cubs, she will nestle them to keep them warm and safe.

Both males and females select their dens before hibernation, but females spend more time improving them. They line the den with cones, sticks, bark, moss, and dried grass to provide insulation. If cubs are with their mother, they will help rake up the bedding, but the mother does the bulk of the work. If they aren't disturbed, bears can spend the whole winter in one den, although they may use multiple dens in one year.

Hibernation has been called "nature's response to food shortages." For many years, bears weren't considered hibernators because they didn't fit the classic description of a hibernator. True hibernators are small, such as bats, chipmunks, woodchucks, and ground squirrels, and they lower their heart rates, body temperatures, and other metabolic processes to extremes. These animals need to awaken periodically, raise their body temperature, move around, and urinate. Some must also eat and defecate.

Bears' hibernation is somewhat different. Like other hibernators, bears dramatically reduce their heart rates by diverting blood to their heart, lungs, and brain. They also cut their oxygen rates dramatically, almost in half, by reducing their breathing. But unlike other hibernators, they only drop their body temperature by about ten degrees and only reduce their metabolic processes roughly by half. As a result, bears don't eat, drink, urinate, or defecate for four or more months, yet can be aroused to respond to danger or nurse newborn cubs. In the Sierra, more than a few people have accidentally documented this rapid response.

In March 1932, in Yosemite, photographer Ralph Anderson tried to get a bear to stick its head out of a den. M. Beatty documented the result in the April 1943 issue of *Yosemite Nature Notes*:

> After setting up both still and movie cameras, every effort was made to get the bear to leave the den but to no avail. As a last resort, it was decided to try a flash bulb picture of the interior by lowering the camera down into the horizontal tunnel. In order to level out a place for the camera, Ralph Anderson cautiously reached down in the vertical opening to remove several uneven blocks of snow. As his hand neared the entrance of the den, a paw reached out with the lightning speed so characteristic of a bear, and Ralph came out with a bloody hand.

In March 2007, Marcia Rasmussen unknowingly entered an occupied bear den in Sequoia while leading a trip for the local chapter of the National Speleological Society. She wrote up the events in her caving blog:

> It took us about three hours of huffing and puffing and grunting up the mountainside to reach the top of Paradise Ridge. At 6,500 feet of elevation, the snow had grown thigh-deep. Near the top of the ridge, one of the people in my group noticed a small hole, which appeared to be a cave entrance. I decided to take a few minutes and check it out. I put on my helmet and headlamp and slithered down into the hole. The cave entrance was small. It was just big enough for me to fit my hips through, fairly easily. Once inside, I found myself in a small room, about six feet in diameter. I sat for a moment and let my eyes adjust to the low light. On the floor of the cave were two small, round nests. They appeared to be raccoon-sized, with no sign of recent habitation. I heard a tiny rustling noise, and decided it was probably a small rodent.

From this chamber, there appeared to be a small passage leading straight downward. I decided to hang my body upside down into the passage, shine my headlamp down there, and see where the passage led. As I peered around the rock, another face peered around the same rock from the opposite direction, and I found myself eye-to-eye with a very surprised bear. Awakened from a winter sleep, his bleary eyes opened wide as saucers. I let out a scream and scrambled for the entrance. My friends heard the scream and then a giggle, but had no idea that anything was amiss. They extended their arms to help me, as I climbed back out into the bright snowy daylight. Seconds later, a bear's head popped out of the same hole. He wriggled a little, and out popped the body of a yearling bear. Without pause, he charged headlong down the snowy mountainside and disappeared. I decided to name the cave "Close Encounter Cave."

Bears' hibernation is made possible by the genius of their unique metabolic pathways. First, the energy they use is derived from stored fat rather than muscle. The fat reserve also provides water so they do not dehydrate, as well as warmth and nutrition for the first few weeks after they emerge. Second, their muscle use is limited to metabolizing fat and producing milk for newborn cubs. Normally, metabolism of protein would produce nitrogen and other by-products that would be toxic to most other animals within days. In bears, these chemicals are reabsorbed and combined with glycerol from fat to form amino acids. Finally, the amino acids form more complex proteins that go full circle and replace the lost muscle and other tissues. This process also provides some heat and has earned bears the title of "ultimate recyclers."

Recycling also protects the bears' bones. Usually, inactivity leads to bone loss or osteoporosis, but bears maintain muscle, which protects bone, and reroute calcium, which creates bone. Rather than going to the bladder, calcium and other minerals are systematically retrieved back into the blood.

Despite the bears' giant fall cholesterol binge, they don't get hardening of the arteries, and despite their feast-or-famine diet, they don't get gallstones. This is probably because, in winter, bears produce bile juice, or ursodeoxycholic acid, that may help them avoid problems with gallstones. When given to people, this acid dissolves gallstones. The demand for bear bile has reached epic proportions in Asia, where there is a three-thousand-year history of using it to cure ailments ranging from diabetes to tooth decay. The demand for bear bile is so high that the black market for their gall bladders reaches all the way into California. There is also a widespread business in Asia of keeping bears captive in bile farms, which animal rights groups continue to fight. This exploitation, along with habitat loss and direct killing, has led to the dramatic decline of the Asian black bear.

Finally, during hibernation, any metabolic processes unnecessary to maintain life are shut down. By December, testosterone drops and testicles ascend into the body cavity. The stomach and intestines cease to function and remain empty, and kidney function is reduced.

At the same time, another process is just getting started. Blastocysts that have been floating freely in fertilized females finally attach to the uterine wall in early December. Embryonic growth then lasts for just two months, and newborn cubs are born in January. By giving birth so quickly, the sow avoids using all the protein that would be required for transplacental nourishment and instead relies on fatty acids to create milk. Limiting the amount of time cubs develop within the sow's body also limits their exposure to the toxic by-products of recycling within her body. So cubs are born tiny and undeveloped. They weigh less than a pound, are blind and toothless, and have just a light covering of fur. A newborn cub is often described as looking like a "pink, hairless rodent." The sow bites off the umbilical cord and licks the cubs to clean them and stimulate defecation. She then eats the afterbirth and feces and begins nursing the cubs, which she keeps warm against her belly.

Cubs don't hibernate; they spend most of their time sleeping and nursing. The mother's milk contains 20 percent fat, five times more fat than human milk, which allows cubs to develop rapidly over the next five weeks. In April or May, when the cubs finally emerge, they weigh between five and ten pounds. Before adults leave the den, they lick off calluses that formed on their footpads from inactivity, and excrete a fecal plug. The fecal plug, also called the tappen, forms in the rectum from feces, dead intestinal cells, hair, pine needles, and bedding material. Once it is expelled, the digestive system starts returning to normal. Bears keep their dens so clean that the fecal plug and shed hair are about the only mess left behind. This contrasts with their day beds, which are generally depressions in the ground surrounded by multiple fecal piles. Because hibernation means bears have a dormant season and an active season, you can age a bear by counting the cementum rings on its premolars, similar to how one would age a tree.

Black bear cubs spend only one additional winter with their mother. The sows can therefore give birth only every other year, but they do so for most of their adult lives. In contrast, grizzly bear cubs spend two winters with their mothers, so the sows give birth every third year. Cubs that survive the first few years of life can live in the wild for twenty-five years or more. In Yosemite, biologists documented that a wild bear they tagged in the park as a subadult lived at least thirty-three years before it was hunted outside the park. In Minnesota, state biologists documented a wild bear that lived thirty-nine and a half years, finally dying of old age in 2013.

## BEARS AND HUMANS

All of these physiological, physical, and behavioral traits bears depend on to prepare for and survive hibernation also allow them to easily find and exploit human food and trash. They use their strength, sharp teeth, and claws to rip open sheds, tip over full dumpsters, and tear into cars. They walk great distances from picnic area to picnic area and are even able to swim out to boats to raid food stashes. They use their paws and prehensile lips to manipulate and open latches, locks, and levers. They see well enough to peer into windows and locate grocery bags, they hear well enough to be alerted to opening bags of chips, and they smell well enough to locate a candy bar wrapper left in one jacket in a pile of gear. They have the dexterity to open one zipper of a backpack and leave the rest of the gear undisturbed. Their curiosity and excellent memories allow them to find new ways to open cars and windows and buildings and remember these techniques the following year. Once bears learn that humans and human structures are a good source of food, they quickly become conditioned to eating it, a result we refer to as food conditioned.

The unique ability of bears to find and exploit human food and their willingness to try new things is difficult for most people to imagine. In addition to obvious items like food and trash, there are thousands of documented instances of bears breaking into property for a variety of other things, including bird seed and pet food (even with Dobermans present); empty coolers or grocery bags visible through windows; unwashed dishes; strong grease odors; children's car seats that appear clean; detergents; insect repellant; various animal poisons; toiletries and ointments; gum, mints, and candy wrappers; air fresheners; and candles. These attractants all have either visual associations with food or have odors, although the odors aren't necessarily food-related and don't necessarily indicate edibility. David Karplus, the current trails supervisor in Kings Canyon who has spent decades in the backcountry, recalls:

> The day after you would use creosote [a toxic by-product of tar that the parks no longer use in this application] to preserve the wood on the bridges, the bears would come in and chew all the handrails off. There was a rumor that a bear once ate five gallons of creosote and was found dead five days later. Another time, a bear came in and ate the ammonium nitrate we were storing to make explosives for blasting trail. We didn't have bears in our camp after that.

Billy Hancock, a recently retired career-long trail crew leader in Sequoia and lifelong visitor to the Sierra, shares another example of a bear testing out a scented item:

> When I was a very young man, my family used to take our vacations at a campground called Carlon Camp on Evergreen Road, just outside Yosemite. So one time, my sister, mother, and father were in a tent, but my two brothers and I were sleeping in a trailer with our heads at the open tailgate. One of my brothers had just gotten a "butch" or "flattop" and he had put what they call "butch wax" on it to make it stand straight up. So he was sleeping on one side, I was on the other side, and my other brother was in the middle. That night, a bear came up and started licking the wax off my brother's head. Neither he nor I woke up, but the brother who was sleeping in the middle woke up and watched in fear that if he did anything, the bear would take a munch out of my brother's head. So he waited until the bear left to wake us up. When he did, we both saw the bear walking off, and then realized my one brother had slobber all over his head.

Bears also occasionally break into structures where there is no obvious attraction, but the structure looks like, or is associated with, one where a bear previously received a food reward. It is simply bad luck when a visitor with a clean red Subaru camps in the same spot where a visitor with a red Subaru containing food camped the night before, or when a visitor with a perfectly clean campsite is using the same location where a visitor spilled fish oil the night before. There are also times when bears are just curious. David Karplus recalls a beautiful moonlit night when a bear walked up to his nearby empty tent, lifted its paw, looked at Karplus, and flattened the tent for no discernable reason.

Since bears are both naturally afraid of humans and opportunistic, they generally wait until humans are out of the way to take the desired item. In some cases, bears easily locate the desired item and only disturb what is necessary to obtain it, such as using a claw to open a zipper on a pack for a forgotten energy bar wrapper. But when there is a generalized scent, a hard-to-find item, or a range of desired items, bears can cause massive destruction. When bears enter tents, cars, or buildings in their search, they may enter and exit the same way, or they may enter one way, rip the place apart, defecate, and then exit another way. When someone tells you a bear "left its calling card" in their car or cabin, they are likely referring to this type of unforgettable experience.

The more time bears spend around humans, the more they become "habituated" to human presence and increasingly mute their normal fear reaction, which would be to flee or climb a tree for safety. Habituated bears that are also food-conditioned bears can become quite bold, taking food items even when humans are present. When they do this, they don't necessarily even cause a stir; the bears can be so quiet they can move through fully occupied campgrounds without being noticed. (I have followed a 400-pound bear through a crowded campground and been amazed that almost nobody noticed the bear until I pointed it out.)

Once bears have obtained the item of interest, they won't necessarily eat it. Caitlin Lee-Roney, Yosemite wildlife biologist, once came upon a locker a bear had just broken into. She remembers that the locker was "shared by two women; one was diabetic and the other wasn't, and the locker was full of candies. The bear ate all the regular candies, but the diabetic candies were spit all over the ground." In 2004, *USA Today* reported that in Washington State, a bear got into a cooler containing both Busch and Rainier beer. While the bear only drank one can of Busch, it drank thirty-six cans of Rainier.

That pickiness seems limited in scope, however. Bears tend to be gluttons. Fortunately, most human food simply bulks bears up, but bears do occasionally consume toxic items such as the creosote mentioned above, gas and oil, cleaning products, and a variety of other chemicals people throw in the trash. In recent years, illegal marijuana gardens have become an increasingly common problem in the parks. The gardens and their open trash pits attract bears, and bears that come in to feed also end up ingesting leftover fertilizers and herbicides. Bears have died after getting stuck in dumpsters and then squished in dump trucks. They have starved after getting their heads stuck in containers. Bears also risk intestinal blockage from consuming plastics. During his research on Yosemite bears in the 1970s, Dave Graber recorded two instances of bears dying from eating freeze-dried food that likely ruptured in their stomachs. Collateral damage includes broken teeth, tooth abscesses, and shredded claws.

Generally though, the most visible effect of bears consuming human food is that they become very, very large. Considering the frenetic way bears eat to prepare for hibernation, one can understand why they don't simply fill up on human food, but instead, gorge themselves to the point where they more than double their weight. Wild female and male black bears generally weigh about 150 and 250 pounds, respectively, but food-conditioned bears weigh much more. The heaviest black bear ever found in California was a male that ate garbage and was trapped in Yosemite's Camp Curry in 1966. It weighed in at 692 pounds. Even larger black bears have been recorded in other places. In 1976, Joseph Allen legally shot a male black bear weighing 902 pounds in New Brunswick, Canada.

The problem comes to a head in parks where bears want our food and are good at getting it, while vacationing humans tend to be distracted and don't always store their food properly. At the same time, black bears are extremely skilled at finding ways to obtain our food without coming too close to us. As a result, low levels of conflict between humans and black bears tend to feel more like a nuisance than a safety risk. Steve Herrero, noted expert on bear attacks and Professor Emeritus at the University of Calgary, explains: "The basic bear survival strategy is to use creative solutions to obtain the basic necessities of life while not pushing the envelope too hard by not dominating the scene with aggression."

Since most park visitors enjoy seeing bears, accept some property damage, have little fear of injury, and don't want bears killed, low-to-moderate levels of conflict are considered an amusing nuisance that is widely tolerated. But over time, as bears become increasingly conditioned to human food and habituated to human presence—while females are also producing cubs every second year—that conflict escalates until it is no longer tolerated and people demand that something be done. This is especially true in the Sierran parks, where summers are hot and dry and both bears and humans are plentiful.

And with that background, I begin our story.

# II

# Creating the Problem

# 3

# ENTER THE VISITORS

Long before the national parks were established and became major tourist attractions, Paiute, Miwok, Monache (Western Mono), Yokuts, and other groups of Native Americans either lived in or traveled through the areas for at least six thousand years. Then, around 1800, disease, including smallpox, tragically decimated their populations. Although they hadn't yet had contact with Euro-Americans in these areas, they likely got infected by coastal peoples who had been infected by the Euro-Americans. It may have happened during trade or after coastal groups escaped to the foothills and mountains to avoid exploitation. Then, when the Euro-Americans did arrive to these areas in the mid-1800s, they attacked or forcefully relocated much of the native populations that remained, although a small number of native people did stay in Yosemite Valley.

The relationships the native groups had with black bears is unknown. There is evidence that while one group used bear hides for warmth, another had strict taboos against eating bear, apparently because the bear's footprint is so similar to that of a human. Since bears and humans relied upon many of the same seasonal foods, it is reasonable to assume bears sometimes raided human food caches, but, whether such conflict was tolerated is unknown. What is known is that when settlers arrived, they described the black bears as uncommon and wild, so any bears that had learned to raid human food caches or had become habituated to human presence must have either already been killed by Native Americans or by the earliest Euro-American settlers.

Therefore, although Native American presence had some important impacts on wildlife—such as through the use of fire to alter native vegetation and therefore natural foods—Native Americans did not likely contribute to the habituation or food-conditioning of the bears in any long-term way. For this reason, I begin the story at the time of the establishment of the parks.

In 1864, the U.S. government granted both Yosemite Valley and the Mariposa Grove of sequoias to California. They were established as a state park that quickly became a major tourist destination. In fact, visitation had already started in 1854, and the first development to serve guests had already been built across from Yosemite Falls in 1857. In 1893, the Sentinel Hotel was built. At the time, both visitation and development were localized at the upper east end of the valley (as they continue to be in present times) and limited to the summer months. To deal with the waste that immediately began accumulating from early visitors and employees, each development started its own dump. At the time, trash was mostly organic; the abundance of plastic came later. So it was appealing, and mostly edible, to wildlife. According to Jim Snyder, retired Yosemite trail crew foreman and historian:

> That is where the bears got into the dump business, from behind the hotels. The bears seemed to get what they wanted from the dumps and stick to them.

The problem was that the bears, although relatively timid and few in number, quickly became conditioned to associate human developments with food. In late summer and fall, after visitation subsided and the dumps were no longer used, they would head to the upper east end to forage at residences. The resulting conflicts could be intense. John Muir, the famous advocate for preserving wilderness and brilliant observer of natural history, wrote jokingly of the bears in 1898:

> He breaks into cabins to look after sugar, dried apples, bacon, etc. Occasionally he eats the mountaineer's bed; but when he has had a full meal of more tempting dainties he usually leaves it undisturbed, though he has been known to drag it up through a hole in the roof, carry it to the foot of a tree, and lie down on it to enjoy a siesta.

Residents, accustomed to hunting bears for sport and meat, responded with shotguns, in effect keeping the conflicts in check.

In 1890, the government established Yosemite National Park (Yosemite) with lands around the state park. In 1906, the state ceded Yosemite Valley and Mariposa Grove back to the federal government that added them to Yosemite National Park. That same year, Yosemite lost five hundred square miles of good habitat along the west and southwest part of the park, probably as a political concession. Also in 1890, the government established Sequoia and General Grant (later expanded and renamed Kings Canyon) National Parks. Once the parks were created, the leadership immediately began to develop them and make them accessible. Since the enabling legislation of the parks specified that the only way the parks could collect income was through the issuance of permits to concessionaires, the parks had a vested interest in ensuring the concessionaires were successful and therefore in enabling visitors to access the concessionaires' developments.

To start, the government built new roads and expanded the railroad service. By 1907, visitors could readily access Yosemite year-round. Camp Curry, which started with a handful of tents on the Valley floor below Glacier Point in 1899, was immediately popular and began to expand. The Yosemite Lodge was built in 1915. At Sequoia and Kings Canyon, tents were available for rent starting in 1899 and the first lodge was built in 1915. Meanwhile, camping became popular. The USFS started developed campgrounds, and the national parks soon adopted them. They provided designated parking, picnic tables, fire pits, and bathrooms. Before designated campgrounds, people camped wherever they wanted.

As development and accessibility increased, visitation and the accumulation of trash increased. Modern garbage trucks didn't yet exist, let alone plastic garbage bags, making trash too cumbersome and expensive to haul out. Instead, employees and residents brought it to local dumps. At first, the concessionaires took care of their own trash and campers took care of theirs, but the campgrounds became increasingly filthy and increasing numbers of bears gathered around the increasingly odorous hotel dumps, so by 1915, the parks took on the collection of all garbage. At centralized dumps, workers burned the trash and then buried the remains.

Over the years, park visitors became more and more intrigued by the bears and started making evening pilgrimages to the dumps to see them.

There, visitors endured the stench of burning trash in the hopes of catching a glimpse of a bear in their lights before it ran off into the woods. The delight of these visitors during the summer contrasted with the irritation of locals in the fall, after dumps closed and bears started creating havoc at residences. Acting Yosemite Superintendent Major H. Benson's sentiment in 1906 that the valley was a "death trap" for wildlife continued to be true up until about 1916. Everyone living there had a gun or a trap and pursued bears relentlessly. For the most part, management approved of that strategy. In 1911, Sequoia Superintendent James Hughes said, "So far as I know, the bear is neither useful nor ornamental, and I recommend that he be terminated." That isn't to say, however, that anyone could kill a bear at any time. In 1909, a soldier who killed a bear at Clough Cave in Sequoia was tried for the crime.

The practice of centralizing dumps that happened in Yosemite, Sequoia, and Kings Canyon also happened in parks throughout the country and beyond with similar results. During the first decades of the national parks' existence, the U.S. Cavalry oversaw operations. They would march to Yosemite every spring from the Presidio in San Francisco to patrol boundaries, catch poachers, put out fires, and keep out domestic sheep. Then in 1914, civilian rangers replaced the cavalry, and on August 25, 1916, President Woodrow Wilson established the National Park Service (NPS) with the mission to "preserve unimpaired the natural and cultural resources and values of the National Park System for the enjoyment, education, and inspiration of this and future generations." Although World War I, a huge influenza epidemic, and the "red scare" delayed the park service era from taking off, Stephen Mather, the first director of the NPS from 1916 to 1929, anxiously wanted to increase visitation. For one, he needed to acquire funding to run the parks. During the first years of the NPS's existence, base funding did not exist. To obtain it, the parks needed visitation, and to increase visitation, Mather decided the parks needed to increase their appeal to the public.

The NPS didn't get a national base of support until 1933, when President Franklin D. Roosevelt consolidated all national parks, national monuments, national military parks, national cemeteries, national memorials, and national Capitol parks into the National Park System, with the National Park Service tasked with its oversight. The combination of places with historic significance such as the Washington Monument, the Statue of Liberty, Gettysburg, and Antietam with places of natural significance such as Yellowstone and Yosemite tremendously broadened the base of support for the NPS.

In the meantime, Mather led the charge to improve roads, facilities, and campgrounds. Sequoia National Park started building the Generals Highway in 1920, and the all-year road (Highway 140) between Yosemite and Merced was completed in 1926. Yosemite Village appeared in the 1920s and is, according to retired Sequoia-Kings naturalist and historian Bill Tweed, likely the first of the strip malls. When World War I ended and the social prosperity of the 1920s arrived, these developments allowed visitation to skyrocket. By the late 1920s, Sequoia averaged well over a hundred thousand visitors per year and Yosemite approached a half a million visitors per year.

But that wasn't enough. Mather believed the parks needed to further increase visitation and that they should do it by providing the public with a variety of attractions. In 1918, a makeshift zoo—more like a collection of cages of orphaned animals—was established in Yosemite Valley with three mountain lion cubs and, later, a bear cub. Other parks also kept zoos to entertain visitors. In 1924, Yellowstone started a zoo. Before that, there were two makeshift zoos in Yellowstone run by the concessionaires.

In 1921, Yosemite introduced Tule elk, a species not native to the Sierra Nevada, into Cook's Meadow. The twenty-eight-acre paddock originally held twelve animals, but management increased the numbers at about 25 percent annually. The state stocked non-native salmonids throughout the lakes, rivers, and streams in all three parks. Yosemite also hosted the Indian Field days, an annual rodeo with native crafts and dances, which ran from 1916 to 1968. The famous Yosemite Firefall, a tradition that ran off and on from 1872 to 1968, featured the nightly exhibition of a simulated glowing waterfall created by shoving embers off Glacier Point to the valley below. The show famously started at nine at night when the emcee shouted, "Hello, Glacier Point!" The fire tender responded with, "Hello, Camp Curry!" The MC yelled, "Let the fire fall!" And then he shoved the embers off the cliff, to the delight of the hundreds gathered below. Throughout this period though, the development of the bear-feeding shows trumped every other attraction in popularity.

# 4

# BUYING OFF THE BEARS

The bear-feeding shows, although developed and promoted as an attraction, arguably came about as a desperate attempt to lure bears out of developed areas and get control of the increasing problem of human-bear conflict. Looking back, it is easy to see why the conflict increased. First, many more people visited the parks and created many more tons of food waste that attracted the bears. Second, in the more developed places like Yosemite Valley, the parks banned visitors from bringing in dogs, so bears that came in to feed on the food waste became habituated faster. Third, after the establishment of the NPS, it became illegal for park residents to kill bears. Fourth, the more bears came around, the more people loved to gather and watch them, regardless of the nuisance bears caused. By the early 1920s, bears were becoming so accustomed to eating at dumps and so habituated to human presence that they no longer ran from visitors, but remained to feed even in the middle of the day, sometimes right from visitors' hands.

At that point, conflict with humans was continual, widespread, and involved hundreds of bears. It had reached a point where even targeted killings and rangers' attempts to chase bears off with dogs and shotguns full of rock salt couldn't solve the problem. Even the construction of incinerators had little effect, since the parks could only burn a fraction of the trash and were effectively just creating another place for bears to congregate. The original hope that allowing bears to feed at the dumps would reduce or eliminate conflicts elsewhere had completely backfired. The parks were at a complete loss of what to do except to continue and even expand the feeding by converting dumps into feeding areas with formal shows. Naturalist and historian Bill Tweed calls the approach "buying off the bears." Sequoia and Yosemite both did it, but approached it in different ways.

In Sequoia, the first bear-feeding area, or "bear pit," began as a garbage dump located in an easily accessible area called Sunset Rock, at the western edge of the Giant Forest sequoia grove. Bill DeCarteret, born and raised in Three Rivers and a lifetime packer in Sequoia-Kings, remembers:

> When we were just little kids, the rangers would tell you to be sure to go around five o'clock to Sunset Rock so you can watch the bears. At Sunset Rock, there was an enormous—well, it looked enormous to me—a big area where they consistently dumped garbage. As I remember, you'd see ten or fifteen bears at a time and they would be fighting over garbage and it was kind of fun to watch because they were active and they didn't seem to bother anybody because that was their main interest: the garbage dump.

The NPS then moved the dump to the more famous location at Bear Hill, right in the heart of the Giant Forest. There the event evolved from an informal gathering of onlookers to a nightly spectacle, with the park even erecting bleachers so several hundred visitors could watch the nightly feeding of more than thirty bears. Leroy Maloy, another local and lifetime packer, as well as a retired NPS employee, describes the area:

> Bear Hill was located just up above the coffee shop. The rangers would drive right up in these little garbage trucks and the place would be completely full of bears and they would throw the garbage down and the bears would gobble it up. They had a grandstand where people could sit and watch the bears eat. There was a little bitty fence you could step over. It wasn't really a fence at all, just a barrier. And there would be bears, lots of bears. The bears would never bother the drivers because they knew they were being fed. I can remember one bear, they called him Scarface, and he was one of the biggest bears. He was a fighter and would be the first one to get food. We would go up there and look for Scarface.

Many retired law-enforcement rangers from Sequoia-Kings remember Bear Hill as a harmless place. In reality, there were a lot of injuries during those years, but it was before society became litigious and focused on safety, so for many people possible injuries were an acceptable risk.

In Yosemite, concentrated bear feeding also started with people gathering at garbage pits, but these pits weren't as conveniently located as they were in Sequoia. Yosemite purposely developed the pits at the lower west end of the valley in the hopes of luring bears away from the developments at the upper east end. Visitors accessed the pits by driving down rough narrow roads to watch the bears amidst the stench of burning garbage. Jack Phinney, recently deceased longtime Yosemite volunteer, recalled:

> We camped in Yosemite every year for about a month and there was on old pit that was excavated for gravel for road construction in the valley. It was then a dump and you could go there any time of the day because the concessionaire dumped his trash; there was always a smoldering fire, and you were guaranteed of seeing a bear or two there. Usually bears would be driven away by bigger dominant bears and so on, and they got pretty big. You wouldn't see bears anywhere else except sometimes you would see cars stopped and there would be a mother bear and one or two cubs. People would get closer and closer until a circle of people would surround the cub with the mother on the outside and she would head for her cubs and knock people down. The bears would go up to the cars and people would be passing out food to the bears and the bears would end up on the car with its nose on the window. At that time, there were no limitations on where you could drive. You could drive right through the forest.

The likely reason Yosemite Valley had more roadside bears than Sequoia-Kings was because Yosemite developed their feeding areas in the lower west end where the valley is narrow and the dumps were, by necessity, near the road.

As in Sequoia, the dumps in Yosemite evolved into formalized bear pits, but in Yosemite, it was the concessionaire, the Yosemite National Park Company (which merged with the Curry Company in 1925 to form the Yosemite Park and Curry Company), which transformed Yosemite's bear pits into a formal affair, and they did it for profit. This wasn't the first time a Yosemite tradition was transformed into a profit-making event. In the early 1900s, the Curry Company reinstated the Firefall, the popular tradition of dropping embers off Glacier Point at night, which had temporarily ended in 1897, to entertain their guests. The transformation of the bear pits, however, had a much more blatant profit motive. In 1923, the Yosemite National Park Company built a feeding platform near the river bend about a mile below Yosemite Lodge on the north side of the river and erected a couple of electric flood lights. They baited bears until they came in on cue every night, at which point they transported up to two thousand visitors for fifty cents to a spot on the opposite side of the river. Once the visitors arrived, they turned on the floodlights so visitors could watch bears for about twenty minutes. If the visitors didn't see a bear, the concessionaire refunded their money. The concessionaire timed the show so the shuttles could leave Camp Curry for the bear pits right after the visitors were awed by the Firefall.

In May 1924, to increase the number of bears at their pits, the Yosemite National Park Company got permission to spread oil from its buses over the government garbage pits, so bears would go to the new feeding platforms instead. It was supposed to happen for only a few days, but they continued spreading oil for three or four weeks until the NPS received complaints from the public and stopped it. After that, the concessionaire started the shows later in the summer when bears were easier to attract. There were a few years in the late 1920s when the park opened the upper end pits since they were close to the incinerator, but due to the unending conflict, the park shut them down in September and diverted all trash to the lower end, in effect luring even more bears to the concessionaire's shows. By 1929, feedings were accompanied by a formal lecture by a NPS ranger-naturalist.

Sequoia and Yosemite were not alone in creating bear-feeding areas. Many parks had bear pits, including Crater Lake, Rainier, and Rocky Mountain. Some, like Yellowstone, even fed grizzlies. Often the rangers themselves fed the bears while visitors sat in the bleachers and watched. Future president Gerald Ford worked as a seasonal park ranger in Yellowstone, where he worked as an armed guard on a bear-feeding truck. Also in Yellowstone, there are photos of Horace Albright, the second director of the NPS, feeding bears during his time as that park's superintendent, and there is a record of President Warren Harding feeding two bears that were treed by rangers.

While the NPS worked to dramatically increase visitation, the bear-feeding program, albeit unintentionally, drastically increased the number of bears concentrated in developed areas. At times, at least thirty bears fed at one time at Bear Hill and twenty-two bears fed at one time at the Yosemite pits. Further, with easy access to increased nutrition, sows had record numbers of multiple births. In 1939, sows in Yosemite had five sets of triplets and one set of quadruplets, while sows in Sequoia had two sets of quadruplets. With so many bears in one area, interactions among them were common. One such encounter reported in Sequoia in 1939 by Ranger Augustine describes two rangers and four visitors witnessing an adult male bear kill a member of a set of quintuplets and then carry the dead cub from Bear Hill to a tree where he devoured it in front of them.

The goal of "buying off the bears" had been an utter failure. Through the 1920s and 1930s, the problems went from bad to worse. Finally, in 1939, a National Park Service report titled, "Wildlife Conditions in National Parks," stated:

> The bear shows had grown to be major attractions and the service found itself unable to abruptly discontinue them without tremendous public protest. Soon bears began to invade campgrounds, break into automobiles, and some bears that were unable to stand the competition around garbage pits became the pitiful "holdup" bears begging along the roadsides. Here and there, an individual becomes surly and dangerous, making control measures necessary.

Black bears weren't dangerous in the sense of aggressively attacking humans, but they were dangerous in the sense of being large, strong animals with sharp claws that were in close proximity to humans and wanted what the humans had. Although to date no one has been killed in the Sierran parks by a black bear, during these early years injuries to visitors were common. In the 1930s, there were dozens of injuries each year at each park. In 1937, sixty-seven people went to the hospital from injuries sustained at bear shows in Yosemite. Most of these injuries resulted directly from visitors getting too close to bears.

A 1937 report from Yosemite perceptively summarized the situation:

> A number of park visitors are clawed, cuffed, or bitten by black bears every few days during the tourist season. Resulting injuries are usually relatively minor ones; scratched hands or faces, nips on the legs or arms, and similar hurts that clear up in about a month. Although these bears could easily maim and kill, there has been no fatality among the tourists—so far. The shock, however, is sometimes more than the injury would seem to warrant, for to be attacked by a large black bear, no

matter how slight the actual damage, is a terrifying experience. If a bear wants a bone that another bear has, he secures it by slapping and biting. Naturally, when a person tantalizes him by holding a chocolate bar just out of reach to snap his picture, the bear tries to grab the candy by the same method. He may even knock a little black camera to the ground because it is disappointingly not edible. A quick motion made by a person or another bear sometimes startles the bear into an almost instinctive attack. Being presented ham sandwiches by one group of people, the bear moves expectantly to the next group. When no food is offered and an attempt is made to shoo him away, the bear may nip and claw to explain what he wants. This may indicate that reports of unprovoked attacks are really very much the opposite from the viewpoint of the bear.

As problems escalated through the 1920s and 1930s, the parks tried a variety of methods to alleviate them while keeping the bear shows open. One method was to keep humans from feeding bears directly. At first, in 1927, the parks just asked visitors not to feed bears from their hands. Then, the parks asked visitors not to feed bears outside of feeding areas. On February 6, 1930, Sequoia Superintendent John White sent a memo to all employees stating:

Obey personally and enforce rigidly at all times the instructions against feeding bears. The only place for bears to receive food from human beings is at the incinerator, and the only person to give them food there is the bear tender.... Be particularly careful this spring, after the bears are out, especially if any appear at Hospital Rock [Picnic Area], to see that they are not fed by picnickers. Also, please place signs freely at places chiefly frequented by bears reading, "It is dangerous and it is prohibited to feed the bears. John R. White, Superintendent."

Although it would have been helpful for the NPS as a whole to ban the feeding of bears, NPS Director Albright, who succeeded Mather in 1929, retained his policies and kept development proceeding. Even during the Great Depression, he did not want to frighten the public or take away any attractions. Instead, the NPS was only willing to discourage feeding, and issued press releases about the potential dangers of feeding bears. For example, on July 31, 1931, a press release stated, "All National Park bears are wild animals. Persons feeding bears do so at their own risk.

Teasing, molesting, or touching bears is prohibited by park regulations."
In fact, the NPS as a whole didn't make the feeding of wildlife illegal
until 1983 when it was added to the Code of Federal Regulations.

Another method to alleviate problems was to try to keep bears from
approaching humans or developed areas. At first, rangers tried hazing. In
Yosemite, there are records of rangers using birdshot on bears in 1910
and, later, "dogging" and "stinging" bears with shotguns in 1917. In
Sequoia, there are records of personnel using rock salt on bears in 1929
and using birdshot on bears in 1931. In 1937, there was research done in
Yosemite on whether electric fences could control bears. Two fences,
each enclosing an area of about twenty-four square feet, were constructed
for the experiment in the lower western end of the valley. In 1939, Lowell
Sumner noted that success was limited, largely due to the extreme dry-
ness of the Sierra that leads the soil to become an insulator rather than a
conductor for electricity.

Rangers also used dogs to run bears out of developed areas. In 1929, a
famous movie star even got involved. According to the Yosemite Superintendent's Report from that year, Rinson, son of canine movie star Rin-
Tin-Tin, came to the park to chase bears. Apparently, Rinson impressed
even the superintendent, who noted that Rimson was "as cool under fire
as Rin-Tin-Tin is in front of the movie cameras, and twice as effective as
his dad when the bears form the supporting cast." Still, the dogs, even
Rimson, were no match for the endless supply of food.

When hazing didn't get bears to move out of an area, the parks tried
moving the bears themselves. Relocation within the parks began in a
meaningful way in 1929 when a ranger in Yosemite named Bill Reymann
developed and started using a portable bear trap. With it, rangers could
catch bears, daub them with paint, and release them at the lower end of
the park. When they used the trap continually, it began to alleviate some
of the problem, but the relief was temporary since the bears quickly
returned. The Yosemite Superintendent's Monthly Report for October
1929, said:

> A new patrol wagon for bears is the latest innovation in Yosemite. A
> large piece of corrugated pipe sealed at one end and equipped with a
> trap door at the other end has been mounted on two low auto wheels
> and attached to one of the Ford trucks; when the alarm is sounded this
> device can be quickly transported to anywhere the bears are reported

as "disturbing the peace." Up to October 26th, fourteen bears have been caught and given "free rides."

According to historian Jim Snyder, serendipity had a major role in this invention:

> It is very likely to have come about because of the ongoing construction of the new Wawona Road where culverts were being set that summer. Somebody put two and two together and got a piece of cut-off culvert down to the blacksmith and machine shop in the valley where the new model was fabricated. Before that construction, I'm not sure anyone had a good idea about how to build a container to trap and transport a bear. The culvert provided a great shortcut.

Throughout this period, some people wanted to get rid of the bears altogether. Not surprisingly, the parks gave some bears away in another attempt to alleviate the problem. The parks sent lots of bears to zoos. Yosemite also transferred several bears to Southern California, out of the black bears' historic range. Between 1933 and 1938, twenty-eight bears were relocated to the San Bernardino Mountains and deposited at the Crystal Pines Park of the Angeles National Forest and in 1938, six bears were moved to the Santa Barbara National Forest. The California Department of Fish and Game (now California Department of Fish and Wildlife) requested these bears in order to promote hunting tourism where grizzlies once roamed. It was a successful transfer, and black bears established a small population there. In 2009, wildlife genetics researcher Sarah Brown and others published a paper in which they examined the DNA of the current southern California black bear population and found that, even today, the descendants of these bears are more closely related to the bears in Yosemite than to any other black bears in California.

Meanwhile, back in the parks, bears continued to eat upwards of sixty tons of food scraps each year, and the problem escalated. So the parks killed bears. Starting in the 1920s, a park superintendent would ask the NPS director for permission to kill bears in groups of ten. When permission was granted, action was taken. In the 1930s, more than one hundred bears were killed in the Sierran national parks. The exact number isn't known, but there were years such as 1939 when Yosemite alone killed at least twenty-five bears. This early solution of killing bears may seem at odds with the NPS mandate to "conserve the scenery and the natural and historic objects and the wildlife therein," but in those days, animals were classified as "good" or "bad." Historian Jim Snyder reminds us:

> When the park service took over, it eliminated the "trouble" animals. We always read the thing in the Organic Act [NPS enabling legislation] about preservation versus use and future generations and all that stuff, but no one ever reads section three, which says that the Secretary of the Interior will have the authority to eliminate problem animals. And it wasn't just predators. We tried to eliminate gooseberries, and we tried to eliminate mosquitoes.

Starting in 1919, the NPS authorized rangers to kill predatory animals and retain their skins until further directed. This authorization wasn't aimed at bears, but at wolverines, fishers, mountain lions, and coyotes. The elimination of predators and other "inconvenient" animals like rattle-snakes and porcupines continued into the 1930s.

Concurrently, the NPS actively introduced "good" wildlife species. In addition to the well-known trout introduction programs of the 1890s, Sequoia introduced Japanese pheasants and wild turkeys between 1906 and 1909 to make the parks more appealing to visitors. Although bears were not part of the early predator-control programs, killing them for nuisance control easily fit this early paradigm. That doesn't mean everyone bought into it. In 1916, biologists Joseph Grinnell and Tracey Storer published an article titled, "Animal life as an asset of National Parks" in the journal *Science*. It held that native predators were no less worthy of protection than other animals.

In retrospect, the futility of these early efforts to eliminate the human-bear problem is obvious, given that literally tons of food was still available to bears. Efforts to "buy off the bears" and keep them out of public areas were simply, as historian Bill Tweed says, "moving bears up and down the food chain" and making the problem worse by creating dozens of food-conditioned and habituated bears as well as increasing their reproductive rates. It is also, in retrospect, difficult to imagine just how bad the problem became, with dozens of bears entering public areas, tearing open cars, and raiding tents. By the end of the 1930s, even the concessionaire was afraid the bear problem was driving tourists away rather than luring them in. It was time to close the shows.

# 5

# FROM BEAR PITS TO TRASH CANS

The impetus for closing the shows started in the late 1920s and gained momentum in the 1930s, when the political and cultural climate started to change from one in which bear shows were fiercely protected to one in which their utility and appropriateness were questioned and even scrutinized. Parks began to emphasize protecting nature in its natural state and weaning the public from many of the artificial attractions. In 1927, Colonel John White, the Sequoia superintendent, ordered an end to the killing of predatory animals. In 1932, the Yosemite Zoo was abolished, and in 1933, the Tule elk herd that was kept in Yosemite was relocated to Owens Valley.

During this period, the parks made their first serious attempt to use science to inform wildlife policy, with most of the effort coming from a few enthusiastic individuals. In 1928, Yosemite Assistant Park Naturalist George Wright offered to personally fund a survey of national park wildlife, which began in 1929. Wright enlisted naturalists Joseph Dixon and Ben Thompson to help expand the survey effort into other parks, and in 1933, *Fauna of the National Parks of the United States* was published. This report, commonly called "Fauna No. 1," said that parks should be managed based on scientific research, restored to their natural state, and then kept there. The authors defined natural as the parks' condition prior to European influence. They also explicitly mentioned bear-proofing campgrounds by providing food safes and bear-proof garbage containers to control campground depredations by bears, and putting food in bear-proof canisters. Wright also recommended patrolling developed areas and enforcing feeding regulations, limiting artificial feeding, and destroying surplus animals. With the exception of a few park employees such as Yosemite naturalist Carl Russell, who understood the problem and wanted to end the bears' access to garbage, the advice was ignored and seemingly forgotten.

That same year, 1933, the National Park Service created a Wildlife Division. This new division would have provided strong leadership on the critical issue that food storage must accompany an end to feeding bears, but in 1936, George Wright died in a car accident. Joseph Grinnell died in 1939. Without these charismatic leaders, the NPS Wildlife Division lost traction. The NPS disbanded the division in 1940, and transferred the remaining biologists into the Department of the Interior's Bureau of Biological Survey. One remaining local voice, Joseph Dixon, continued to push the idea, but he was largely ignored, and there is evidence that even he had a limited understanding of the problem. In a 1940 report, Dixon suggests that the main feeding area be closed, but a smaller one be developed in a less public location to appease park visitors. As he explains in the report, "The bear could be fed just enough to attract him and could be fed cleaner food, under more wholesome conditions."

Regardless, the call to end bear feeding continued. Biologists both within and outside the NPS warned that bear pits and feeding programs on the one hand, and relocating and destroying bears on the other, greatly altered natural bear ecology and behavior and posed a threat to visitors. But even those calls were shelved until there was a change in overall leadership.

Finally, NPS Director Albright, who opposed closing the feeding grounds, retired in 1933 and Arno Cammerer took over. In 1938, Cammerer implemented a system-wide regulation forbidding the public to feed, touch, tease, or molest bears in any manner. Concurrently, the NPS benefitted from New Deal programs implemented between 1933 and 1940 to build additional larger-capacity incinerators in the parks, therefore lessening the need for dumps. In 1940, when Newton Drury succeeded Cammerer as the next NPS director, he finalized the process by ordering that all bear shows be closed. Finally, after two decades of hosting bear shows, Sequoia-Kings closed Bear Hill, and Yosemite closed its west-end bear-feeding show.

But bears were still getting human food. In 1942, an open pit remained in use in the Cedar Grove subdistrict of Kings Canyon where people gathered, and garbage dumps remained in operation in all three parks. In other words, while the timed feeding shows ended and many feeding pits were closed, other dumps remained in operation for another 30 years. In 1943, Yosemite Superintendent Frank Kittridge tried to revive the Yosemite bear show. Naturalist Dixon reported that a secret feeding platform had been set up at the base of El Capitan. It had a concrete feeding platform about one hundred yards from the highway, and water was piped into a concrete and rock bear's bathtub. A flimsy barrier of crisscrossed logs kept humans and bears separate. The hidden show only lasted that one summer.

In the park archives, there are letters between the regional director and the Yosemite superintendent discussing preparations for closing the bear pits. In them, the regional director repeated the recommendations of Fauna No.1, pushing for bear-proof lockers and trash cans in all of Yosemite's campsites. The superintendent replied that this just wasn't feasible and did nothing to bear-proof them. Not surprisingly, when the parks diverted the trash to incinerators rather than bringing it to the feeding platforms, bears immediately looked for other easy sources of food. While the feeding pits were closed, the dumps were not, so they provided one easy source of food. The campgrounds provided the other. Unprepared, the parks needed an immediate plan to keep bears from entering the campgrounds en masse.

In 1940 and subsequent years, Yosemite's plan involved trapping all of the bears in the valley before they denned and moving them to controlled feeding stations (i.e., new bear pits) above the valley at Gin Flat to try to get them to hibernate up out of the valley. The first year, they caught and moved thirty-nine bears, and when the bears returned, they caught them and moved them again. In the end, it didn't work because no matter how often they were moved, the bears would return. Sequoia simply had no plan for keeping the bears out of the campgrounds. Although the bears primarily shifted their focus to the dumps, they also went straight into the campgrounds, hotels, inholdings, and pack stations where nothing was bear-proof, and there was no plan to make anything bear-proof, and the problem quickly became acute. There are accounts of bears suddenly appearing in developed areas en masse, entering buildings and tents, easily ripping into the soft-tops cars had at that time, and scratching up lots of people. Old-timers like Earl McKee remember bears being "all over Giant Forest." At his family's nearby pack station, they kept their trash outside so bears wouldn't come into the house, and kept a dog outside to scare off the bears. Sometimes, the rangers would come and get Earl's dad and their dog to go after some of the bears and have the dog, as McKee recalls, "tree the bear so they could extinguish it."

Similar scenes happened all over the country at parks that also rapidly closed bear shows without bear-proofing anything in preparation. The lack of preparation wasn't because anyone thought the bears would simply shift to the remaining open dumps, which the bears only partly did; it was because most parks simply didn't know what to do. With the only proposals for solutions being farfetched ideas such as fencing campgrounds and booby-trapping them with pit traps, park managers had no tangible solution. Instead, NPS Director Drury approved the shooting of all problem bears. In the 1940s, more than one hundred bears were killed in Sequoia-Kings and Yosemite combined. Old memos refer to the killing as successful management. On October 10, 1945, Sequoia Superintendent John White wrote to the regional director:

> Disposal of vicious and undesirable animals as control measures has been gratifying this season. Three habitual camp-robbing bears were killed, and one trapped and hauled away from the camping area.

This killing was fairly consistent with nonpark policies in California at the time. The state treated black bears as undesirable pests until 1948, when the state reclassified bears as game animals and they became subject to hunting restrictions.

Parks with grizzly bears had a more tenuous situation. In Yellowstone, you could once watch large numbers of grizzlies at feeding areas just like how you could watch large numbers of black bears at feeding areas in the Sierran parks. When Yellowstone closed its last bear show at Otter Creek in 1941, like the Sierran parks, regardless of the fact that dumps were still open, Yellowstone hadn't bear-proofed anything in preparation for the closure. The bears came flooding in, problems ensued, and in the 1940s, the park killed dozens of grizzlies and hundreds of black bears. Worse, in 1942, visitor Martha Hansen was mauled to death by a grizzly in the Old Faithful Campground. Two years later, Martha's family was awarded $1,895 in damages, which is the first record of a financial settlement to a family injured by a bear in a national park.

To support Director Drury's decision to end the bear shows, in 1943 wildlife biologist Olaus Murie began the first research on bears in Yellowstone. He found that while the problem of bears being conditioned to human food was widespread, human food comprised only a small percentage of their diet. He also disproved the belief that these bears needed human food; they foraged on enough natural food to survive. Murie found that punishing individual bears was ineffective, and he echoed George Wright's recommendation that campgrounds be bear-proofed with "bear safes" and bear-proof refuse containers. He also recommended that the parks study human behavior to find ways to motivate visitors to store their food properly and stop feeding bears. His findings and recommendations were spot-on but completely ignored. There would be no additional research in Yellowstone until 1959. Instead, Yellowstone focused on killing.

How did the parks get away with this killing? It was simple. The end of the bear feeding shows and subsequent killings coincided with the war years. Between 1942 and 1945, gas and tire rationing meant almost no automobile tourism. Although open, the parks had low visitation, and many facilities were closed. This would have been the ideal time to bear-proof facilities, but instead, the parks focused entirely on killing bears, which park managers kept hidden from the public eye. In 1945, Yosemite's chief ranger wrote to the superintendent:

> Although our endeavor is to kill quietly and secretly, word gets around quickly; but to date, no unfavorable comments have been heard by me.

# 6

# FROM TRASH CANS TO CARS

When World War II ended, so did gas rationing. People had newfound freedom and prosperity and were finally able to return to the national parks. The new wave of tourism in 1946 and 1947 totally overwhelmed park facilities. Even though hundreds of bears had already been killed, the new influx of food and trash, along with the lack of bear-proof facilities or trash storage, combined to form a disastrous situation. Bears roamed all over developed areas. Although they focused on open dumps, open trash cans, and unattended food; property damage, nuisance behavior, and injuries skyrocketed.

Park managers frantically tried to tackle the problem from several angles. One approach was to increase public education, teaching visitors to avoid feeding or approaching bears. But they couldn't effectively educate the public about how to keep food and trash from bears when there was no bear-proof place to put it. Vehicles certainly weren't bear-proof. It was a mess with no clear solution; at times it seemed like the only option was to laugh.

The cartoon characters Yogi Bear and Ranger Smith from Jellystone Park were instantly popular when they appeared on *The Yogi Bear Show* in 1961, probably because so many visitors could relate to their dilemma. Much later, in 1985, Yosemite gained its own comic when the late cartoonist Phil Frank created *Farley*, a syndicated comic strip about a part-time park ranger at the fictional Asphalt State Park. Farley's adventures included many interactions with the local community of bears that ran a restaurant called the Fog City Dumpster. Phil got the idea for Farley from his neighbor, who just happened to be the brother of bear researcher Dave Graber. Dave recalled:

> In the 1970s my late kid brother lived on a Sausalito houseboat adjacent to Phil's boat, and they became friends. My brother visited me in Yosemite and found everything about my bear research and the park's bear management hilarious. He recounted his twisted version of the bear stuff to Phil, and voilá.

Rangers knew garbage was a large part of the problem, but it was difficult to do much about it because the types of trucks and roads needed to collect trash and haul it out of the parks still didn't exist. In 1947, some campground problems were alleviated when rangers began collecting trash and taking it out of the campgrounds before dark, when most of the bears came in. Still, the trash was just brought to a central incinerator where it would be partially burned and then thrown in the dump, where bears continued to congregate and feed on the remaining tons of garbage. Bears even got used to the dumping schedule and learned when to come in to feed.

Looking back, it seems that people just didn't understand that the need for everything to be bear-proof really meant *everything*. In 1952, social scientist Donald Brock from the Colorado A&M School of Forestry conducted "A Survey of Public Opinion Concerning the Yellowstone Bear Feeding Problem." He found that Yellowstone visitors knew bear feeding was wrong, but they didn't know why. Or maybe they were overwhelmed by the thought of bear proofing everything, a daunting task even in later years.

In the mid-1950s, the NPS again had a chance to bear-proof facilities when Mission 66 was implemented, and again they missed it. Mission 66 was a ten-year program with the goal of dramatically expanding visitor services by 1966, the fifty-year anniversary of the NPS. Although Mission 66 provided federal funding to develop national park facilities, neither bear-proofing of facilities nor trash were included as part of the effort. It seems the parks' emphasis was still on the enjoyment part of the NPS mission rather than the preservation part. While frustrating to us today, current Sequoia-Kings Superintendent Woody Smeck points out, "It is easy to find fault with decisions made in the past." He elaborates:

A superintendent's job is to juggle and manage and triage multiple things with finite resources, and when you are in that situation, you have to set priorities and acknowledge that you can't do everything you would want. You have to set priorities in how you are going to invest your people, your money, your time, and managing people and bear interactions—I'm certain in the past it was a concern, but so was building roads, maintaining facilities, putting out wildlife fires, educating visitors, promoting tourism, working with partners and communities.

At that time, instead of bear-proofing, the parks turned their emphasis to relocating bears. In the Sierra, this led to the very beginnings of thoughtful research questions about bear management. In 1951, Harold Basey started working at Sequoia-Kings on the backcountry trail crew, becoming the Colony Mill ranger in the mid-1950s. Each week, he received one or two bears in traps from rangers who had caught them in developed areas. The rangers had started spray-painting these bears through holes in the traps in 1948 because they wanted to know if the ones they caught and relocated were coming back. At the time, they had no other way to mark them. They wanted to know if relocation worked. Harold Basey remembers releasing those bears:

> There was no immobilizing of the bears. The rangers just marked them with spray-paint through holes in the trap. To release the bears, you had to stand on the trap at the back. Every once in a while, we had a ranger who didn't know that and would lift up the front gate and the bear would knock him over. Sometimes when they were marked, it was noted that they either occurred back in the Giant Forest area within a week, or we never saw them again. That was kind of the beginning of the research job that I did that showed that translocating bears wasn't the best solution.

At some point, Basey asked to be allowed to use ether but was told no. Al Erikson, a game biologist with the Michigan Conservation Department (now the Department of Natural Resources), was pioneering ether as a way to immobilize bears for research. There is a vivid description of this early work by Peter Steinhart in a 1978 issue of *National Wildlife*:

> It was rough and tumble work. Trapped bears were anesthetized with ether while inside the culvert trap. To contain the ether, the trap was

unventilated. Erikson and his helpers could not always predict the size of the bear, and sometimes the only way to be sure the ether had taken effect was to wait until the trap began to shake, indicating the bear inside was undergoing the muscular spasms that usually precede unconsciousness. Bears trapped with foot snares, on the other hand, had to be wrestled to the ground by a gang of men wielding chains and chokers until someone could leap on the restrained animal and clap an ether cone over its muzzle. Care had to be taken lest too little ether leave the bear wide awake or too much could cause respiratory failure. More than once, Erikson and his crew had to give the bears artificial resuscitation by rhythmically applying pressure to their chests. The bears paid dearly. . . .

During this period, hazing was not a major tool, but it was used. In the 1940s, some rangers used shotguns with pellets on bears, and in 1957, the parks experimented with the rodent repellent called Cefro. In 1963 in the Enchanted Valley in Olympic National Park, there are records of a ranger, Bill Lester, attempting to condition bears to avoid the sound of the whistle by throwing rocks at them while he blew the whistle. Retired ranger Dick Martin recalls that, "It didn't work and was kind of pitiful in retrospect, but at least he tried something." Instead, bears that caused problems were killed. Leroy Maloy, whose family owned a pack station in Sequoia, remembers:

> If we used anything to haze bears, it was lead. The dogs would tree 'em, then we would call the rangers if it was a really bad bear. I mean, they wouldn't just shoot a bear if it was the first time I don't think. But if it had paint on them, they would.

The law enforcement rangers who worked in Sequoia-Kings remember doing the killing fairly quietly. One, Bruce Black, who passed away in 2011, shared his recollections:

> Do you want me to be real candid? We would trap them and we would take them down to where the cliffs are above the Kings River—you know the old CCC camp? There is an abrupt drop-off just beyond there—I am being extra candid here—then we'd shoot them and kill them and drop them off down toward the river. I could make a wild guess that two or three were killed each summer. I can't say that was

well accepted, but the rangers would not make any public display whatsoever.

The law enforcement rangers who worked in Yosemite have similar memories. One, Jack Morehead, who was later Yosemite's superintendent, recalls how, in the absence of a management program, the killing was routine:

I was a seasonal in 1955 in Yosemite. Our bear management was absolutely nothing. When you had a problem bear in the campground, you put out a bear trap and caught it and our normal routine was to try and relocate it at least two or three times into the backcountry. But if it came back, well, we killed it.

Retired naturalist and historian Bill Tweed describes this period as one with some educational efforts, but mostly of "collecting garbage while letting trash cans roll," with a steady quiet removal of bears. And it wasn't always hidden from the public. As Tweed describes:

I remember one incident in the '60s when one of the rangers took out a bear in Round Meadow in the morning, in full sight of the breakfast windows of the dining room. It got him in a little trouble, but there wasn't really an objection about the necessity of killing bears, it was about doing it with so little discretion.

In the Sierra, things got worse when there was a major drought from 1959 to 1961. Bears were so desperate to find food in those years that they ranged far into the foothill towns of Visalia, Farmersville, Exeter, Porterville, and even Orinda, located one hundred and fifty miles to the west near the San Francisco Bay. In Sequoia, more than sixty bears were killed during this period, and about thirty more were shot just west of the park in the town of Three Rivers. Bill DeCarteret, who was packing in Mineral King during the drought, remembers:

In Mineral King, the native bear feed was very scarce and the bears were walking up and down the middle of the road in broad daylight. Along toward fall it would get worse and they would even get in the corrals. What a mess. We were up half the night trying to keep these villains out. It got so bad we had to leave a bale of hay out every night and they would eat almost all of it. It was a really tough summer. It

even got worse as the year went on. They were just terrible lookin',
and you'd find a bear out in Three Rivers in January and February just
all scraggly. A lot of bears were killed.

The same desperate situation was occurring in Yosemite. On July 5,
1962, the *Star*, a local newspaper, published an article called, "Yosemite's Frustrated Bears." It said that bears were so desperate they were
chewing on wooden signs, and the park had to switch to making signs out
of metal.

The bear situation deteriorated further as the parks entered the 1960s,
but then for the first time, bear-proofing began in a meaningful way. In
1963, all thirty-two-gallon garbage cans in the Valley were fitted with
bear-proof lids. These lids, invented by Yosemite maintenance employee
Merv Cross, now deceased, opened like mailbox slots and were said to
look like Half Dome from the side. The lids swiveled on a metal pole that
was set into a concrete base upon which the whole can sat. There was also
less open trash in the towns in and around the parks because by this time
they were no longer burying it, but hauling it to nearby dumps.

Unfortunately, now that open campground trash was less accessible to
bears, they became more focused on the structures that held visitors'
food: the cars. As Bill Tweed describes:

> We locked up the garbage and started educating the public, so the
> bears started going to the cars. Bears are intelligent, flexible scaven-
> gers and they learned cars weren't much harder to break into than big
> logs. With safety glass in the car windows, I would always joke that
> there wasn't even much downside to breaking into cars.

So while the number of recorded incidents didn't increase much between 1959 and 1976, the cost of the incidents nearly quadrupled as bears
shifted from feeding out of trash cans to ripping into cars. It was also a
change that visitors found harder to tolerate. Meanwhile, most dumps
remained open, perpetuating the creation of more and more food-conditioned bears. But visitors and employees alike still didn't fully understand
the connection between cause and effect.

Steve Thompson, sales manager for Bear Saver, a company now spe-
cializing in bear-proof trash cans and food-storage lockers, remembers
being part of the problem:

Even though we were city boys, we vacationed in the Sierra since I was little. We were those bad kids who were throwing donuts and cookies at bears to see what they would do. We would do rock-paper-scissors to decide who had to go to the dumpster, because inevitably there would be a bear inside who would get ticked off after you dropped a bag of trash on its head. Then we would all run away laughing and screaming. That's how things were in the '60s and '70s.

That type of story makes one wonder: who was in charge or accountable? In those days, no one officially oversaw bear management at the park level. It was a collateral duty based on personal interest. In fact, there was almost no natural resource program in the parks; in most parks it was simply a minor subset of the ranger program. This was true in both Yosemite and in Sequoia-Kings. In Sequoia in the 1950s and 1960s, Harold Basey went from being the Colony Mill ranger to the supervisory naturalist in Lodgepole and Giant Forest and became the interested person who took on bear management as a collateral duty. He was a naturalist by day and spent his nights managing bears. He was, for many years, the park's leading expert on bears. In Yosemite, the bear lead was Neal Guse Jr., although he wasn't actively engaged with research or program improvement like Basey and at some point was reassigned to a post in Washington DC.

At a regional level, the NPS didn't provide much direction to the parks until the 1950s, when the regional office made a push toward developing modern bear programs. Out west, the region instructed the parks to install bear-proof garbage cans, provide public education, and experiment with repellants, while continuing to use destruction as a major tool. From the national level, some direction came in 1960 with the creation of a service-wide bear management plan, but there was no direction to close the dumps.

Meanwhile, Secretary of the Interior Stewart Udall knew oversight and guidance were needed and appointed five scientists to make recommendations about wildlife management in the national parks. Starker Leopold chaired the committee and the resulting report, completed in 1963, is referred to as the Leopold Report. The report recommended that the parks base their management on research, with the goal of maintaining or re-creating biotic associations that represent a "vignette of primitive America." It also said that "Fed bears become bums and dangerous," and recommended the dumps be closed. That same year, the National Acade-

my of Sciences published the Robbins Report, which also said that research was critical for sound management and clarified that the protection
of the natural condition meant allowing for natural processes.

These reports resonated with the NPS, and parks started to develop
management plans emphasizing the maintenance of nature in a natural
state, though "natural" still meant pre-European, and it would be years
before natural processes were included.

# 7

# CLOSING THE DUMPS

In the 1960s, the environmental movement brought greater awareness and interest in protecting the natural world, and the decade's social movements brought the courage and desire to make change. In 1968, the Yosemite Firefall was abolished for good, and in 1970, the eastern third of the Yosemite Valley and Mariposa Grove were closed to private automobiles. The dumps, however, stayed open, though this was no longer due to inadequate technology. By the late 1960s, all of the technology and infrastructure—dumpsters, trucks, and roads—necessary to close the incinerators and haul trash to landfills outside the parks was in place. The limiting factor was a lack of political willpower. The parks needed a final push. That push finally came in the form of two significant events in two famous and important parks in the Rocky Mountains.

First, there was a bewildering tragedy in Glacier National Park. On one night in August 1967, two grizzly bears attacked and killed two college girls, Julie Helgeson and Michele Koons, in separate and unrelated incidents at park campgrounds ten miles apart. Prior to that, no one had ever been killed by a grizzly at Glacier even though about thirty thousand backpackers visited the park each year. But in 1967, in addition to the lodges providing food scraps to the bears and women sleeping in sleeping bags outside their tents, there were lean berry crops. The story is documented in haunting detail in the book *Night of the Grizzlies* written by Jack Olsen.

In retrospect, the maulings seem clearly linked to food conditioning, a lack of availability of natural foods, and close proximity of bears and humans; but at the time, leadership searched for other answers. The public information officer at Glacier found that both women were menstruating, which brought about the hypothesis that menstrual blood brought on the attacks. At Glacier, women rangers were switched to office duty while menstruating. Female visitors were given government brochures called "Grizzly, Grizzly, Grizzly," cautioning them not to travel in grizzly country during their menstrual periods. Dave Graber, now retired chief scientist for the Pacific West Region of the NPS, remembers being reprimanded for writing a memo about the absurdity of this theory. In 1988, Lynn Rogers and others finally tested this theory by conducting experiments on black bears at a garbage dump. They offered the bears used tampons, unused tampons, tampons with nonmenstrual blood, and tampons soaked in rendered beef fat. Menstruating women were interspersed with the habituated bears. The researchers found that the bears basically ignored everything except the beef fat and published the results in 1991, finally putting the issue to rest. Since then, women are no longer advised against backcountry travel while menstruating, but are instead advised to take proper precautions, such as using unscented tampons and storing used tampons and pads properly.

The second event leading to dump closures occurred in Yellowstone National Park. It was precipitated by a falling-out between Yellowstone park management and grizzly bear researchers John and Frank Craighead. The Craigheads were independent researchers who secured their own funding to study Yellowstone's grizzlies from 1959 to 1971. The Craigheads pioneered the use of many kinds of technology during their study that are now central to bear research. As Lance Craighead, the son of the late Frank Craighead explains:

> [John and Frank] were twins that worked together most of their lives. My dad was the older one, but no one really knows who was oldest because when they were babies and had little bracelets on their wrists with their names on them, one of the nurses took the bracelets off to give them a bath and then couldn't figure out which one to put which bracelet back on. They were the first to use radio-collars on bears or any other large animals. A ham radio operator named Hoke Franciscus and an electrical engineer called Joel Varney developed the transmitters. The Craigheads were the first to experiment with trapping and drug administration and dosages with Sucostrin.

In 1967, the Craigheads issued an interim report titled "Management of Bears in Yellowstone National Park." They said the Yellowstone population had become garbage-dependent, but they were afraid that if the park closed the dumps all at once, the bears would go straight to the campgrounds. John Craighead predicted that such a rapid switch would be catastrophic, even leading to human fatalities. The Craigheads urged the NPS to close the dumps slowly while providing bears with an alternate food source. According to Lance Craighead:

> One of their ideas was to provide the bears with elk carcasses. At the time, elk were being rounded up and slaughtered outside the park to reduce their numbers, but the idea of providing carcasses was not adopted by the park service. The Craigheads' biggest concern was that once the dumps were shut, bears that were used to human food would find it where they could, which would be in the campgrounds—and which is exactly what ended up happening.

The Craigheads were widely considered brilliant, but they clashed with park administration. In 1969, the NPS Natural Sciences Advisory Committee led by Starker Leopold released "A Bear Management Policy and Program for Yellowstone National Park." Like the Leopold Report and the Craigheads' report, it recommended gradual closure and carrion feeding. Other scientists also weighed in against abruptly closing the dumps, but the Yellowstone leadership didn't agree. In 1968, the NPS, including Yellowstone's head research biologist Glen Cole, disputed the Craigheads' claim that all Yellowstone bears were garbage-dependent. They said the Craigheads were only trapping at dumps and therefore not catching and studying the wild bears that they presumed were also in the park. Also, the Yellowstone superintendent made an issue of the researchers using ear "flags" on the bears, which may have been more about getting the Craigheads to leave than about the visual impact of the ear tags.

Soon after, in 1968, the NPS began to close the Yellowstone dumps and in 1969, the park began a no-feeding policy. Although the process of dump closures took twelve years to complete, each dump was closed abruptly. The already deteriorating relationship between Yellowstone and the Craigheads was now beyond repair. The Craigheads' study came to an end in 1971, and the NPS immediately removed the ear streamers from marked bears, making it impossible for anyone to track what happened to individual bears as a result of the dump closures.

The rest of the NPS followed Yellowstone's decision by abruptly closing all garbage dumps, including those in Shenandoah, Glacier, Mount Rainier, Rocky Mountain, and the Tetons. The same thing was happening concurrently in Canada. For example, the Lake Louise dump in Banff National Park closed in 1971. In 1969 and 1970, Yosemite closed the open dumps at Tuolumne Meadows, White Wolf, Crane Flat, Yosemite Valley, Wawona, and those in the valley and adopted a solid-waste collection system. All garbage was hauled out of the park and either incinerated or taken to the Mariposa County landfill. There were some exceptions; a few park dumps stayed open until the late 1970s and early 1980s. Sequoia-Kings closed all of their dumps in 1971.

After the abrupt closure of the dumps, one might wonder what happened next given the continuing lack of bear-proof facilities. According to Dave Graber:

> All hell broke loose. The claim at the time was that food dumps were creating garbage bears, that then became problems. In hindsight, this was partially true and partially not true. There is no doubt that the dumps were attractants to bears. There is no doubt, in retrospect, that all that additional nutrition was making more bears. The part that didn't quite hold was that those bears at the dumps were then interacting with people. But, after the dumps were closed, both grizzly and black bears began appearing in campgrounds as the next-best place to get easy-to-obtain high-calorie food from people. That's when they really began interacting with people. And so whether you were in Shenandoah or Yellowstone or Sequoia, bears were suddenly present in big numbers in campgrounds and the number of interactions with people, including injuries and damage to property, skyrocketed. Things got very bad.

It was like a repeat of the closing of the bear pits—on steroids. The campgrounds still weren't bear-proof. In many parks, trash containers weren't even bear-proof. Dave Sampietro, a retired Sequoia maintenance worker, remembers those years:

> I was on a garbage run in Lodgepole in 1970, and we didn't have bear [-proof] tops. We had to stop and pick every can off the ground and pick up the garbage that was spread all over by the bears. Every can.

That's how it was. Bears were everywhere making a mess just constantly.

Even more than before, bears were breaking into cars and buildings.
As Bill Tweed remembers:

It was a whole other world out there in the housekeeping cabins and
other buildings in Giant Forest. Bears were all over, and those cabins
were not bear-proof. There wasn't a building built in Giant Forest that
a bear couldn't open in ten minutes.

In Yellowstone, this same behavior was happening, but with grizzlies,
and there was no backup plan. The dump closures coincided, for unrelated reasons, with years of poor natural food crops, which exacerbated the
situation. In 1972, John Craighead's prediction of a human death came
true when an adult female grizzly killed a man after he returned to his
camp and surprised the bear while she was feeding on his unsecured food.
Yellowstone's response was to kill all bears in the park that were using
human food, or were habituated to human presence, while strictly enforcing proper food storage. Since the killing was done quietly behind the
scenes and without a paper trail, no one knows exactly how many bears
were killed, but according to Graber, "It was likely as many as thirty or
forty in just a few years."

As a result, the grizzly population was dramatically reduced, reaching
a low in the early 1970s and then taking thirty years to return to earlier
numbers. Lance Craighead explains that even though the population has
since rebounded in terms of numbers, it is less robust:

Even now, with numbers back up, the level of genetic variability within the Yellowstone bear population is now lower than before. You can
tell by comparing it to the closest population up in the Bob Marshall
Wilderness and in Canada. If the park had closed the dumps gradually
and also had a program to lock up all the food in the campgrounds at
night like they do now, some of those bears could have survived to
have offspring that wouldn't have learned the food conditioning from
their parents.

The drastic reduction in grizzly numbers in Yellowstone contributed
to the listing of the species as threatened in 1975. Lance Craighead also
reminds us:

While the controversy at Yellowstone centered on grizzly bears, hundreds of black bears were also killed, and that was in addition to those killed prior to the dumps closing. In the late 1950s and early '60s, there was a concerted effort in Yellowstone to get rid of the black bears that were begging along the roads and that were getting trash in the campgrounds. I don't know how many were killed, but when we were kids, we would often see black bears in those places and by the time the grizzly bear study ended, you never saw any.

We will never know exactly what happened, or how many bears were killed, because many killings were not recorded, and that wasn't just true in Yellowstone. Dick Martin, a ranger in Rainier during those years, remembers:

> Those bears I dealt with, there wasn't a single piece of paper done on them. I remember killing a bear in Mount Rainier that was bothering camp. We tried to translocate it, and I finally just got impatient. I was on the radio one night with one of the rangers who worked for me and he said, "What do you want me to do with this bear?" And I said, "Well, we've caught him a couple of times, and he's screwing things up and making a lot of work for everybody, so let's just overdose him with Sucostrin," and I said that on the radio. Other times, I remember just free-range shooting them.

The same was true in Yosemite and Sequoia-Kings Canyon, where more than a hundred bears were killed in a just few years. During this period, although the methods were modernized, killing nuisance bears and dumping the carcasses was standard procedure for field rangers. In Sequoia-Kings, Andy Ringgold remembers how the rangers worked:

> Typically when we killed bears, it was with one of two means. We either shot 'em or they were trapped and overdosed with Sucostrin. I think most of the bear carcasses went to the Wolverton dump. And that was consistent with the policy at the time, minimal as it was.

At Yosemite, where Jack Morehead was a ranger, things weren't much different:

> By this time, things had gotten more sophisticated. Instead of a ranger just whipping out a pistol and shooting the bear after it had been trapped, they were euthanizing bears with a drug. They usually shot

the bear in the trap because free-range could be pretty chancy. You didn't want to wound the bear. Then you didn't want to just dump it in the dump because the public goes to the dumps, so it wasn't written protocol, but we would haul the dead bear in the trap up to Big Oak Flat Road, which is off Highway 120 and dump it off. There was a perfect spot. It was the top part of the second tunnel. There was a spot where you could back the bear trap up to the guard rail and the bear would fall over this cliff.

When the dumps were closed, just as when the bear pits were closed, the parks again responded by killing a lot of bears, but this time, the political fallout was completely different. This time, as opposed to the early 1940s, there was no war to hide the killing. Also, U.S. culture had changed. The 1970s was the baby boomer generation, and neither the boomers nor the new generation of rangers would support the indiscriminate killing of bears. Not surprisingly, controversy quickly developed at the three parks, but was centered on Sequoia and Yosemite, each in what would become their trademark style: Sequoia's controversy was a mostly internal affair, while, relatively speaking, Yosemite's was a high-profile political media frenzy.

# 8

# TWO STYLES OF CONTROVERSY

In Sequoia, the controversy over killing "problem" bears was triggered internally. On October 5, 1973, a seasonal ranger from Lodgepole could no longer stomach the killing and wrote an anonymous letter to Assistant Secretary of the Interior Nathaniel Reed. He said he kept his name anonymous because of threats by his superiors to keep quiet or lose his job. In the letter, he listed a range of practices implemented by the two lead permanent rangers in the Giant Forest area that resulted in bears being "disgustingly mistreated and mismanaged by National Park Service personnel." He wrote that unidentified bears, including cubs, were secretly killed at night without any procedural review or documentation. The carcasses were then either dumped over the cliff at Little Baldy or skinned and kept as trophies, and there was at least one case of rangers eating a bear they had killed. He described bears that were shot openly, instead of being trapped before they were killed, resulting in some being only painfully wounded before running off. Other bears were trapped and relocated against policy onto USFS lands. While some other seasonal rangers also objected to these practices, he claimed that supervisors had threatened them to keep quiet. He alleged that there was no oversight from the superintendent or chief park ranger, who either "did not know what is going on in the park they administer" or were "ignoring it," or from the head biologist, who, he said, claimed he was either "too busy" to do anything or "on vacation." Finally, he wrote that an environmental impact statement on bear activities was needed to figure out the impact of the killing on the bear population.

The letter was truly anonymous; from later writings, it is clear that park management had suspicions about who wrote it but wasn't sure, and it had quite an impact. An investigation headed by the regional office led to one ranger being transferred and the other fired. As former law enforcement ranger Andy Ringgold recalls, "The controversy caused such a stir in Washington that somebody did an investigation and two rangers got their butts in major slings over the perceived indiscriminate killing of bears."

In Yosemite, on the other hand, the controversy was instigated from outside the NPS. In 1972, a woman named Ursula Faasii from the National Coalition Against the Poisoning of Wildlife started criticizing Yosemite for killing bears. At first, the park just ignored her because she had no background in wildlife management. According to longtime ranger George Durkee, "Even though it was the 1960s, the parks weren't used to citizen activists who were right."

But then famous photographer and climber Galen Rowell got involved, and the controversy quickly gained traction. Local residents told Rowell about the secret place the park dumped bear carcasses off Big Oak Flat Road, so he rappelled down to the spot to check it out. He found the spot after descending about thirty feet down a vertical cliff, where the cliff ended in a boulder field. Since the rangers had been dumping carcasses there for fifteen to twenty years, it contained a very large pile of decaying carcasses and bones. Rowell knew the park had been telling the public what it wanted to hear, that it was relocating all these bears to the high country to "live happily ever after," but here they were: dead. Finding this pile of bones pushed him into activism. Rowell's son, Tony, explains:

> In the late 1960s and early '70s, my father visited Yosemite National Park hundreds of times to climb on all the different routes, and on many of those trips he brought his family. He felt strongly about putting a better bear management program in place. When he felt strongly about something, he would immerse himself in it completely. He encountered many bears and to see them tortured and killed—he just wanted a change. So he spent time observing the park service's horrific treatment of these bears, and then he put lots of his time and energy into making a change.

In 1974, Galen wrote an article about his find and observations for the *Sierra Club Bulletin* titled "The Yosemite Solution to *Ursus American-us*." The article described:

> . . . a ghastly spectacle. A ranger, inexperienced with the use of tran-quilizer guns, used the wrong charge on a small cub in a tree. Instead of piercing the skin, the entire dart blew a large hole in the side of the cub. It fell from the tree, writhed and died in view of its mother and twin, who were subsequently captured and placed in a metal bear trap on wheels. The dead cub was thrown into the bed of a truck, the trailer was attached, and the whole procession was driven to Happy Isles Visitor Center, which was closed for the season. The dead cub was unloaded...In the circular confines of the culvert trap, the mother and cub went nearly berserk. Flashes came rhythmically from the rotating emergency light on top of the truck, like a torture scene from *Clock-work Orange...* I saw the cub. His body lay on a rock below the cliff where more than twenty bears have been dumped by rangers in the past two years. Carcasses and bones dotted the scene, invisible from the highway through the closed-canopy oak forest. Except for the smell.

Galen used the media attention garnered by his article to point out three big problems with park management. First, rangers were telling visitors that bears were being moved into the backcountry when they were actually being marked for death. Second, the number of bears killed in any given year depended on which "regime" was managing the park at the time rather than being dictated by an approved protocol. And third, the park didn't even know if the problem was related to a small number of rogue bears or *all* bears due to a complete lack of research. He also pointed out that while visitors used a variety of methods to keep bears away, many methods were downright cruel and that while most visitors wanted to stop the killing of bears, others wanted more bears killed. He said one problem was that rangers weren't holding visitors accountable; not one visitor received a warning or citation for improper food storage in 1973. Meanwhile, Galen's pictures went to media outlets like the *San Francisco Chronicle* and *Los Angeles Times,* where they were published with statistics about rangers killing more than two hundred bears between 1960 and 1972.

As a result, the public became furious with the park, with activist Ursula Faassi right in the middle of the firestorm. Jack Morehead, Yosemite's chief ranger at the time, was also thrust into the limelight, but as the reluctant defender of the park's policy. He remembers the fallout:

> Ursula Faassi was one of those dedicated spirits. I'm sure she was a lovely lady, but boy, she was on a mission and she just could not stomach the idea that we were killing bears. They were God's wonderful creatures. So she started on a huge campaign press and rant. She had an organization down in Oakland, and they kept getting interviews and coming up and photographing us. It finally got to the point where a major television station in Oakland wanted to do a huge production on the rangers euthanizing bears. Superintendents aren't dumb people and ours didn't want to be the one interviewed. So he must have thought, "Throw old Jack in there." So I went down and appeared on this evening program. We gave our two sides. Ursula presented hers—that bears were warm, fuzzy, lovable, cuddly, magnificent creatures. Although they were eating food and harming property, it was not their fault. Her main point was that the euthanizing drug we were using must have caused them immeasurable agony. She went on and on. I reiterated that we were using the best drug possible, that bears weren't cuddly and cute, they were wild animals, and that they were causing immense property damage.
>
> I thought the television announcer was doing pretty well trying to be neutral and that we were both holding our own, but toward the end, Ursula and her buddies had planned a trap for me: they brought a live bear cub into the studio. I had no advance warning, and here came a trainer with a bear cub. It was probably twenty pounds, and they were trying to explain how cute and wonderful and lovable this little bear was, and this little bear, thank God for me, got pissed. It didn't like being in the studio, with the hot lights and people, and it started squirming. It scratched the trainer, twisted out of her arms, got on the floor, and started crashing around. The camera people were scurrying. The announcer was screaming. Ursula was saying, "Oh my word, calm down," and I just sat there and laughed. It was hilarious. So I just made my final point that bears are wild animals, not pets, and that they could be destructive. I said we tried to keep them wild, but when we couldn't, we did the best we could. Then I said that if people had better ideas on how we could euthanize them or teach them to not come near people and destroy property, we were open to that. So that is how it ended. I don't recall ever hearing of Ursula after that interview. Well, I'm sure Ursula would have a different account.

# III

# The Aftermath

# 9

# RESEARCH IN YOSEMITE

It was clearly time for a change. According to Jack Morehead, shortly after his interview with Ursula Faassi, Yosemite's superintendent got the staff together, including Dick Riegelhuth, chief of resource management, and said, "We are indeed giving the public the wrong impression. We've got to figure out how to do this right." The problem was, the parks simply didn't understand the problem sufficiently to know how to develop and institute the necessary reforms. Was it merely a subset of "rogue" bears that were causing the problems? If so, those bears could be targeted. On the other hand, if *all* bears were involved, the solution would be much different. But with the spotlight on the parks, the leadership could no longer continue doing business as usual and had to make a move.

The responsibility to lead the charge fell upon Dick Riegelhuth, who, as Dave Graber recalls, "was a pretty smart fellow and knew he was cornered." Riegelhuth decided Yosemite would start a research program to find out whether the park had rogue bears and, if so, how to stop their behavior so the bears didn't have to be killed.

It wasn't that there wasn't already any research going on. Harold Basey, the ranger who marked bears with paint to study translocation, began a more formal research project in 1968 on black bear ecology that lasted until 1974. Although denied permission to use ether in the 1950s, he received permission in the 1960s to use the Sucostrin, the drug pioneered by the Craighead brothers in Yellowstone. With Sucostrin, a bear is not tranquilized, but is immobilized through paralysis; the bear is awake and aware, but can't move its muscles. Since Sucostrin is nonspe-

cific and acts on all muscles, including the diaphragm, the dosage has to
be accurate; if a bear is overdosed, it can suffocate and die. Basey recalls
the delicate balance:

> We had to give resuscitation to a number of bears, but if you under-
> dosed the bear, they snapped at you. Many times we underdosed, and
> sometimes we overdosed. The bears came out of the Sucostrin very
> quickly, so that was kind of exciting. And just to be honest, we lost one
> bear and felt very badly about that. Everybody involved tried very hard
> to save the bear. It caused us to be more careful.

All of the bears marked by Basey were originally called "Basey
bears." They put visible ear flags in the bears' ears—similar to those used
in Yellowstone—so at night, rangers could either photograph or describe
the tags. They then put a more permanent aluminum tag in the other ear
with a number. The bears' movements were tracked with observations
and recaptures. Right before Basey left his job at the park, he proposed
that security cameras be installed at certain garbage sites to photograph
the bears coming in, but the project wasn't funded. (These wouldn't have
been the high-tech digital cameras available now, but 8mm motion picture cameras.) Regardless, Basey increased the park's understanding of
bears greatly just by switching from spray-painting bears to marking
them with individually identifiable ear tags. Basey recalls:

> Before, people at the Giant Forest Lodge would say, "Oh yeah, we
> have Pete and we have George." When I started marking the bears, it
> turned out that they had about three or four Petes and about three or
> four Georges. They didn't know which bears they had at all, and the
> bears came in a lot more often than they thought.

Basey also learned that bears move around a great deal more and a
great deal faster than previously assumed. Rangers would see bears in
Giant Forest that would then beat them down the two-and-a-half-mile
road to Crescent Meadow. Rangers were learning the same thing in Yosemite. There, rangers would record a bear in the valley and see the same
bear at Glacier Point—a steep, uphill, four-mile walk—that same evening.

Unfortunately, Basey's research was limited; park leadership was
barely involved and Basey had to take care of most details himself, in-

cluding purchasing basic equipment such as stretchers for weighing the bears. Furthermore, in those days, rangers did everything. Basey gave campfire programs on bears, trapped bears, managed bears, and did law enforcement, in addition to his regular ranger-naturalist job. In winter, he taught at Modesto Junior College. As a result, he was only able to dedicate part of his time to research and never had time to analyze his data or write it up.

After the controversy hit in 1973, Riegelhuth needed a full-time bear biologist. Since Basey was the only one who had done extensive research on bears, Riegelhuth asked him to take on bear management as a full-time position, but he declined. Basey remembers:

> My supervisory job as a ranger-naturalist was, I thought, a more enjoyable job in the summertime, so I backed out of all bear research. They told me, "Either you take charge or you stay out." And so that ended my era of marking bears.

The primary bear research hub therefore shifted from Sequoia to Yosemite, where Reigelhuth was managing the higher-profile end of the controversy. In 1973, Yosemite contracted UC Berkeley's Starker Leopold, the wildlife expert who oversaw the Leopold Report, to provide the ecological data necessary for the professional management of bears. Thus began a period of intensive applied bear research that continued into the mid-1980s.

The largest and most comprehensive project in Yosemite was the one Leopold oversaw. It went from 1974 until 1978 and was led by Dave Graber, who at the time was a graduate student at Berkeley. Graber got involved in the fall of 1973, right after starting graduate school at Berkeley under professor Starker Leopold. Graber recalls:

> Leopold called me into his office and said Yosemite had gotten itself stuck between a rock and a hard place. They needed some research in a hurry to show they cared and were doing something and contacted Leopold to "do a study." I asked him why he thought I was a good fit and he said, "You are the only graduate student that I have who doesn't have a project and is big enough to carry one end of a bear." Really. That is exactly what he said. So since the park was being squeezed in both directions—from the public for better safety and better protection of their property, and now from conservation groups that heard about the Rowell report saying that killing bears was not an

acceptable solution—I got graduate research in Yosemite and eventually a career in the park service trying to figure out how to get the park out of this mess.

When Graber got to Yosemite in 1974, he recalls finding there was no history and no paper trail, so he started by interviewing a lot of park service people to ask them what they thought was the root of the problem. As he recalls:

> Different people had different versions of reality, but the general theme was that there was this cohort of rogue bears that had bad values and took food and injured people, and if those bears could somehow be gotten rid of, the problems would somehow go away. Interestingly enough, no one mentioned food as the cause of the whole problem, even though people like Joseph Dixon had long ago discovered it.

So Graber began his research on the behavior and ecology of black bears in the midst of this "maelstrom" of concern and attention. He continues:

> The newspapers and television were always coming up to Yosemite to see what was going on. In today's terms, there were probably a half a million dollars in property damage in a given year in the mid-1970s. Originally there were two of us. Later there were three. I started off with Keith Aubrey, who is now a big fisher expert, as my first technician. Then I had Pete Stine as a technician who, for a period in later years, ended up being my boss. So we were chasing around trying to put together a population study and make sense out of the mess while my study subjects kept getting moved or killed by park management. It made it really hard to do the numbers, but by the end of my first season, it was pretty obvious to my technicians and me that the problem was all about food. It wasn't really very subtle. Bears came around when there was food and, when food wasn't available, they wouldn't come around. I originally planned to simply discover who the bad bears were and why they were bad, but I found out early on that at that time in Yosemite, nearly all the bears in the park interacted with people and their food to some extent. They were either in developed areas like Yosemite Valley or in the backcountry, which by the mid-'70s was absolutely teeming with backpackers and bears.

Graber found bears in areas where they had never been reported before. Bears were at nine, ten, and even eleven thousand feet in elevation, well outside their normal range, but where the backpackers like to camp. The bears were following backpackers up above tree line, and there was nothing the backpackers could do to defend their food from bears. He explains:

> By the end of 1976, I was prepared to tell the park service that food was the beginning, middle, and end of the problem, but my professor said, "Yeah, but your population data aren't good enough yet. You've got to collect more information." Also, Dick Riegelhuth really wanted to know how many bears there were. At the time, we didn't have any of the DNA techniques available today. All we had was Jolly-Seber catch and release [a population estimation method based on the recapture frequency of a marked subset of the population] and since we knew our data were nonrandom because bears are either trap-happy or trap-shy, we had to do exhaustive sampling. We simply marked every single bear in Yosemite Valley. I later did the same thing in Giant Forest. In five years, we caught almost six hundred bears, which made for a lot of long nights.

For many of the rangers who helped Graber, those nights left a big impression. One, George Durkee, provides a vivid description:

> There was this huge male that we darted at dusk down the Merced River from the Little Yosemite Valley ranger station. The bear was huge. We later weighed the bear and he was 620 pounds. We called him BFB for Big Fucking Bear. He was too big to carry back to the ranger station, so we wrestled him onto a litter and floated him up the river at dusk. It was something out of *Apocalypse Now*, because we were these shadowy figures coming up the river. All you needed were jungle sounds and distant gunfire.

Graber took the data and built a population profile of the bears and found that humans were the principal cause of mortality for the bears. Says Graber:

> Once they reached about the age of four, the only way they seemed to die was if we killed them. After that, they lived for a long time. I met one wild bear that was twenty-seven.

Graber also got good estimates of fertility and growth. The bears that ate human food had higher reproductive rates than anything recorded in the literature. Female bears were reaching puberty at age four and having cubs. Males were growing until they were eight or nine. Interestingly, the nutritional benefits of consuming human food were not equal among the bears. Some bears were more successful at obtaining human food than others because of boldness, strength, aggressiveness, cleverness, or the ability to avoid being captured by park staff. Graber says:

> The flip side of saying that almost every bear in Yosemite used human food was that almost every bear in Yosemite also ate mostly natural foods. They hadn't forgotten how to forage on natural foods; they were just taking advantage of the higher-calorie human food that was also easier to get. To analyze the bears' diets, I analyzed 1,405 bear scats with Howard Quigley, drinking a lot of Rainier ale [like the bear from Washington] and listening to loud rock and roll. It was really tedious.

They found the majority of the bears' diet in spring and summer consisted of plants, and in the late summer and fall they relied on nuts, berries, and acorns. Pine nuts were another important fall food. In Yosemite Valley, bears feasted on apples and pears from historic orchards. As for animal foods, ants and mule deer (mostly fawns) were the main staples, along with a variety of other insects and all types of rodents. Birds were less important and fish were only occasionally found. On average, 15 percent of the bears' diet was food of human origin. The actual percentage fluctuated both annually and seasonally based on weather, park management, and fire activity. Hot fires reduced snag (dead tree) availability and therefore insects, whereas moderate fires increased berry production.

Through the course of his study, Graber became interested in a variety of related issues and kept expanding into different areas:

> I had a good friend who worked at San Francisco General Hospital, and he said he could run blood tests if I wanted to learn something about physiological status. So I started taking blood samples and learned that young bears were often grossly malnourished and anemic in the spring and continued to lose weight until about June, which probably aggravated the problem. I also learned a lot about behavior. Bears generally treated people as dominant bears, including sometimes testing their superior status. Injuries however, were rare.

In 1974, a group of undergraduate students from UC Berkeley were also in Yosemite, working on another, smaller research project on bears funded by a one-year "Student-Originated-Studies" National Science Foundation Grant under the advisement of Professor John Parmeter. They conducted intensive observations to help ensure only nuisance bears were relocated. The students compiled a master list of bears, collected incident data, conducted behavioral observations, and collected scat (feces). They found garbage in 38 percent of scat samples and estimated the population of Yosemite Valley bears at thirty-two, Tuolumne bears at twenty-six, and White Wolf bears at thirteen.

# 10

# RESEARCH IN SEQUOIA

**A**lthough smaller in scope, new research also started in Sequoia in 1974, with a two-year black bear ecology project headed by Berkeley graduate student Michael Walraven. Walraven wanted to determine the relative importance of various foods to bears by comparing their seasonal abundance with their relative contribution to the bears' diet. He estimated seasonal abundance by sampling the vegetation, and he estimated the relative contribution to the bears' diet by sampling their scats. He measured the abundance of human food as that which was available in developed areas in various seasons. He then developed a computer model to determine if seasonal changes in the quality and abundance of natural bear food could be used to predict the magnitude of human-bear problems in developed areas.

To test his model, he caught bears to determine which habitats they were actually using at what times. If a bear used a habitat type, he theorized it was due to a combination of the quality and abundance of the food within that habitat. The actual bear location data showed trends similar to the simulated distribution, including finding bears using developed areas when the human food therein had greater quality and abundance than natural food available elsewhere. He also used his research to explain that relocation should never be expected to work unless bears are moved to areas with excellent natural food supplies.

In 1979, Maurice Zardus, a resource specialist at Sequoia-Kings, tried to analyze Walraven's location data in more detail to learn about relocation success rates, but the tracking data were too inconsistent. He therefore hired Audrey Goldsmith as a seasonal employee to acquire additional data by aerially tracking collared bears for the summer. Although her sample size was only five bears, none of which were moved further than about thirteen miles, and she only had twelve hours of helicopter time, she determined that all five bears returned home and that "relocation is time-consuming, expensive, and may be more population control than rehabilitation." Still, she didn't recommend an end to helicopter relocation (which started in the mid-1970s), but rather that it be limited to aggressive bears due to the cost. Also around this time, there was a one-season project in which a graduate student from California State University at Fresno spent the summer of 1979 measuring black bear dens in Sequoia and Kings Canyon.

Meanwhile, Graber wrapped up his work in Yosemite and accepted a job as an NPS researcher in Sequoia-Kings. In 1980, Graber started a study in Sequoia with the goal of comparing the behavior and diet of backcountry bears, or those with little human interaction, to front country bears. Graber recalls:

> I really wanted to do a backcountry study. I remember Les Chow and Lee Anne Ayres, the project technicians, and I marching all over Sequoia and Kings Canyon looking for the right site. They wanted the most romantic place they could go, and I wanted a place where we could get a lot of data without spending a fortune. So we ended up picking the Colony Mill area because it was nearby, and our initial trapping data indicated that there was no movement of bears back and forth between there and the front country site in Giant Forest. I didn't know why. I still don't know why.

In Giant Forest, the researchers could dart bears to mark them as they did in Yosemite, but in the Colony Mill area, the bears were too wild; the researchers couldn't get near them. Since Graber wanted to get ear tags on every bear and record the seasonal weights of as many bears as possible in spring, summer, and fall, the researchers started using snares. Graber traveled to Washington to learn how to use snares from a trapper named Ralph Flowers. He then worked with Les and Lee Anne back in Sequoia to perfect their technique. At some point, Les took over much of the snaring program. Les remembers the workload:

We had something like fifteen snares out there for ten days at a time. For a while we had "Bambi." Bambi was a dead deer fawn we found and used as bait in the snares. We didn't want her to get taken, so we carted Bambi around with us for about a week. We made regular rounds to check the snares for trapped bears, but we did have two instances of snared bears being killed by other bears. We felt really bad about it. After tagging a bear, we tried to never leave until the bear was responsive and could defend itself, but it was tough because we were really busy. One day, I worked four bears by myself. There was one bear that had trouble staying out of snares. I think we caught her like four times in one week. That is the problem with snares—they are nonselective. I don't know if I would necessarily do it the same way now.

One of the key technological differences between Graber's Sequoia study and his study in Yosemite was the use of a lot more radio collars, plus the funding for weekly flights to track the bears. Graber put collars on roughly fifty bears, allowing him and his team to study the bears by observing their movements and activity patterns. Les Chow explains:

One of David's burning questions, was "What happens to the two-year-old males?" If you look at the demographic data, they just sort of evaporate and you never see them again. So our emphasis was to collar those yearling males and see what happened to them over the course of the next few years. It turned out they would usually disperse to places outside park boundaries and end up getting shot. It became more obvious that in the protected Giant Forest area, the bears were mostly females with really small home ranges in fantastic habitat. The males that came through were usually just wandering through, checking out the females.

In Sequoia, since so many bears had radio collars on, the researchers could also find dens. It turned out that dens were in a wide variety of substrates and habitat types. Dens were in chaparral, rocky talus, cavities at the base of trees, and cavities high up in trees. Researchers found a den adjacent to the highway that was used in two years by two different bears. They found siblings denned together, but apart from their mother, who denned alone, fifty yards away. Their most interesting finding was that some bears were active all winter. Within every age class in both sexes, there were individual bears that skipped a year of denning. The exception was with pregnant females, who always den because they give birth to altricial (immature and helpless) young that need to be kept warm and secure in the den while they grow fur and continue to develop. When bears were winter-active, they tended to use lower elevations where there was less snow, access to herbaceous foods, and acorns on the ground.

In Yosemite, Graber knew that bears were occasionally active in winter from superintendent's reports from 1929, 1936, and 1937. He also received reports from Yosemite Valley lodges during his research that bears were "ravaging and pillaging" behind their restaurants in December, January, and February. But since there were no radio collars on the bears, Graber, who was in school at Berkeley most of the winter, didn't know if those bears were active all winter or just occasionally active. It wasn't until the Sequoia study that he could be sure some bears were active throughout the winter.

Graber also found some illuminating differences between the Sequoia bears and the Yosemite bears. In Sequoia, the age structure of the bear population more closely resembled a natural population than the population he studied in Yosemite. That meant Sequoia had more old bears and a lower fertility rate. Why the difference? Two reasons. One, the population Graber studied in Sequoia had more fully wild bears than the population he studied in Yosemite due to the inclusion of the Colony Mill bears. Second, during the short time lag between Graber's Yosemite study in the late 1970s and his Sequoia study in the early '80s, food-storage advanced so much that even food-conditioned bears were getting less human food. Graber surmises that by the 1980s, the Yosemite bear population likely resembled what he found in the Giant Forest; and likewise, had he studied the Giant Forest population in the 1970s, it likely would have resembled what he found in Yosemite. Graber remembers:

> In the 1970s, Giant Forest was just as bad as Yosemite Valley. It was horrible, in fact. I don't think you can imagine how horrible things were. I came to Sequoia a few times from Yosemite for joint research meetings and one time I went out chasing bears with Michael Walraven and we would see fifteen different bears in two hours in Giant Forest. The campground was just a catastrophe.

Carrying out these intensive research projects required dedication. Les Chow remembers:

A research day started for us at six o'clock [a.m.]. We checked traps. We processed bears. We checked snares. We probably did that until around eleven or twelve and then came back to process blood and check data sheets. Then we had lunch and went radio tracking. After that, we took a nap, checked snares again at seven o'clock, and then went into the campgrounds until, I don't know, midnight. We were primarily researchers, but part of our investigation was to look at what impact human food had on black bear behavior and biology, so of course we were often in the campgrounds. We would try to make sure the campgrounds were clean by visiting every site and talking to everyone. We did it early in the evening when visitors were cooking dinner and then again late at night. We'd spotlight every picnic table and every car and wake people up to make them put their food away. It was hard work, and we worked a lot. It was probably the reason for the breakup of my first marriage because we were gone sixteen or eighteen hours per day. I have to give my field partner at the time, Lee Anne Ayres, most of the credit because she was relentless. She was the toughest person I have ever met. She could do things like going twenty-four hours a day for two days straight. She was amazing. She kept us going. And David Graber was inspirational. We had some great days.

During the course of their work, the researchers noticed that while the literature said bears were primarily morning and evening animals, the campground bears in Sequoia were nocturnal. Then the researchers put collars on the Colony Mill bears and found that they were primarily morning and evening animals. Graber recalls:

When we realized that, we thought, "Whoa." So Lee Anne had this idea, because she could take more pain, that we would do twenty-four-hour shifts—eight hours each—with the three of us, sitting out on Moro Rock and listening to the activity sensor every fifteen minutes. It was basically a mercury sensor embedded in the collars. Active. Inactive. Active. Inactive. We could then build an activity profile of when the bears were awake or asleep. I don't know what it had to do with management, but it was interesting and it showed us that when bears were around campgrounds, they became nocturnal and avoided contact. Lee Anne also documented that sows without cubs had a midday rest while those with cubs remained active.

The research not only inspired interest in bears and their proper management, it also inspired interest in the researchers. To some outsiders, the act of researching bears was dangerous, glamorous, and apparently even sexy. In 1987, a Harlequin Romance was published called *Earthly Treasures*. On the back cover, the book is described with the following quote:

> When Jordan McKenna arrived at her sister's lodge in California's beautiful Sequoia National Park, she was surprised at her attraction to Ben Gerard, a dedicated naturalist. And when she saw his "little black book" filled with women's names, she wondered just what sort of man he was. When the women turned out to be the black bears Ben was studying, she was disturbed at her overwhelming sense of relief. . . .

Clearly, the book is about Graber's research and his charismatic personality, although the author wants us to believe otherwise. On the copyright page, there is the following disclaimer:

> All the characters inside this book have no existence outside the imagination of the author and have no relation whatsoever to anyone bearing the same name or names. They are not even distantly inspired by any individual known or unknown to the author, and all incidents are pure invention.

# 11

# BEING PROACTIVE—FOOD AND TRASH

**W**hen Starker Leopold agreed to mentor bear research in Yosemite, Graber recalls that he did so on the condition that the research be accompanied by the development of a proactive bear management program driven by a proactive bear management plan. He also demanded the total cessation of the use of Sucostrin. Leopold's intention wasn't to stop Yosemite from killing bears, it was to ensure that each decision to kill a bear followed established policy, the actual killing followed established protocol, and the results were documented in a report. The report had to detail the history of events and the rationale for the decision, and it had to be available to the public. Since Leopold made Dave Graber's research conditional on Yosemite developing a coordinated policy, and since Yosemite needed the research, Dale Harms, the Yosemite biologist, quickly wrote an updated bear management plan in 1975. Shortly thereafter, Sequoia wrote a similar plan. Until that point, there had been no coordinated policy. That was true on both a park level and on a national level. Decisions were often made on the spot based on the responding ranger's personal assessment of the situation.

The human-bear management plans showed guidance on a range of topics broken into three categories: proactive management (education, food storage, law enforcement); reactive management (control of bears); and research and monitoring. The distinction was important because, for the first time, the parks focused on being proactive versus simply reactive, and on managing humans versus managing bears. The plans also designated who would oversee each aspect of the program, and put general program oversight under resource management. Over the years, the plans were then tweaked and updated based on research results and field experience.

At first, the plans had three stated goals: (1) maintaining the black bear population at a sustainable level, (2) planning park development and park use to minimize conflicts, and (3) ensuring that bears lead natural lives. By 1982, there was just one goal: "to restore and perpetuate the natural distribution, ecology, and behavior of black bears free of human influences." The previous three goals were modified into objectives that then fell under that umbrella goal. Although there was some resistance to taking the decision-making away from the field rangers, most park employees welcomed the plans. Rick Smith, a retired Yosemite law enforcement ranger, speaks to the relief felt by many employees:

> Having a bear management plan that was sensible and defensible stopped putting the rangers in the indefensible position of having to make decisions about whether or not to kill a bear—at least then we had some criteria and if we had to kill a bear, it was because the bear had met some criteria in the plan.

The most basic element in managing bears proactively was the provision that the parks had to end the availability of human trash and food to bears. This meant closing all remaining dumps, bear-proofing all trash and all facilities, and providing visitors a way to bear-proof their food in campgrounds. In contrast to the first attempt at closing the dumps, these changes didn't occur all at once, but were phased in as money and technology allowed. But since each new bear-proofing initiative had unexpected challenges, three steps forward was often followed by two steps back, with the entire process taking decades to complete. Luckily, the rangers kept stepping, and the bear-proofing initiatives kept evolving until they finally worked.

From the late 1930s through the 1950s, dumps were slowly replaced with incinerators. Then in the 1960s, the emphasis turned to actually removing trash from the parks. In the '60s and '70s, all thirty-two-gallon trash cans in all three parks were bear-proofed with the mailbox-style lids invented by Merv Cross. This was made possible not just because of the invention of the lids, but also by the invention of plastic trash bags, which made it possible to pull garbage up and out of these cans. Overnight, the parks moved three steps forward in managing bears. At first, these lids seemed like a perfect solution, but soon, problems appeared. First, once the cans were full, visitors piled additional trash on and around them that rewarded hungry bears when they came in the evening. Second, some maintenance employees strained their backs when they lifted the heavy lids to empty the cans. Also, the amount of trash increased continuously and the parks never seemed to have enough cans to accommodate it all.

As bigger mechanized trucks allowed trash removal to become increasingly sophisticated, the parks moved to using dumpsters. The first dumpsters weren't bear-proof though and provided bears with a windfall of food. In 1975, Yosemite maintenance worker Tolleman Gorham retrofitted their dumpsters with the same mailbox-style tops as the trash cans. Yosemite's dumpsters are front-loading, meaning the garbage truck drives up to the dumpster, inserts the metal forks into the metal sleeves on the dumpster, lifts the entire dumpster over the front of the garbage truck, and dumps it. When the dumpster is tipped, the lid hangs free. The Sequoia dumpsters are largely rear-loaders. Rear-loaders are tipped into the back of the garbage truck, and the lid bangs into the back of the dumpsters. They are used in places that have low overhead clearance. Since rear-loading dumpster lids got banged around, they couldn't be retrofitted with the mailbox tops, so Sequoia maintenance had to invent a different solution.

Jack Fiscus, a retired Sequoia maintenance worker, remembers retrofitting a lot of dumpsters and using a lot of trial and error:

> We started with the ones with the two rods and you turn the center handle. But, there were a lot of moving parts, and it just didn't work with the public. It's got to be simple. If they didn't lock it, well, it didn't work. I think the next generation was the rods that went from one end to the other, but the visitors would just leave them lay. They couldn't get them through. So we retrofitted those with little doors with doorknobs.

Jack's colleague Dan Whitehair adds:

> It was something the public knew. The doorknobs closed automatically when they dropped shut. We had to keep it simple. We needed at least two movements to outsmart a bear, but two or less for humans. If there was an open, broken, or unlatched dumpster, bears got food.

Retired Yosemite biologist Steve Thompson (unrelated to Steve Thompson of the company Bearsaver), who tragically died in an automobile accident in 2014, explained it all very succinctly with a quote that, to his embarrassment, was picked up by the *New York Times*. He said simply, "Bears are smart, and some are very smart. My problems start when the smarter bears and the dumber visitors intersect."

At first, Yosemite seemed to have it easier than Sequoia-Kings with their simple retrofit of the mailbox-type lids on the dumpsters. But eventually, the bears started mailing themselves. Biologist Steve Thompson explained:

> These dumpsters were in the park for ten years, and then all of a sudden, all over the park, bears learned to get into them. We observed bears putting their body in with their feet hooked over the sides of the chute. That way, they could get an armload of trash and get back out. But the strategy was not without risks. We got a lot of bears trapped in dumpsters. One year, it happened over fifty times. Then a visitor would go to put trash in a dumpster and open it and there would be a bear in there lunging, trying to get out. We got a lot of bears out of dumpsters, but some also got crushed in garbage trucks. We had one bear that ended up in dumpsters five times in one year. Two times he got out after the dump truck came by and dumped it in the morning. Both of those times, he got out of the back of the truck and came over the windshield and slid down and scared the driver. The other three times, we let him out. There was also a bear that got out of a truck and stayed on top as the truck drove past Yosemite Lodge toward El Capitan. When an employee drove by, they pulled the truck over and the bear jumped off.

During those years, Kate McCurdy was often Steve's only employee. She recalls:

> I would have to get up at the crack of dawn and drive around to let the bears out of the dumpsters before the trash guy got there. If I took a few days off, I would come back and there would be a few bears missing who had been taken away in the trucks. So we would come up with a new latch and a volunteer and I would go out and weld them on, but until you put the new latch on every dumpster, it wouldn't get tested because bears would just go to other dumpsters. Then you would find out it didn't work.

In 1992, Kate McCurdy lived in the Valley next door to J. R. Gheres, foreman of the concessionaire stables. J. R. got so tired of hearing bears banging around in the dumpster between their houses that he went out there one day and just stared at the dumpster to figure out how to make it stop. Then he drilled a hole that went through both the side of the dumpster and the door, placed a carabiner through the hole to keep the door closed, and chained the carabiner to the dumpster so that no one would steal his carabiner. It was brilliant, cheap, easy, and bears couldn't get into it. Since you would use the carbiner as a handle once you unclipped it, it was easy to remember to reclip. McCurdy says:

> So this cowboy figured it out because he wanted to get more sleep. In 1997, all the park dumpsters were retrofitted with a carabiner on a cable. It cost about four dollars a dumpster. I would say it is one of the most successful cheap things the Yosemite Fund [now the Yosemite Conservancy] ever got to buy for the park.

Ironically, while the Sierra parks were frantically developing better ways to store trash, the USFS was preparing a document called "Animal Resistant Garbage Containers," published in 1995, that acknowledged the Sierran biologists for their input and gave summaries and blueprints for many of the designs the Sierran parks already phased out. The lesson here is twofold: first, that communication among agencies had a long way to go, and second, that the level of food conditioning among bears, and therefore the sophistication of trash storage needed among areas, varied widely.

Unfortunately, in the Sierra, even after converting garbage cans to three-cubic-yard dumpsters and finding ways to bear-proof them, the availability of overflowing trash to bears often defeated the purpose of bear-proofing. Night after night, there would be visitors who dumped all of their trash from a week-long vacation into the dumpsters and others who filled them with packaging from bulk food or new camping gear. There was no end to the trash. Then, regardless of signs and other public information efforts, late night visitors would have no place to put their trash, and often piled it on and around the dumpsters. Overfull and overflowing dumpsters also tended to get particularly filthy and sticky. To avoid touching them, people threw their trash on top, furthering the problem. Where dumpsters overflowed, bears got food.

Solutions to overflowing trash included limiting visitor numbers to that which the facilities could accommodate, scheduling additional trash pick-ups, and scheduling trash pick-ups to occur after dinner: after most people dumped their trash, but before most bears came in looking for it. (For the parks and all other areas, a reduction in packaging throughout society would also help.) While all of these solutions are simple on paper, in reality they are expensive and politically challenging.

Storage of the garbage trucks—especially once they were full—provided the parks with another challenge. When the garbage trucks were parked within the parks, bears would rip up protective fences and sheds to get at them. Although bears could only access a small bit of trash from the trucks, they got enough of a food reward to keep coming back. Solutions included surrounding trucks with electric fences, building garages, and driving the trucks out of the parks for storage.

The great irony of the parks finally closing the dumps and finding solutions to most trash problems was, as noted before, that the bears increasingly turned their attention to cars and flimsy buildings. It explains why, in the early 1970s, while incident numbers didn't increase by much, damage costs skyrocketed. The need to provide the public a place to store food outside of their vehicles became urgent, but as of yet, the parks had not developed a solution. It wasn't because bear-proofing was a new idea. In the 1930s, George Wright had suggested using food safes and bear-proof refuse containers, and Joseph Dixon brought up the idea in the 1940s, but, outside of trash containers, no one ever acted on the issue until Dave Graber came to Yosemite.

Fairly early on during his time in Yosemite, Graber proposed that the park should build bear-proof boxes and put them in the campgrounds for people to store their food. He suspected that once human food became unavailable, the bears would go away. Since the boxes had to be made of steel to withstand the bears' strength, the estimated cost to build them was high, but in 1977, Yosemite got the money to try it in one campground. Graber selected White Wolf Campground in Yosemite because it had only eighty-five sites. Also, it wasn't in great bear habitat, so he surmised that once human food was no longer available, the bears would leave the area. Graber describes the experiment:

> They closed the campground for five days to put in the lockers. People wouldn't use them. They sat on them. But there was an authoritarian

ranger up there named Bob—I don't think I'll say his last name—who cooperated, if you can call it that, by driving around the campground with a loudspeaker yelling, "Put your food away" and terrorizing campers into storing their food. So there was almost 100 percent compliance. The four or five bears that were using the campground spent about four or five days pounding on the boxes, meaning, "Oh shit," and moaning a lot. Then they left to go pillaging elsewhere. So it was a huge success, and people celebrated that. I'm pretty sure the White Wolf bears headed north into good bear habitat. We will never know for sure because although we had caught and marked all the bears at White Wolf, we couldn't afford radio collars. And I learned something important about government psychology, which is, since Yosemite and the regional office were so thrilled with the lockers they immediately wanted to spend what I thought was a gazillion dollars to put lockers in all the campgrounds in Sequoia and Yosemite. I was at Sequoia by this time and thought, I don't know if they are going to work everywhere and if they don't, my name will be mud and I'll be run out of the service and be humiliated. So I tried to stop them. I'd say, "Let's do some more experiments," but they weren't listening. They said, "Grab all the money you can and put in the lockers."

The second installation, in Sequoia's Lodgepole Campground, was much more difficult. It was closer to good bear habitat, the bear population was bigger, and the campground was larger and therefore harder to get full compliance. When a campground is near good bear habitat, there will always be bears in the area, so good compliance isn't enough: it takes perfect compliance. Graber found that even at 95 percent compliance, bears still visited the campground. That last 5 percent provided enough food to make it worthwhile to the bears to make a quick trip through the campground. If they found food, great; if not, they just continued on their way. As a result, Graber found that while lockers improved the situation, there continued to be some bears in Lodgepole Campground. So Graber considers the big lesson learned to be that bears will keep coming back, even for an incredibly small reward.

Those first lockers, referred to as "footlockers," worked well. The front door had a hinge at the bottom and opened downward. When closed, the door was secured at the top with two thumb latches. Visitors could close them, and the bears couldn't open them. But as more lockers were installed and more visitors began using them, it became increasingly obvious that the lockers had a big problem: they were too small. They were less than ten cubic feet, and people were bringing more and more food and bigger and bigger coolers. Harold Werner, the Sequoia-Kings wildlife biologist at the time, decided to find out what size lockers were actually needed. In 1989 and 1990, he conducted a food volume monitoring study in Lodgepole Campground and found that the original footlockers only held a third of what people were actually bringing. Former bear technician Sherri Lisius remembers trying to make the footlockers work:

> People would say, well, I can't store my food in this stupid little locker, so we would spend hours searching for lockers that weren't completely full, looking for little openings where we could put people's food.

Since partial food storage is ineffective, larger or additional lockers were needed. But the design for the small footlockers was not transferrable to a larger size, and it was not perfect anyway. Since the hinges were down in the dirt, they would get wet and rusty and people often dropped the doors on their feet when they opened them quickly. A larger locker required a door that would be too large and too heavy to open downward. A larger locker needed doors that opened from the center out, like kitchen cabinets. Thus began a seemingly endless cycle of developing a new design, learning that either the visitors couldn't (or wouldn't) close them or that the bears could open them, then frantically looking for a solution—without adequate time, money, or personnel. Meanwhile, employees scrambled to keep the failed designs working with homemade retrofits.

The first real try at a new design happened in 1990 when the California Prison Authority designed the SecureStore locker. It was twenty-three cubic feet and made of ten-gauge steel. The closures were two spring-loaded knobs that had to be pulled at the same time. It failed within a week because bears figured out how to open the knobs using one paw and their mouths.

Jill Oertley, the wildife biologist in Sequoia-Kings at the time, remembers her and Harold's relief and optimism when the USFS's San Dimas lab got involved:

> I remember people from the Forest Service's San Dimas lab stopping by the park to show us some bear-proof ideas. Harold about wet his pants he was so excited. They showed us the handle they designed that

hung on a chain and was used to open a spring-loaded latch. The latch moved vertical rods in and out of position. The rods secured the door to the locker by fitting through holes in the top and bottom of the locker. We explained that people would never take the handle out of the hole where the latch was, because it would make it easier for them to open next time. They listened to us and took our suggestions to heart and even made some changes, although we were still concerned about the handle.

Park biologists spent weeks retrofitting the SecureStore locker latches with the new San Dimas modification. It took only a drill to do the retrofit, but the work didn't happen overnight. Bear technicians and biologists often had to work overtime to get it done with inadequate tools and little rest. Former Yosemite biologist Tori Seher recalls the long days of drilling. "It seemed like it took forever to retrofit those damn things."

Then San Dimas made a whole new locker that measured thirty cubic feet, called the Boxmaster locker. It was made of steel and had an improved latch and an inside escape handle in case kids climbed inside and got stuck. The company said the lockers had been "retrofitted with a proven bear-proof latch." Unfortunately, problems developed. You still had to take a handle that hung from a chain, put it into a socket, and turn it to release the long rods. It failed in 1991 because, as Jill and Harold had predicted, some visitors would leave the handle in the socket and bears could turn it. It was also easy to damage. The rod would bend, and worse, the metal holes where the rods inserted would get jammed and have to be redrilled repeatedly.

So the parks kept looking for partners to develop new locker designs, while simultaneously working frantically to retrofit existing lockers and manage the bears. Finally, a metal company called McClintock got in the game and came up with a redesign of the handle on the chain so that it was spring-loaded and couldn't be left in the socket. Eventually, due to failures, McClintock designed a new latch that one opened by pushing one's hand up into a metal housing. At first, the housing wasn't designed deep enough to keep bears from opening them with their paws. To block the bears from entry, a metal bar had to be welded under the housing. Finally it worked; a human hand could bend and gain entry, whereas a bear paw couldn't. Unfortunately, they were installed on lockers without solid frames and made of thin steel, so if they weren't installed perfectly plumb on a concrete pad with metal shims under their legs, they wouldn't close properly. With bears working over them nightly, the lockers had to be checked daily and shims added or removed for them to latch correctly.

Meanwhile, there was the continual slog to get funding for initial purchases and installation. Funds were pieced together from the National Park Foundation, the Yosemite Fund, the Sequoia Natural History Association, and the NPS's regional budget. Once lockers were installed, money was needed for maintenance: cleaning, oiling, and painting, as well as for equipment for retrofits. Kate McCurdy, former Yosemite wildlife biologist recalls:

> Bear boxes were not glamorous, and the Yosemite Fund likes glamorous projects. Bob Hansen was the executive director and went out on a limb to promote the bear box project. But you couldn't just go to GSA [the government supplier] and pick out a bear box. McClintock was the only company that you could go to and buy a bear box—and they didn't work. So we had to manufacture our own. Thank God Hansen had a contact with Herrick steel and they could make a box without overcharging for it.

In fact, Herrick did better than not overcharging. Herrick donated a few hundred lockers to Yosemite. Their lockers had a clever new design for a latch where a metal lever holds a locking mechanism in place (at least it did after the first retrofit). Grateful as the park was, and continues to be, for this generous donation of lockers, as with all designs, even the retrofitted design had an issue. In this case, it was that visitors would pinch their fingers in the mechanism or skip closing it to avoid the pinch. To deal with this, the bear techs added reflective tape to the mechanisms in such a way that it only showed when the latches were open. Then they could just shine their flashlights at the lockers at night to quickly determine if they needed to be latched.

Since funding came in fits and starts and designs were continually evolving and needing retrofits, the installations weren't systematic, but also came in fits and starts. Jeff Keay, former Yosemite wildlife biologist remembers:

> It was kind of piecemeal. We hit the hotspots. And when we started a campground, we wanted to make sure we could do the whole campground. White Wolf was first because it was so difficult to manage. Yosemite Valley was last because it was so huge. We could make

more progress if we took care of Tuolumne Meadows and White Wolf first.

Since the lockers went in piecemeal, the bears didn't give them a good try until they were all in. Before that, the bears would just go to campgrounds without lockers to access food. Kate McCurdy explains:

> So it wasn't until we had bought hundreds of lockers that we started figuring out which latches didn't work. Then we would have to go back to the Yosemite Fund and say, "Thanks for spending hundreds of thousands of dollars on the lockers, but they don't work." It is a pretty nice funding agency that doesn't walk away at that point. It was not a fun time. We would put together a committee of really smart people to come up with gizmos and knobs and spring-loaded latches that could keep bears out, but that people could figure out.

For both the public and the employees, it was a love-hate relationship. The public wanted to use lockers to keep bears out of their cars and tents, but missed seeing bears in the campgrounds and found the problems with lockers frustrating. The employees knew the lockers were needed, but were exhausted from trying to fund, design, install, and maintain lockers while managing the bears. Regardless, the situation with bears in campgrounds was so chaotic by this point that the lockers had become a necessity. Harold Werner remembers:

> There were a few times in Cedar Grove, especially in the '80s, when we actually had people camping together in circles for protection. It reminded me of the old wagon trains circling around to protect themselves. Those were dramatic years.

In most cases, the public was desperate to use them. Kate McCurdy remembers:

> Steve [Thompson, NPS] finally got this big stack of lockers from the Yosemite Fund, and we started in the Valley and did Upper Pines and Lower Pines and pretty much all the campgrounds. People were all excited, so the Yosemite Fund came through with one more shipment of lockers to take to the Tuolumne Wilderness Trailhead parking lot, where the ground would just glitter with glass from broken cars. It was like Oz. So we got this shipment right before Labor Day weekend when all the trailheads were full, and Steve, who I think was going to

the Strawberry Music Festival, knew there was no way to get those lockers installed before the busy weekend. So the truck came and they offloaded the lockers at the edge of the parking lot. People were so desperate to use lockers that they were climbing this six-high stack of lockers and putting their food in any locker they could access. The rangers called the next morning, furious because the bears had climbed up on the stack of lockers and were pulling the lockers down and launching them off the stack and made this huge mess. It was so indicative that we couldn't work fast enough to get those lockers installed.

# 12

# BEING PROACTIVE—EDUCATION AND ENFORCEMENT

Food storage is only effective if people know when, how, and what to store, so in the 1970s, the emphasis on education increased. Signs, public programs, and leaflets had been used for decades, but by the 1970s there were additional creative outlets for the information, including local radio stations. In addition to the expansion of messaging, there was a change in the tone of the message. The parks had already gone from killing bears secretly, to being open about killing bears, then, in a brochure called "The Bears are Not to Blame," the parks make it clear the bears, and not the humans, were the real victims. But it wasn't until 1977 that the parks bluntly told the pubic that they were part of the problem, with the new campaign phrase "A Fed Bear is a Dead Bear." It turned out visitors responded strongly to that emotional appeal. Dave Graber describes how the change came about:

> In 1977, a bear we knew really well named Mr. Stubbs came back down to Upper Pines Campground after spending the summer in Little Yosemite Valley. He had been caught and handled a few times and weighed over five hundred pounds. He was about as ferocious as a rutabaga, but he could just squash coolers and rip the entire tops off them. We knew that was the end of Mr. Stubbs. I got the call. My technician Howard Quigley got the call. And a ranger named Ginny Rouseau got the call. We were all upset because we knew we were going to have to kill the bear. The people were all standing around ga-ga eyed because we darted Mr. Stubbs and we had him on the stretcher

and it took forever because he was so big. And we were collecting data and putting him in the trap while the parents were telling the children that the rangers were now going to take the bear far away so he wouldn't bother people and Ginny looked at them and said, "No, we're not. We are actually going to take him over there and we are going to kill him. And do you know why we are going to kill him? Because people like you and you and you let this bear have your food over and over and over and you turned him into a bear you can't live with and you won't let us live with and so you are all responsible." She could be really ferocious, and the effect was unbelievable. People were just absolutely shook up. They were so upset. Then we went through our business and everybody was absolutely silent. And then we took the bear and we killed him. And as the weeks and the months went on, we kept talking about it and Yosemite started adopting the phrase "Feed a bear—Kill a bear." And I realized it was the only way to go. We were all desperately trying to figure out how to convince people to be more responsible.

In later years, even that slogan had growing pains; "Feed a Bear—Kill a Bear" became "A Fed Bear is a Dead Bear," and as Kate McCurdy says with frustration, "[B]ut then people thought a fed bear meant a bear living on federal land. We heard it so much we removed all the 'Fed Bear is a Dead Bear' signs and literature from Yosemite." Yet, the switch to talking about the visitors' role in the killing of bears stuck, and when Sequoia ranger-naturalist Malinee Crapsey wrote an article called "The Death of #583" that detailed a true story of a bear that went from wild to dead after becoming conditioned to human food, it was reprinted widely. Then in the 1980s, there was another spike in environmental education. There was a larger staff of ranger-naturalists who presented thousands of bear education programs, the NPS created standardized outdoor wayside exhibits about bears, and in 1984, former Yosemite ranger-naturalist Bob Roney made a 16mm film called *Bears, Forever Wild?*

Bob made the film after an influential day at work in 1979. He was working at White Wolf in Yosemite and did a ride-along with Gary Tenaka, the local bear technician. That night, Gary had to kill a bear, and when it was done, Bob remembers Gary saying, "I wish the people responsible for this bear being killed could see what their actions just did." So Bob decided to make a film, and it ended with just that, it actually showed the killing of a bear at the end. Former biologist Jeff Keay says,

"I thought Bob Roney's movie was a milestone for us. We were motivating a change in behavior from an emotional side." Although the film was mostly shown in Sequoia-Kings, and rarely in Yosemite, it did have a great impact on those who saw it, as did the hundreds of heartfelt walks, talks, and evening programs led by ranger-naturalists who embraced the need to educate the public.

By the 1980s, bear education was coming from more than just the NPS; the concessions employees often joined in with "Save-a-Bear" campaigns, educational pins, and T-shirts and even proved to be a great source of volunteers to educate park visitors. In 1994, Yosemite launched a "Don't be Bear Careless" campaign that Sequoia-Kings soon joined. Around 2000, Yosemite changed it to "Keep bears wild," to provide a positive message. The Yosemite Association then started a campaign with this logo and donated the money to the canister rental program and the development of two movies designed to educate visitors about bears. The Sequoia Natural History Association started similar efforts in the 1990s. Over time, the parks realized successful messaging required repeating the same message multiple times, but in fresh and appealing ways—and in multiple languages. Fliers were even placed over the urinals and in the women's bathroom stalls, the one location the park had visitors' undivided attention. Linda Wallace, a ranger in Sequoia, remembers designing cartoons to reach people. "You can't just say it once and everyone gets it. People are coming and going all the time so you must say it over and over and over in different ways that appeal to different people."

Education, particularly one-on-one education, works. Once most people receive a personal lesson about how access to human food can harm bears and make them vulnerable to property damage or personal injury, they will store their food and trash. At least, it works for most people. Not all people. Some people don't believe it. Some people don't get it. Some people forget. Some people enjoy the craziness of bears running through camp. These people need more than education to store their food and trash. They need laws. Until 1976, although feeding was prohibited, there were no regulations about food storage. Since rangers had no authority to make people put food in their trunks, they would, as Dave Graber succinctly puts it, "just fake it."

In fact, there was hardly any specificity at all about laws in the parks and there was minimal specialized law-enforcement training. The only requirement for law-enforcement authority in the NPS was forty hours of training. But that was about to change. In 1970, the "Fourth of July Riots" in Yosemite came about after rangers asked a group of about four hundred young adults that were illegally camped in Stoneman Meadow to leave. After the crowd refused, mounted rangers rode into the crowd carrying clubs, and the situation immediately deteriorated into a riot that continued through the night. In the morning, the park called in the National Guard and 135 people were arrested and thirty went to the hospital with injuries. These were the first riots in the history of the NPS.

A helpful explanation of what led up to the riot—from both perspectives—can be found in a July 25, 1971, *New York Times* article titled "A report on the range war at generation gap." According to the article, thousands of young people showed up in the valley every weekend to panhandle, blare music, have visible sex, openly do drugs, be naked, and circle the campgrounds on motorcycles. One ranger reportedly said, "Look at 'em. These hippies are getting to be just like the chipmunks and bears: depending on the tourists for their food." It is no surprise the "hippies" clashed with traditional users looking for quiet such as families with young kids. On the other hand, again according the article, it was the height of the anti-Vietnam era and the "youth" were angry with the government and establishment in general. Also, since park lodging facilities were designed for the financially well-off, some of the younger generation couldn't afford to stay anywhere in the park, including in the campgrounds, and therefore descended on the meadows.

After the riots, Yosemite closed Stoneman Meadow to use and the NPS decided to try to work with the younger generation. According to an August 4, 1971, article in the *L.A. Times* titled "Personnel shifted to change the image of Yosemite National Park," after the riots, five rangers were transferred out of the park and four were transferred in, along with a new superintendent named Lynn Thompson. The idea was to "accommodate rather than harass longhaired youths" by curtailing aggressive law enforcement and instead focusing on environmental education. As Graber puts it, "The director hand-picked people and brought them in and the ranger division in particular became this group of big men with giant egos and a lot of talent."

Partly as a result of the riot, along with the changes to Yosemite park management, changes came to the way the NPS handled law enforcement. On a national level, the General Authorities Act was passed in

1976. It established a minimum level of training required for all commissioned law enforcement officers. That same year, the first federal regulation allowing the NPS to make visitors responsible for protecting food and waste from bears, referred to as the first food storage order, became effective. The first year, rangers only issued warnings. Enforcement with citations, violations, and impounding food began in 1977. The general rule for the NPS is found in Title 36 of the Code of Federal Regulations. In its current form, 36 CFR 2.10(d) reads:

> The superintendent may designate all or a portion of a park or area where food, lawfully taken fish or wildlife, garbage, and equipment used to cook or store food must be kept in a sealed vehicle, or in a camping unit that is constructed of solid, non-pliable material, or suspended at least ten feet above the ground and four feet horizontally from a post, tree trunk, or other object, or shall be stored as otherwise designated. Violation of this restriction is prohibited. This restriction does not apply to food that is being transported, consumed, or prepared for consumption.

Title 36 of the CFR, specifically 36 CFR 1.7(b) also gave each park's superintendent the authority to write park-specific food-storage orders in a Superintendent's Compendium. Of course, enforcement was still dependent on each ranger's personal initiative to clearly document a case and enforce the new order.

Another new legal authority (36 CFR 13.50) allowed superintendents to implement area closures. Closures work best when dealing with temporary issues such as closing a campground for a few weeks to install lockers, or keeping people away from a major food crop while it is in season. In parks with grizzly bears, closures are often used for safety issues, such as when a sow and cub are hanging out on a popular trail. In parks with black bears, it is harder to get closures approved, but they can be used for short-term management.

# 13

# BEING REACTIVE—TRAPPING, IMMOBILIZATION, AND MARKING

Ideally, a proactive program would prevent the problem. All facilities would be bear-proof, everyone would be educated, law enforcement would be consistently applied, and the bears would be wild. Realistically, however, even when an excellent proactive program is in place, there will always be a need to manage the few bears that slip through. In the twenty-five years following the events of 1973, there wasn't just a need to manage a few bears, there was a need to manage dozens of food-conditioned and habituated bears that continued to obtain tons of human food while the parks struggled to piece together their proactive programs. During that period, the reactive tools of trapping, relocating, and killing remained major tools of the trade, albeit ones that evolved as the proactive tools were developed and put in place.

Trapping for marking, hazing, relocation, and destruction remained central to bear management, but it became increasingly professional. Steel foot traps were never really a part of bear management; they were phased out of Sequoia in 1920 and Yosemite in 1932. The basic trap during this period was, and still is, a culvert trap. Today's culvert trap is very similar to the original style. It is made from a piece of metal culvert pipe with a door welded on one end and a metal cap welded on the other end. Bait is hung near the back on a trigger. When a bear pulls on the bait, the trigger causes the door to close. Until the 1980s, the traps had a guillotine-style door that came straight down from above. Occasionally, bears were injured or killed when the door came down before they were all the way in. Yosemite has records of a bear being killed by a door in 1974 and of a bear being euthanized after a door smashed its paws in 1982. It was also a potential hazard for children. In 1985, Sequoia-Kings maintenance worker Jack Fiscus, now retired, modified the trap to have a swinging door. Yosemite then borrowed the design and by 1992, all traps in Sequoia, Kings, and Yosemite were retrofitted.

In addition to culvert traps, rangers occasionally used dart guns, sometimes without approval. Andy Ringgold, a former ranger who darted for the first time in 1969, remembers feeling justified to dart, regardless of his lack of experience. "I figured why the hell do they make us practice with this thing? If all they make us do is shoot it through a porthole in a trap, you don't need target practice."

However, overconfidence paired with inexperience could lead to tragic outcomes. Former ranger Joe Abrell recalls one incident:

> Because the sow had already been captured or killed, someone [tried to capture the cubs by shooting them] with a dart gun. The darts had actually gone into the body cavities and I remember seeing the dead cubs lying on the ground in the maintenance yard. You know at that time, people just didn't have the knowledge about how to load a dart [to ensure the correct powder charge was used] given the distance to, and size of, the bear.

One of the biggest problems with darting is that between the time you dart a bear and the time the drug has gone into effect and you find the bear unconscious, you have no control over the animal. In 1982 in Yosemite, three bears fell out of trees after they were darted and died from their injuries. Steve Thompson (NPS) described another incident when a bear fell from a tree, but with a much different outcome:

> I had two sisters visiting just after I got the job, and we were in Curry Orchard. There was a bear we were trying to catch, and we darted it and it went up a pine tree. We were taught in training to then hold these nylon parachutes under the tree and wait for the bear to fall into it. So we ran under the tree and my sister says, "Is it raining?" and then all of a sudden, this bear that was urinating on her, since one effect of the drug is that bears empty their bladders, came out of the tree like a rocket with a rain of branches. It was like a pinball bouncing off tree limbs, and it ended up hitting beyond us. It survived, but we changed our policy after that because the bear could've killed someone if it

landed on them. Once I caught a fifteen- or twenty-pound cub from a tree that ripped some of my fingernails off when I tried to catch it in a parachute.

Although darting has a lot of risk, it can be necessary when bears can't be caught with other methods and is often used during research. That doesn't mean there aren't problems. Kate McCurdy tells of a time she and others darted a bear in Tuolumne Meadows and even after hours of searching, couldn't find it and went home. It wasn't until the next day that she and her coworkers found out what happened when some campers reported being trapped in their tent the night before by a large bear that passed out on the zippered door of their tent. They said it snored loudly for hours while they hunkered inside, terrified.

Luckily, the technology has come a long way. The earliest dart gun, which was pioneered by the Craigheads, was actually just a bow and arrow. Retired ranger Rick Smith remembers shooting bears in Yellowstone with a bow and arrow to drug the bear, the arrow retrofitted with a syringe of drugs on the tip. Then there were rifles that required .22 charges. Newer dart guns use air canisters, are easier to load and aim, and have adjustable tensioning to change the power of the propulsion depending on the distance to the animal. They therefore allow the user to be gentler on the animals. At the same time, there has been an evolution in all the associated equipment that has made everything simpler and more efficient.

Regardless of how they were caught, almost every bear was then drugged so it could either be marked and released or "humanely" killed. The drugs that were used changed a lot during this roughly 25-year period. Before the 1970s, rangers used Sucostrin. As noted earlier, with Sucostrin, it was easy to overdose an animal, which led to some deaths and near deaths. Pat Quinn, former Sequoia-Kings trail crew supervisor, will long be remembered for his response to one overdose. He recalls:

> The trail crew had just completed a first-aid course a week or so before the incident, so certain procedures were fresh in our minds. Billy Hancock, Dave Sampietro, and myself were working in the Sycamore warehouse when Mike Chin brought in a darted bear to be processed. After the bear's weigh-in, Mike became visibly anxious because of the bear's shallow, labored breathing. Mike was concerned because he had discovered that she was a lactating female and may have overestimated

her weight before darting and drugging her. Then the bear stopped breathing. I don't remember any further conversation, but I do remember the urgency I felt and the shock on the faces of the other employees. I contemplated my next move while consciously overcoming the bear's strong body and breath odor. I grasped her snout with both hands, closed her mouth, and began mouth to nose respirations. I remember the bear's nose being wet and her eyes fixed and unresponsive. Later, others told me they thought I was nuts and were already discussing how to dispose of the carcass. However, after the fifth or sixth breath, the bear exhaled, groaned, sneezed, and shook her head— all at about at the same time—projecting oral and nasal mucus in many different directions, including my hands, face, shirt, and pants. We all quickly moved away and then came the spontaneous laughter... Mother and baby bear survived the ordeal... and a group of trail crew leaders left for the Sequoia backcountry later that season feeling ready to address any emergency and confident in their ability to use unusual techniques for unusual circumstances. We even coined the phrase, "Think outside the bear."

Of course, the other big problem with Sucostrin, as noted earlier, is that while a drugged animal can't move, it can hear and it can feel pain. That was why, when Leopold got involved in 1973, he decided Sucostrin was too cruel and made the NPS switch to a new drug called Sernylan. Yosemite switched from Sucostrin to Sernylan in 1974, and Sequoia switched in 1978. Sernylan was phencyclidine (PCP), also known as angel dust. The parks used it for a while, but it was later banned for use because it was addictive to humans. Longtime ranger George Durkee recalls:

> With Sernylan, once you darted a bear, some would get sleepy and fall right over in camp, and we would do the whole thing right there. But a lot of times, the bear would be totally amped up, and if we started chasing it, there was the general glee and excitement of the chase and they would run forever. We learned that if they had adrenalin in their system, the drug wouldn't take effect, but if you let them graze peacefully and wander around, they would just clunk over.

In the 1980s, two new immobilization drugs became available. One was an opiate called M99 (etorphine). It was useful for sedating bears quickly and could be reversed with M5050 (diprenorphine). In about

1976, Graber tried using M99 as a replacement for phencyclidine, but since it is a narcotic, the regulatory burden was too complex for field use. Also, M99 is lethal to humans, so Graber's team had to keep a loaded syringe of M5050 in a holster on their belts. They soon switched to the other new immobilization drug, which was ketamine (ketamine hydrochloride). Ketamine is an anesthetic but can cause rigidity and seizures and requires a high dose to take effect. Also, ketamine is in a class of drugs called cyclohexamines. Cyclohexamines cannot be reversed. Luckily, if one mixes ketamine with a tranquilizer called xylazine (xylazine hydrochloride), the amount of ketamine needed is greatly reduced, as are the side effects. Once a bear processes the ketamine and only xylazine is left, the xylazine can then be reversed with yohimbine, a drug more commonly known for its use as a treatment for human impotence.

Occasionally, the xylazine is processed before the ketamine and the bear can become rigid and, as Dave Graber describes, "go ballistic," but usually, the ketamine/xylazine works well. Yosemite and Sequoia-Kings have since switched to an even newer drug called Telazol. Telazol is made of tiletamine and zolazopam. Tiletamine, like ketamine, is an anesthetic and a cyclohexamine and therefore cannot be reversed. Zolazopam is basically diazepam and acts similarly to the xylazine. Telazol is incredibly safe, but has no reversing agent, so the bears often take several hours to wake up.

Along with the changes in trapping and drugging, there was also a shift in how bears were tagged to ensure they could be identified properly. At first, Jeff Keay's wife, Judy, sewed colorful ear streamers with unique symbols similar to those used in Yellowstone by the Craigheads. In 1976, biologists added small metal clips to the other ear as a backup identification system for when the streamers were lost. In 1991, biologist Steve Thompson replaced the handmade streamers with commercially available plastic numbered cattle tags to save on labor. Bears' lips were also tattooed in case the metal tags were lost. In later years in Yosemite, tattoos were phased out and identifying microchips were implanted instead.

Importantly, there was in increase in professionalism. Harold Werner remembers things being "a bit loose" when he arrived in the fall of 1979. He remembers stories of "bear technicians lobbing darts over the tops of tents and things like that." Dave Graber more bluntly recalls it being "a disorganized mess." Harold Werner understands why lots of beginners think they know everything about handling bears. He remembers being the same way:

> I first worked up a bear nicknamed Slim Pickens with Mike Chin. Slim was an old, arthritic, half-blind bear. We had to replace the collar on her so we radio-tracked her and darted her, and she fell right over and we replaced her collar. Since then, I've never seen a similarly easy bear.

The truth is that bears behave differently and metabolize drugs differently depending on a variety of factors including age, weight, and disposition. Learning the nuances and best ways to approach a variety of situations takes training plus experience. It took experience for Graber to learn how to handle cubs. He explains:

> With family groups, we learned to always try to sedate the cubs first because then the mother wouldn't go anywhere. If you sedated the mother first, then the cubs would go up a tree and then you couldn't leave until the cubs came down, which was often all night long.

So the biologists instituted a field training course on capture and handling and began retaining a veterinarian to oversee the handling and drugging. Through trial and error, the biologists learned to balance encouraging broad involvement in the program with keeping tighter control over the program. Graber remembers this balancing act well:

> I was given clear orders to allow the rangers to help work on the bears so they would get practice and stay involved, which drove me crazy because you couldn't rely on them. They would leave halfway through when something interesting was broadcast over the park radio. If you needed someone to help you carry a bear or go through an entire sedation, you needed someone to be there and stay there. So I gradually hand-picked a few rangers that were very professional and that I could count on to stay through the entire process.

The participants also remember. Bob Roney and Dean Shenk both attended the two-week class. The first week occurred in the classroom and the second week was all field time. When they were done, they got to be called black-bear control-action technicians. Dean remembers being taught to go to the Ahwahnee to pick up scraps of food for bait. One night when he hadn't eaten dinner, he was given a tray of perfectly cooked prime rib. Only part of it went to the bear.

The increasingly professional treatment of bears during handling was also reflected in the decision to end the publicizing of the bears' nicknames, a practice that was very popular with the public. Kate McCurdy describes one reason why:

> In the early '90s, we were still allowed to give bears nicknames in addition to numbers. My sister announced her engagement at the same time we caught this one family of bears, and so I nicknamed the cubs Jack and Meredith after my sister and her fiancé. And for years I had to deal with Jack and Meredith because they knew how to get in and out of dumpsters and were such pain-in-the-ass siblings. And that is when we realized that it was a bad idea to nickname bears, because you had to kill your sister and then her fiancée gets squashed in a trash compactor.

There were also bears with nicknames like Sunshine and Sugarplum, and when they were killed, it was a media disaster, even though Sugarplum's name hardly fit her temperament. The AP quoted Reigelhuth as describing Sugarplum as the "feistiest nastiest bitch we've had in years." He clearly attributed her popularity with the public to her name, as the AP also quoted him as saying it was just "blatant foolishness" to name them in the first place. But visitors really did love to know the bears by name, as did many of the rangers and biologists. Harold Werner easily remembers Beach Boy jumping from car roof to car roof and collapsing convertibles, and he remembers the antics of Zimbabwe, Mrs. Jones, and Jennifer, while the behaviors of numbered bears just run together in his memory.

When funding allowed, bears that were caught and tagged were also fitted with radio collars. By tracking bears with these collars, researchers learned a lot about bear movements and behaviors. Unfortunately, the early models had a huge liability: there was no way to remove them remotely, so the bears had to be recaptured to remove the collars. Researchers were starting to experiment with breakaways made of nylon webbing, but they weren't available yet, so some of the collars never came off, leading to some terrible tragedies. In 1981, bear #207 was collared in Sequoia weighing only sixty-one pounds. In October of 1986, Bill Smart and his son Tommy legally killed this same bear in Eshom

Valley weighing two hundred and fifty pounds. The collar was so tight that it was choking the bear. Underneath, the skin was raw with maggots eating through the flesh on the bear's neck, and they described the stench of rotting flesh. Once breakaway collars were available in the late 1980s, the parks switched to collars that had this feature, although even these breakaways would occasionally fail and stay on too long. They also retrofitted all their existing collars with three-inch sections of old canvas fire hose that would rot away faster than the collar. And they became much more careful with how tightly they applied the collars. Kate McCurdy remembers how this would backfire on them:

> Because bears' heads are basically the same size as their necks, while we put them on, we used to debate about how tight to make the collars so they wouldn't be too snug but also so a bear couldn't pull it over its head. Due to our caution, it was not uncommon for us to release a bear from a trap after it recovered and find its radio collar in the trap.

# 14

# BEING REACTIVE—RELOCATION, HAZING, AND AVERSIVE CONDITIONING

**O**nce a bear was trapped, drugged, and tagged, something had to be done with it. From the invention of the trailered culvert trap onward, the habit of relocating bears increased steadily over time until it became standard, unquestioned protocol. Trapped bears that were known to be problems were relocated to far corners of the parks. Between 1938 and 1986, over five hundred relocations were documented in Sequoia-Kings and Yosemite. It didn't matter that Harold Basey suspected relocated bears returned to their home range from his time spray-painting bears or that Audrey Goldsmith documented it in 1979 when she spent the summer aerially tracking relocated radio-collared bears. The perceived success of relocation was so powerful, and there were so many rangers doing it that it took decades to convince the NPS that in reality, it wasn't working.

Graber, for one, wanted relocation to end. He recalls his frustration from a research standpoint: "They were literally moving bears by the hundreds out of Yosemite Valley, which I hated because it made understanding bear populations miserable, but there was nothing I could do; it was the hand that I had been dealt." Graber was also convinced it was a bust. As more bears were marked, it became obvious that regardless of whether relocated bears returned or stayed put, they were almost all killed by legal hunters or poachers, hit by cars, killed as nuisance animals, or even killed by other bears. He gives an example:

Female 188 was only three years of age when she was released in May 1975. In September, she was observed one hundred and forty-one kilometers north of the release spot, near South Lake Tahoe. She adapted to her new environment, because next summer, she and her three cubs of the year became nuisances around cabins there until she was finally destroyed.

In 1987 in Minnesota, biologist Lynn Rogers was interested in the same thing and found during his research that when bears did return, they navigated home in a direct path.

Since relocated bears were often moved as far as possible, while staying in the park, in the hopes they wouldn't come back, they were often moved right up to the park boundaries. When the bears became nuisances elsewhere, it was not unusual to have it happen in another agency's jurisdiction, and that was often a disaster. Kate McCurdy describes how angering another agency actually increased their workload:

> More often than not, bears that were relocated to the edge of Yosemite came back, but not always. Right before Fourth of July weekend, we moved one bear because we couldn't deal with it over the busy weekend. I don't know why we thought if we moved it we wouldn't have to deal with it. The bear went right into a USFS campground near Hetch Hetchy. The way the [U.S.] Forest Service was set up, they didn't have any means to deal with bears in their campgrounds and they didn't have anything bear-proofed. All the Forest Service could do was call [California] Fish and Game and then Fish and Game would have to deal with the bear, but they didn't have enough wardens to deal with it. So we got a call from a really pissed-off warden that didn't have a problem killing it, but had no time to deal with it. He requested that we either come and get the bear or euthanize it ourselves. It was too smarmy to say that it was no longer our responsibility since it was outside the park. So we went out on the night of the Fourth and found the bear wandering through the campground site to site while fireworks were going off and people were following us around and threatening to shoot it. So we caught it and brought it back to the park and euthanized it.

There was also the problem of accidentally introducing bears into regions where they didn't normally occur or only occurred as occasional transients. This happened in 1975, when Graber recalls the California

Department of Fish and Game reporting that "bears with Yosemite tags were showing up in resorts and campgrounds on the eastern slope of the Sierra Nevada, where no breeding population was known, and only rare transients previously had been seen. Female 307, for example, was killed fifty kilometers east of her release site at Red's Meadow. A few years later, the first known reproduction on the east side started."

Occasionally, other agencies dumped *their* bears at the edge of *their* jurisdictions, next to the boundaries of the parks. Kate McCurdy illustrates the frustration and irony associated with those events:

> At that time, Fish and Game didn't mark the bears that they moved from private or [U.S.] Forest Service lands, so every once in a while, a bear would show up that was untagged, but clearly habituated. We would have to hit the ground running with those bears. It was a little maddening that the [U.S.] Forest Service and towns like Mammoth created as many bad bears as Yosemite, but since theirs weren't marked, the park service took all the bad rap for creating all the bad bears. I'm sure you've heard that everyone in Tahoe that has a bad bear thinks the park service trucked it up there. The reality is that anyone can create their own problem bears if they have a trash issue.

Since he had access to radio collars and airplanes, Graber, like Basey and Goldsmith before him, studied whether relocation was a viable management tool. He too found that once bears were relocated, they either returned and were killed by park management or went someplace else and were killed by hunters, poachers, or on a depredation permit. Graber, however, had a larger data set than Basey or Goldsmith, which, combined with park data, detailed the outcome of the relocations of more than forty bears. He studied it with Harold Werner, the wildlife biologist at Sequoia-Kings who oversaw bear management, and together they determined that relocation was delusional, expensive, and pointless. Retired biologist Harold Werner found the results unequivocal:

> We had no successes. Either they came back or they died. If you are going to kill a bear, you might as well do it yourself so you can do it humanely.

There were multiple reasons for the failures; ecologically, there were population pressures and resident bears in the new locations; biologically, relocated bears have a homing instinct to return; and politically, the parks didn't own areas with good habitat that were far enough away. In Glacier National Park, Kathy McArthur (now Kathy Jope) studied the relocation outcomes for ninety-two black bears and found distance was one of the most important predictors of success.

In the 1989 Sequoia-Kings bear management plan, there is finally the admission that "[o]ur best evidence suggests that long-distance relocation is a euphemistic way of killing bears." Finally, Sequoia-Kings managers changed their approach: they largely abandoned relocation and redoubled food storage efforts. Largely, but not completely. When long-distance relocation mostly ended in the mid- to late 1980s, it didn't end completely, even in Sequoia-Kings. When it was used, however, it was usually for reasons other than anyone thinking it actually worked. It was done to sort out which bear was doing something intolerable when several were in an area, to get a bear out of an area long enough to bear-proof an area, or to provide relief over a busy holiday weekend. Not surprisingly, in Yosemite and less often in Sequoia-Kings, relocation was also still done for political reasons, mainly when the public (or even the park staff) wouldn't tolerate a particular killing. This was especially the case when cubs were involved.

While these management decisions may have been easier on the public, they were rarely easier on the cubs. Sherri Lisius, a former biologist in all three parks, provides an example:

> C91 was breaking into the cafeteria and other buildings, and she wasn't afraid of people. We didn't want to kill her because she had three cubs, so we decided to catch them all and helicopter them into the backcountry. We set a culvert, and she and one of the cubs went into it. We then spent almost twenty-four hours trying to catch the other two cubs. We even built barriers out of orange construction fence around trees the cubs were in, thinking we would catch them when they came down. It wasn't that bright when you think about it because the cubs would just crawl out from under the fences. I remember Harold running through the woods with a butterfly net, trying to catch the little cubs. He did end up getting one that way. They were tiny. They weighed something ridiculous like ten or fifteen pounds. Finally, we got them all and took them to the helibase.

Jill Oertley, Sherri's supervisor at the time, recalls what happened next:

Linda Wallace and I then flew with them into the backcountry. C91 had two girls and one boy. The boy wouldn't leave her side. We stayed in the area a few days until we lost her radio signal. Back in the front country, we found out that instead of staying in place or going back to the Giant Forest, the bears headed south and were being seen by people just outside the park. We went to the Forest Service lookout down there and got a fix on them to confirm. For a few weeks, they stayed out of trouble, but then I got a call from a California Fish and Game warden who was really mad because they had to kill one of our bears for breaking into cabins. I asked him what happened to the three cubs and he got really quiet and said, "What cubs?"

And once in a great while, after a bear was relocated, it would return to its original range and resume its original nuisance behavior, but at a level that was tolerable enough to let it live to old age and die a natural death. "We have had some bears die of old age," said Harold Werner, "and some stay at just low enough of a level of a problem that we could live with them until they died of old age, but it was rare."

This isn't to say there are no places that use relocation with some success. One of them is Great Smoky Mountains National Park, where bears can be relocated much greater distances than is possible in the Sierran parks and into areas with excellent bear habitat. But even there, relocation was, and still is, only used as a last resort and when it is used, there is no tolerance for bears that return and resume their previous nuisance behaviors. Bill Stiver, wildlife biologist at Great Smoky Mountains National Park, explains the situation:

> We have a cooperative agreement with the [U.S] Forest Service and the state of Tennessee to relocate park bears out to [U.S.] Forest Service land, and so we have done it and still do it. It's nice to have that in our back pocket. We do that with maybe five to ten bears a year, but we are very careful about which bears we move. We don't do it with bears that have entered a tent, car, or structure, or that are overly aggressive. We go at least forty air miles. Some do come back, but once they become day-active or walk into a picnic area and try to get someone's food, we don't wait. The bear is gone. It's gone.

Then there was hazing. Hazing has been used in one form or another throughout the history of the parks. And not only on bears; in the 1930s, lots of different repellants were also used on deer. But early hazing methods were generally piecemeal and halfhearted, and food rewards were still widely available, so although no one knew exactly why hazing didn't work, it was generally agreed that it didn't work. When bear research and management started up in earnest in the mid-1970s, front country hazing was largely set aside. Although, as Graber remembers, there were a few side experiments:

> In Yosemite, they would do things like pound on a bear trap to make the bear inside absolutely miserable before releasing it. But there wasn't a lot of effort. We tried repellants. That was a joke. I remember Dale ordering African Lion poop from the San Diego Zoo. It arrived from UPS, and even though it was double-wrapped in plastic, it stank to high hell. The UPS man said, "If you ever try this trick again, you will never get another delivery to Yosemite." For our test, we had this red cooler. We put food in the cooler and then Dale laboriously put little stakes all around it with little sacks of lion shit. It stank awfully. Then we waited in Tuolumne Campground for a second and this huge bear nicknamed Ralph showed up almost immediately. He walked up and smelled the sacks for a minute or two and knocked a few over, then he walked right in and emptied the cooler, and then walked out and knocked over a few more, and then that was that. Visitors also tried a variety of repellents including mothballs, bleach, and ammonia. I never saw evidence that any of it had any effect, but we weren't focused on it. We were mostly obsessed with lockers, canisters, and making people put all their food away.

In the early 1980s, there was renewed interest in hazing, largely from Mike Coffey, a new bear technician at Sequoia-Kings, who tried adding consistency to hazing trials to see if it would increase their effectiveness. The superintendent allowed Coffey to use projectiles under the direction of supervisory wildlife biologist Harold Werner, as long as he kept it out of sight of the general public. Coffey recalls, however, that the basic problem of widespread food availability was still there:

> We tried homemade shotgun shell cases loaded primarily with rock salt. We would go set up a dirty cabin and cook food and purposely try to lure bears into them. Then we would shoot them with rock salt and thirty-five minutes later get a call from the other end of Camp Kaweah that the same bear was down there, getting food off somebody else's porch.

Rock salt had other problems too. The effective distance was only five to twelve yards. Closer than five yards was dangerous to the bear. Farther than twelve yards made the salt pattern too wide. Due to the close range required, a backup person was always needed for safety. "And most importantly," adds Werner, "there was one bear the rangers think they might have killed using rock salt because the salt embedded and led to an infection."

So Coffey switched to using darts without drugs to sting bears and then to the soft rubber bullets that had been used for hazing trials on grizzly bears by John Dalle-Molle and others in Denali in the late 1970s. But again, the bears came right back and, again, not without a cost. Werner says:

> In 1988, we caught a bear with a Ferret soft slug embedded in soft tissue that a ranger shot. We then stopped using them because we decided it was too difficult for people to judge the correct distance to use them safely.

At the time, some managers argued that the hazing was working. Mike Coffey, however, insists that it didn't work, at least in terms of extinguishing a nuisance behavior altogether:

> When you say, "It doesn't work," that doesn't mean you don't have a success story. But how often? One in a hundred? One in a thousand? I don't consider that to be a success. The bottom line is that it didn't work.

The only time Coffey and Werner thought they were successful was when they hazed naïve bears that were new to the campground scene. They believe they never saw many of those bears again. But most of the time, they hazed the "regulars." Those bears were so used to humans and human food that it was almost impossible to make the risk of coming into developed areas outweigh the reward of getting human food. With many of those "regulars," hazing just made the bears harder to trap.

Then between about 1985 and 1990, Werner and Laura Thompson tried food aversion. Instead of harassing the bears, they tried to make them associate human food with being miserably sick. They started with lithium chloride, which affects a bear's electrolyte balance. According to Werner:

The first problem was that it had such a strong taste that to get bears to eat it, we had to put it in capsules and then put the capsules into food. Once bears bit into a capsule, they would never touch that food item again. So it worked as a taste avertant, but we couldn't get them to eat enough to get sick. And as a taste avertant, it had limited applicability because while you could get them to quit eating biscuits or prunes or whatever three-dimensional item that had hidden the capsule, the bears would never generalize. So we switched to an emetic, apomorphine, to try to actually get the bears physiologically sick. The goal of an emetic is to get the animal to feel sick, but not sick enough to vomit and get relief from the nausea. The problem with apomorphine was that we couldn't give the bear a high enough dose. We increased the dose until we were giving the bear something like twenty-five times the dose the veterinarian thought would be adequate. The bear looked groggy, but kept downing the stuff.

Harold Werner's notes on feeding a bear they called Buckwheat prunes with apomorphine from August 7, 1986, illustrate his point:

- 1447 Ate 6mg apomorphine with prune.
- 1448 Are 6mg apormorphine with prune.
- 1454 Gagged.
- 1518 Ate 12mg apomorphine with prune.
- 1522 Gagged.
- 1523 Sat down.
- 1524 Gagged.
- 1526 Gagged.
- 1528 Gagged.
- 1531 Laid down.
- 1533 Laid head down.
- 1534 Ate 6mg apomorphine.
- 1538 Laid down and gagged.
- 1539 Gagged.
- 1541 Appeared drowsy.
- 1551 Ate 6mg apomorphine.
- 1552 Gagged.
- 1553 Ran down slope and up stream.
- 1553-1604 Drank from stream.
- 1604 Gagged.

- 1615 Harold left site.

Later that night, bear tech Jeff Drum recorded that Buckwheat was hand-fed by visitors from their car. That was the root of the problem. Regardless of what aversion methods were being applied, the bears were still getting almost continual food rewards.

Still, there were other experiments. In Sequoia, Werner and his staff conducted several trials with electricity. First, they tried shocking the bears with electricity. In 1988, Harold Werner tried an electric collar on bear #496. It was a standard dog-training collar mounted on the bear's standard radio telemetry breakaway collars. Harold sat in a car and waited for the bear to approach. When it did, Harold pressed a remote control to deliver a shock. Werner recalls what happened next:

> The bear thrashed violently and reached for the collar. Even though the shock was momentary, the bear worked on the collar until it pulled the collar off an estimated fifteen seconds after the shock was delivered. While thrashing, the bear caused a small dent in a government vehicle. Once the collar was off, the bear walked off casually. The bear was back in the developed area the same day.

Werner decided the bear's response was too violent to continue using the shock collar, especially for developed areas around park visitors. So he next tried electrifying the food. According to Harold:

> There was one day we put a plate of food on a picnic table at Buckeye Campground and electrified it with a fence charger. The bear came in and bit the food and got zapped. It ran up the hillside briefly but then it came back, circled around the picnic table a few times, followed the wire from the food down to the battery charger, and then walked off. In 1992, we tried electrifying dumpsters and garbage cans. We even used different garbage cans to create a degree of uncertainty. Bears quickly learned to avoid electrified sites.

Then in the late 1990s, Harold had an employee who wanted to try electrifying a car. It wasn't Harold's favorite experiment:

> I think the bears got a few shocks off it, but quickly learned to avoid the car. That was kind of a waste of time and then we had the hassle of

getting rid of the car. It was kind of an expensive experiment, although
it did educate the public.

In addition to the continual food availability, another problem with all
these hazing and aversion methods was that they were only being applied
by a limited number of people, all of whom were wearing uniforms and
driving marked vehicles. The bears quickly learned to avoid patrol cars
and uniformed employees by continuing with the same behaviors, but at
different locations or different times of day. So employees started wearing different clothes and driving different vehicles to try to get bears to
generalize the negative experience to all humans. It didn't work.

There was then the thought that everyone, including visitors, should
take part in hazing the bears. In 1987, Yosemite and Sequoia-Kings
adopted a policy of "mild aggression" in which they encouraged campers
to be bolder in their attempts to get bears out of camp. That included
throwing objects, yelling, clapping, and banging pots and pans. These
methods did get bears to move onward, but usually only as far as the next
food source, which was generally the next campsite over. So it didn't
change bear behavior, but it did, and still does, allow people to get bears
out of their sites long enough to put away their food.

In the early 1990s, with so many doubts about its effectiveness accompanied by concerns about safety and the required time commitment, hazing was largely abandoned and attention was redirected toward installing
bear-proof systems and educating visitors about the bears.

There was one exception, and that was to make one more try at using
dogs. In 1997, Yosemite decided to contract with Carrie Hunt of the
Wind River Bear Institute to bring her Karelian bear dogs, or KBDs, to
work the black bears in Tuolumne Meadows. Carrie Hunt first brought
her KBDs to the United States in 1992 to chase grizzlies out of developed
areas in Montana and was having some success. This wasn't the first time
dogs were used in Yosemite; after all, Rinson, the son of Rin-Tin-Tin,
had been a bear-chaser. It wasn't even the first time dogs were used in
Tuolumne; rangers kept three dogs there just for that purpose back in
1932. It was, however, the first time dogs were used that were trained
explicitly to chase bears.

Carrie and her dogs came for seven weeks of intensive work that
summer. The idea was to step up the park's efforts from hazing to aversive conditioning. Hazing is the situational use of deterrents to get a bear

to stop an undesirable behavior at a particular moment or to get it to move on. Aversive conditioning is the consistent and continual use of hazing to get a bear to stop the behavior in general. Working full time, they were successful in keeping bears out of Tuolumne's developed areas. The problems were that the dogs didn't help the rest of the park, including the more problematic valley, and that they didn't have long-term effectiveness; when the KBDs weren't there the following year, the bears came back. It seemed that to be successful, Yosemite would need several full-time teams of dogs and handlers running and barking their way through all the developed areas of the park all the time. Since that wasn't a financial or logistical possibility for even one summer (let alone the longer term), Yosemite stopped the experiment when the contract ended. The basic problem was, as was the case with so many other trials, that there was still food available all over and the KBDs didn't even have a chance of being successful. However, Carrie and her KBDs were enormously popular with the public and the media.

Kate McCurdy, the biologist at the time, decided to capitalize on what the dogs did best, which was public relations, and got one KBD from Carrie named Logan to use on patrols. She also hoped Logan would be good at tracking bears in order to avoid another darting fiasco, but as it turned out, he was too easily distracted. However, Logan was brilliant in the role of ambassador for the bear management program. Kate and Logan would rove the campgrounds together for miles each night, talking to endless numbers of people, with Logan and his wagging tail, happily making friends while finding all the improperly stored food. Sometimes Logan chased bears out of developed areas. Other times he slept in the office or chased squirrels. Eventually, when Kate left for another job, Logan left too. At that point, biologist Caitlin Lee-Roney says, "we became the dogs."

# 15

# OVERSIGHT AND IMPLEMENTATION

After 1973, all employees were expected to share the responsibility of keeping bears wild, but oversight and development of the program was placed with the natural-resources management staff. Direction came from the wildlife biologist who in turn consulted with the superintendent. With that change, the program began to take on a more scientific approach, as well as becoming more coordinated and professional. One place this oversight was clearly needed was with the trapping and handling program.

Most employees accepted that the biologists were in charge of handling, but others resisted and even resented their authority. This was partly because it took away some of the autonomy certain employees were used to having. It was also partly because, despite their educational and experiential requirements, wildlife biologists were hired at GS levels (government pay grades) well below that of colleagues with equivalently complex jobs. This affected where the biologists fell within the parks' pecking orders. In Yosemite, Steve Thompson (NPS) recalled his struggle to find his voice:

> I was by myself in the winter, but in the summer I had a seasonal employee. The leadership was not very supportive of our program, so if a conflict came up, we would find ourselves going toe to toe with the chief ranger, basically a GS5 and GS7 up against a GS14. We often got our butts kicked, but we had to try because nobody else was willing to do anything about it.

It wasn't until the late 1990s that biologists were put into a profession-al work series. That change not only gave them appropriate pay, but also a louder voice in park management decisions.

Another change that came with putting biologists in charge of bear management was a new emphasis on data collection. In 1978, Jean Ka-pler-Smith developed the Bear Incident Management System, referred to as the "BIMS" system. The idea was to get several parks, including Glacier, the Great Smoky Mountains, Sequoia-Kings, Shenandoah, Yel-lowstone, and Yosemite, to collect data in a consistent manner. Unfortu-nately, glitches in the early years caused several parks to stop using the system, but the Sierran parks used the BIMS system until they developed a more modern database about thirty years later.

The last big change to the structure of the bear management program was the formal designation of the bear technician. Bear technicians (bear techs) appeared in 1975 as field employees who fully focused on bears. Mike Coffey was one of the first bear technicians in Sequoia-Kings. He described the primary purpose of the bear tech as to "provide public education and information and enforce food storage regulations within the park. Bear techs primarily work nights and weekends and holidays because that is when most of the bear activity occurs." In addition, bear techs set and check bear traps, haze bears, track radio-collared bears with telemetry, assist with research, train and supervise volunteers, make signs, maintain databases, pick up trash, patrol campgrounds and picnic areas, respond to emergencies, check cars for food, and educate thou-sands of visitors a year about food storage and bears. Bear technicians (officially titled biological technicians) also attend to other park wildlife issues.

The bear techs didn't just educate millions of visitors about bears, they were also in charge of educating fellow park employees, concessions employees, contractors, pack station employees, and neighbors from local communities, which amounted to thousands of people each year. Luckily, bear techs are joined by a myriad of other current employees in this task, as well as by the many former bear techs and other long-term employees who still live in these areas. Some park visitors even take the initiative to rove the campgrounds and educate others about the bears. Jill Oertley always appreciated the help:

> People that had worked in the parks for many years generally took ownership of the bears and the bear program, and would provide helpful peer pressure to the other employees to store their food. It was better coming from them than from the bear-lady.

With the wide range of interests among park users, bear techs faced unusual challenges. For example, what does one do with one's food while climbing? Climbers are just like any other visitor when in the campgrounds, but when they go hiking, it is vertical. Since climbers aren't allowed to camp at the base of most walls, they often hike in, preclimb two pitches, rappel down, leave their ropes in place so they can get an early start the next day, and head back to the campground. At first, they would leave the haul bags with food for the trip at the base of the wall overnight, but the bears (and rodents) got into them. So the bear techs got involved and wilderness managers like Yosemite's Mark Fincher got involved and they started teaching people to actually haul their bags high up on the wall so bears couldn't get them. But, as it turns out, bears are good climbers; they can climb up the first pitch on one of the popular climbs on Half Dome, and they can climb up fifty feet or so on some of the harder walls. The task therefore became educating climbers about how high up the wall the food needs to be hung.

In general however, the bear tech was a lot like the town mayor: trying to get everyone excited about bears and bear management. Without full buy-in, everyone would fail. Sometimes fellow employees wouldn't want a bear tech around until they had a substantial problem. Jill Oertley recalls that they would then "scream for immediate attention and think their problems were worse than everyone else's." Sometimes longtime residents of local communities didn't want to listen to a new person. Steve Thompson, NPS, remembered being that new guy in Yosemite:

> I stepped in it right after I got here. It was in 1989 or 1990, and we had people in [a community adjacent to the park] who were keeping refrigerators on their porches and bears were getting into them, so I wrote a letter for the *Daily Report* that said, "Please don't put refrigerators on the porch, they should be inside the building in a secure location where a bear can't reach them." Ohhhh. It was a like a mushroom cloud. Like I was accusing them of being a bunch of hillbillies that were marrying their cousins. I met with the county supervisor and the superintendent

and they said I should have made it applicable to the whole park and not just focus on El Portal.

Sometimes it didn't matter if locals ignored the bear tech, because they had already learned from their own mistakes. Three Rivers local Earl McKee was one:

> We had bears twice spend the winter in our cabin and only found them when we came back in the spring. They would bite a hole in all the canned goods and suck the contents out. What a mess. Bear crap everywhere. We stopped leaving canned goods up there after that.

Other locals ignored the bear tech *and* refused to change their ways. Leroy Maloy, lifetime packer, local, and retired NPS employee told this story of defiance:

> Dick Riegelhuth said there wasn't a bear he couldn't catch and there was a problem bear at the pack station and the trap sat there stinking for days and so I shot the bear, put it in the trap, and sprung the trap. Then I called Dick and said, "Dick, you caught the bear." I would love to have a video of the ranger that came to spray-paint the bear and [release] him over Deer Ridge when he looked in the trap to see why the bear wasn't coming out. Anyway, that was not a good situation, but in the old days, that was how we did it.

Regardless, the bear techs had to keep trying to educate and motivate because there was a huge payoff for good relations in the form of cooperation, fundraising, and volunteering, and there was a huge penalty for poor relations. This was true in the campgrounds, in the communities, and in employee housing.

Trying to be proactive and professional while constantly reacting to chaos was hard. At times, there were even gunshots in the campgrounds from people chasing off bears. Former bear tech Sherri Lisius describes the continual frantic pace:

> I felt like I was working constantly. I was getting paid for forty hours a week but I was probably working sixty or seventy hours a week because there was always something crazy going on. The bears were always out and there was always a problem. They'd be in the picnic areas in the middle of the afternoon and then in the campgrounds until

three o'clock in the morning. We were always running place to place and could never respond to anything before something else would start, and that's why we recruited those humungous hordes of volunteers.

Sherri continues:

One of the first times I got bluff charged was during my first summer. I was with Michelle [Monroe] at Beetle Rock and we were chasing one of the female bears and the bear busted out the window and went into the building as we were chasing her and then busted back out through another window and we were chasing her some more and then she bluff charged me. I was like, "Oh my God, I don't make enough money to do this job. I can't believe I got bluff charged." I was making about eleven dollars an hour, and it seemed shocking so I was cussing, and Michelle calmly said, "Sherri, you can't cuss when you yell at bears because the visitors hear."

One may think that with so many responsibilities, including crisis management, there would have been base funding for the bear tech position. But while the work was regarded as important, funding for the position was always unpredictable and bear management was always understaffed. Often, positions weren't funded until a crisis was underway and there was little money for equipment—even safety equipment like flashlights.

As a result, there was, and still is, a huge reliance on volunteers. Volunteers come from all around the country and abroad. They are student interns, retirees, off-hours concessions employees, and park visitors who decide to stay. Like any paid employee, they need training, housing, vehicles, equipment, keys, background checks, and computer access. Unlike paid employees, they generally work fewer hours a week, or fewer weeks a summer, and have no obligation to stay. Since they require more training and supervision, relying on volunteers puts a greater burden on the biologist than the full-time staff. There are exceptions. Every year, some volunteers are already full performance and work full time for the entire summer. Regardless, volunteers were, and still are, instrumental to the program.

Former Sequoia-Kings biologist Jill Oertley remembers the political conflict between filling in the void with volunteers and letting the program suffer to show park leadership the extent of the need:

We never did have as much money as Yosemite. We were always struggling to fund bear techs and get equipment. I would freak out when we didn't get enough money for bear techs because you can really lose ground quickly. We used a lot of volunteers, and I had good luck with them. Sometimes I got chastised for using volunteers when there was no money because it showed we could do our job with nothing, but it wasn't worth it to me to make a point while sliding back several years in progress and recruiting a lot more problem bears.

# 16

# FROM CARS TO PEOPLE—INJURIES

**W**ith all this chaos, one would think there must have been a lot of injuries. Were there? Yes. And no. In the 1920s and 1930s, most of the injuries occurred when people interacted with bears at the feeding pits. During that time, there were dozens of injuries per year, but most could be described as minor scratches. When the pits were closed, bears mainly turned to dumps where there was less interaction with humans, but the bears also came into campgrounds and other developed areas, where the potential for injuries increased. As Kate McCurdy summarizes:

> Bears are very easy to get along with. If people are hurt by bears, they are generally doing something really stupid, there is food involved, or a bear makes a mistake.

"Doing something stupid" includes visitors who knowingly take a risk and those who are honestly shocked that they could be hurt by a wild animal in a national park. In 1989, law enforcement ranger Robert Bowen took an injury report that documented a visitor's reaction to getting struck and injured by a bear after luring it to his picnic table with food:

> I asked the visitor if he had read the signs saying not to feed the bears and to stay away from bears. He said yes, but assumed the bear wasn't dangerous. He didn't understand why dangerous animals were allowed near the picnic area or why someone wasn't there to keep them away if they were dangerous. He did not comprehend that bears in the park are wild and should be avoided.

Other visitors get used to being around black bears, forget they pose a risk, and feel safe just shooing them away. This is even true of visitors who greatly fear grizzlies. Filmmaker and former Sequoia employee Steve Bumgardner summarizes the feeling:

> You feel more alive in grizzly country because you might die. Your ears are always alert in grizzly country, but in the Sierra, you see people listening to an iPod with earphones while they hike.

More often, visitors get close to bears despite knowing there is a risk. The same is true of bear techs, whose job often involves getting close to bears. Former bear tech Jeannine Koshear recorded this statement in 1990:

> I heard a commotion up in the Crescent Meadow Picnic Area and upon investigation found bear #505 skirting the edge of the parking lot waiting for her chance to make a run for one of the laden picnic tables. I tried to chase her with all the standard techniques, and she ran away while circling around to get closer to one of the picnic tables with food on it. She halfheartedly climbed one of the trees, but decided she would challenge me, climbed down, and bluff charged to within three feet. She was obviously peeved at my audacity in standing between her and her food. The second time she bluff charged, she did not stop, but stood up and put her left paw on my right shoulder and her right paw on my upper left back. I did not realize until later that she had broken the skin, leaving several superficial scratches. She was probably as scared as I was. I continued to chase her. . . .

There are also records of injuries that seem to stem solely from a bear's curiosity. There is a description of an injury in the Sequoia files of a woman who met a bear on a trail and moved upslope to let the bear pass. It followed her up, then back down to the trail. She sat down on a rock to let the bear check her out. It skittishly approached and bit her below the knee. She tried to scream, but was just getting over a case of laryngitis and her scream only confused the bear who backed off a little. This gave her time to flee. (Coincidentally, my two-year-old daughter did the same thing to a stranger's baby. We were taking a walk when we met a mother pushing a stroller. My daughter was curious about the baby and bit her knee.)

Unbelievably, there is even a record of a bears getting bitten by a human. Lifelong packer Earl McKee recalls one of his favorite stories:

We were packing a party to Big Arroyo over Kaweah Gap in 1948, and we came back through Alta Meadow where there was a really huge deer population. And we had this young guy who was the cook and he slept in the kitchen. That night, this old doe kept coming in and trying to eat the soap to get the salt in it, and I'd hear Bert yell. I'd say, "Bert, you all right?" And he'd say, "Yeah," and this happened a couple of times and then about one o'clock in the morning, I heard a commotion like all hell broke loose, and I yelled down, "Bert, what happened?" and he stuttered, "I just bit a bear." Well, when he woke up, he thought it was the old doe, and he just rared up in his sleeping bag and put his mouth against the animal's side and ended up with bear hair in his mouth. Well, you can imagine the bear didn't expect that and took off across the meadow.

What is striking, though, is that whatever the circumstance, the injuries to humans were almost always minor and, in the Sierra, no one has ever been killed. This was true even after most bear-proofing was done and the bears were approaching the humans themselves for their food. According to retired newspaperman Gene Rose, "[t]he only fatal attack that we have had in the Sierran parks by [a mammal] that I know of is a young child that was gored by a deer in Wawona in 1977 when he tried to retrieve his bag of potato chips." (In Yosemite's early history, there were two fatalities by nonmammals: one from a rattlesnake bite and one from a spider bite.)

Regardless, in the 1970s, the public perception of acceptable risk changed. There was less of a tolerance of injuries and more of an emphasis on safety. Why? Partially, it's because lawyers got involved. Dave Graber explains:

There were many more hospitalizable injuries in the '20s and '30s and into the '40s, but the difference was that in the '70s, people were starting to sue when they got hurt or when their car got broken into, whereas in the '30s, people just shrugged their shoulders and said, "Oh well, nine fingers is good enough."

Harold Werner remembers a case based on an injury that wasn't even directly caused by a bear:

When I first came here, we were involved in a court case where a human jumped through a window in a Giant Forest cabin because she saw a bear coming towards her and ended up breaking her wrist. It is unfortunate we settled, because there was no reason for her to do that.

Kate McCurdy adds:

One of the most dangerous animals in the parks is a tick carrying the Lyme spirochete. Of course bears are dangerous, but if you start worrying about liability and minimizing risk, bears and mountain lions are going to make any manager uncomfortable, especially when they are near children.

Thankfully, black bears rarely kill people. When they do, it is usually a predaceous attack, which is extremely rare and has never happened in the Sierran parks. However, it has happened in other public parks, including Great Smoky Mountains National Park. Steven Herrero, the recognized expert on bear attacks, summarized the correlates of such attacks:

We looked at all fatal attacks by black bears, and it appeared that they were disproportionately more in Canada and Alaska than in the rest of the U.S. One possible reason is that they are more commonly food stressed, but there are a whole bunch of others. Another is that most bears in the north don't have as much experience with people as those further south.

Even less common are the occasions when food-conditioned and/or habituated bears kill humans, but to date, this has never happened in the Sierra Nevada. Herrero wonders if we have destroyed the aggressive tendency in Sierran bears:

Assuming there is a genetically determined variance in aggressiveness that is subject to natural selection, it is possible the bears that are more aggressive toward people have simply been eliminated from the population. If that is true, and I believe it is, and the selection pressure is strong enough, then in not all that many generations, you would see a change in aggression.

Many bear managers, including Kate McCurdy and Harold Werner, agree.

Steve Thompson, NPS, thought the change was for a much more basic reason:

> I think bears in the Sierra have so much exposure to humans from a very young age that they learn humans aren't food. Most predatory attacks by black bears on humans occur in remote areas where their experience with humans is limited.

# 17

# CONTINUED PROBLEMS, CONTINUED DESTRUCTION

Although most injuries were minor, the possibility of major injuries or death is real. It should be no surprise that, into the 1970s and 1980s, destruction was still a major tool. Dave Graber refers to that period, particularly between 1975 and 1979, as a "bear-killing orgy." Fortunately, the killing, like the trapping and handling, became increasingly professionalized after 1973. Important changes included the development of criteria for when and how to kill a bear and guidelines on what was to be done with the carcasses.

The criteria for killing were that bears either caused excessive and repeated property damage when food was stored properly, or they injured or threatened people without provocation. At first, animals that fit the criteria had to be captured three times before they were destroyed. Then there was a period when they were relocated and only destroyed if they returned. Then in 1978, it was shifted to a case-by-case determination whether to keep the bear alive, relocate it, or kill it. To use the criteria effectively, a bear had to be caught, marked for unique identification, and then caught in the act to confirm its bad behavior.

Protocols for the way bears were killed reduced accidents and suffering. Free-range killing was phased out. After the mid-1970s, bears were captured before they were killed so they could be drugged before being shot or given an injection of succinylcholine, and later potassium chloride, into the heart.

To avoid another public-relations fiasco like that in 1973, there were also protocols for carcass disposal. Mass bear graves no longer existed in either park. A handwritten note from 1988 in the files from the SEKI Superintendent to Harold Werner says, "Please be certain that no more than one bear is disposed of in any one location regardless of how remote." Sometimes, dead bears were skinned so the skins could be used for educational purposes by interpretive rangers. Occasionally, Yosemite donated bear parts including claws and skulls to Native American communities for ceremonial use.

Meanwhile, one would think the switch from reactive to proactive management, the introduction of the bear technician, increasingly effective bear-proofing, education, and law enforcement, plus the removal of severely food-conditioned bears, would have quickly led to some improvement. Yosemite biologist Jeff Keay analyzed BIMS data from 1975 to 1986 to find out. Keay found that bears were getting less human food and having smaller litters but that bears were also getting closer to humans to gain access to their food, incidents were more expensive because they now involved more buildings and cars, there was less tolerance for injuries, and the situation was still a chaotic mess. In 1989, the SEKI Wildlife Management Plan described the human-bear problem as:

> . . . probably the most troublesome of all wildlife problems in these Parks. The problem is geographically extensive, long-lived, the source of considerable economic and safety concern, enveloped in diverse public sentiment and opinions, and has considerable potential for ecological disturbance.

In 1995, Sequoia-Kings biologist Jill Oertley recalls trying to manage problems in all five front country subdistricts at the same time.

Why were things still so bad? First, although bear-proofing was in progress, the parks were far from bear-proof. As Dave Graber found when lockers were installed in Lodgepole Campground, bear-proof means 100 percent of food and trash must be stored properly, not 95 percent. That meant finding the funding, technology, time, and political will to bear-proof dozens of picnic areas, hundreds of buildings, thousands of campsites, and millions of vehicles. It also meant going back and retrofitting all the installations that didn't quite work. And it meant thinking creatively about all the places a bear might break into to obtain human food. Carrie Vernon, former helicopter superintendent in Sequoia-Kings:

We came to work one day and could see trash spread all over the helibase. The door of the tail compartment on our helicopter was open, and we realized that we had left a large bag of trash in the tail that came from a back haul from a trail-crew camp. The bear managed to open the door and get the bag of trash without scratching the paint or doing any damage to the aircraft. I think he was after a jar of pickle juice.

A second reason things remained so bad was that some types of food were impossible to store. In Yosemite Valley, there are nearly five hundred fruit trees, mostly apple, in historic orchards that pioneers James Lamon and James Hutchings planted prior to the park's establishment. These orchards, ranging in size from scattered groups of trees to the 143-tree orchard that lies within the largest parking lot in Curry Village, attract bears like magnets when the fruit ripens in the fall. Not a new problem, there are notes in Superintendent's Reports dating back to 1925 about dozens of bears eating apples in these orchards. Kate McCurdy explains the scope of the problem:

One night we counted twenty bears in the orchard in the Curry Village parking lot eating apples. There were sows and cubs and big boars and yearlings, and there didn't seem to be any defensiveness or territoriality going on. It was just free feeding in the orchard. Since the apples ripen when the park is busiest, the bears would then wander into Curry Village where there would be open trash cans, food in tents, and food in cars. It had the surreal atmosphere of trying to keep the lid on something that was limitless. People were running around with cameras, and no one was afraid of these animals. I remember feeling a mix of excitement, disgust, awe, and fear. I knew this was so wrong, but the solution was so expensive, and it was so hard to know what to do besides sit and gawk at all the bears in the parking lot like everybody else.

From a wildlife perspective, the solution is clear: remove the orchards. Steve Thompson, NPS, for one, would have loved to "take a chainsaw to that place." The issue is that the orchards are historic, and protected by the National Historic Preservation Act. Although interestingly, it is the trees that are of value historically, and not the apples. The recently signed Merced River Plan allows for the removal of the trees, but before that can happen, the park must consult with the State Historic Preservation Officer

on how to proceed. In the meantime, biologists must continue to be creative. Kate McCurdy explains:

> We thought, how can we deal with all these apples without cutting the
> trees down? In the mid-1990s, we got into the apple business when I
> asked Larry Castro, one of the tree crew, to go out and prune one of the
> trees that made the most apples. I thought it would have fewer
> branches and make less apples, but instead it produced like a million
> little crabapples and park administration didn't like us pruning the
> trees. So in 1992, we tried to get rid of the blossoms by having the fire
> crew, for their annual training, use their fire hoses to blast the blos-
> soms off of the trees at the Curry Orchard in the parking lot. They had
> all kinds of fun and it looked like it was working, but it turned out we
> just thinned the blossoms and the third that remained used the million
> gallons of water to produce much bigger apples. So that failed miser-
> ably.

Kate continues:

> The only alternative we had left was to go out and pick the fruit. I
> learned a lot about apple picking. Apples are really hard to get off until
> they are almost ripe. Then you can shake the tree to get them to fall
> out. But the bears start eating the apples months before, when they are
> still green. So we went out early to pick the apples and made an event
> of it. In fact, there was a whole public apple-picking event and bear-
> awareness day starting in 1998. It wasn't a perfect system, but at least
> by reducing the available apples, the bears were there for less time. It
> didn't matter that the bears were eating apples. It mattered that the
> apple trees were in Curry Village parking lot, where both food-condi-
> tioned and wild bears that came to feed on the apples were now [sur-
> rounded by cars] and a stone's throw from open trash cans.

Along with the slow development and installation of food-storage
facilities and dealing with orchards, there was a third challenge; the seemingly endless number of people who needed to be educated and convinced about proper food storage. It included every visitor, every employee, every concessionaire, and every contractor. It included people who
had been in the area for decades and people who were new to the park. It
included people who spoke a myriad of languages and had a variety of
ideas about how to vacation in a national park. It included day-users,

campers, and backpackers. It included small groups who used camp-grounds for quiet visits in nature. And it included very large groups who increasingly used campgrounds for more raucous family reunions and holiday celebrations. That meant making an enormous and continuous educational push and a continual rethinking about how to present the information. The increase in larger groups also forced park management to rethink traditional campground designs and develop more group sites with enough trash cans and lockers to accommodate more people.

A fourth reason problems continued to be so bad was that until the late 1980s, relocation was still frequently being used. In Yosemite, the prac-tice continued well into the 2000s, long after it had been abandoned in Sequoia-Kings. Kate McCurdy remembers those years:

> I spent a lot of time catching and moving bears. I got to see every corner of the boundary of the park where the roads go right up to the edge, and it was really fun for me because I got to meet all these people in other districts. But I knew that for every gallon of gas we put in the truck, it was less money in the budget for my winter salary. Once in a while, the superintendent would request that we helicopter families of bears far into the backcountry. So we would put all this time and effort into catching a whole family and then they would have to lay me off for a month during the winter to pay for it. Meanwhile, the bears would be back in like two weeks.

Kate continues:

> I think everyone agreed translocation was ineffective, but it bought you a couple of extra days to make a decision. There was also always the hope that you would let the bear go at the boundary and never hear from it again. A lot of bears would be hit by cars coming back or just get beaten up by other bears and come back with wounds all over their faces from fighting. Translocation was such a lame method of dealing with problems.

A fifth reason things were still so bad was that there were already dozens of extremely food-conditioned and habituated bears that were increasingly sophisticated at getting food. The more sophisticated the parks got with their bear-proofing, the bolder the bears became and the closer the bears came to humans to get their food. The reality was, until food storage was more complete, if these bears were killed others would quickly come in and take over their niche. Since it was easier to deal with a known bear, when food storage wasn't in place, the relief from killing a "nuisance" bear was generally very short-lived.

A sixth reason things weren't improving faster was the seemingly endless barrage of administrative hurdles the staff had to clear to get anything done. These hurdles, documented in stacks of memos requesting waivers from them, included things like a requirement bear technicians work Monday through Friday, eight o'clock to half past four, when problems mostly occurred at night during weekends and the institution of daily mileage limitations that precluded bear techs from driving all the way to problem campgrounds. Dealing with these types of administrative hurdles, while being expected to continue using politically popular, yet ineffective methods like relocation, all while continually being short on funding, made an already frantic job exhausting and demoralizing. The field staff desperately needed help, and the message was not getting through to management.

Exhausted, Steve Thompson, the biologist at Yosemite, finally decided to take a stand:

> When I first came to the park, I blindly accepted the policies of bear management which were very much focused on Yosemite Valley. The policy was that any bear seen in the valley would be caught and relocated. So we kept bears on this relocation treadmill. Eventually I came to the conclusion that I was spending all of my time catching and relocating bears without working on the long-term solutions to the problems. That is when I started spending more time in the office and letting some of the nighttime situation go. There was a lot of property damage, but in the meantime, we got bear-proof lockers in the campgrounds and better dumpsters with latch systems.

Kate McCurdy remembers it as a really painful time, but one that had to happen:

> I really hand it to people like Steve Thompson, who refused to do bear management the way it was always done. And he was trained by somebody who was trained by somebody who was trained by somebody to just catch and kill and move bears and not deal with the reasons they were so problematic. He was the one who refused to keep doing that. That meant that instead of reacting to everything, my job was to document. In the morning I would spend hours driving through

the valley and documenting how many break-ins there were, how many bears were in dumpsters, how many trash cans were overflowing, and how many bears were cruising around Curry Village. It was so unpleasant. I would start my shift at five in the morning to call in the license plates of cars that bears had been broken into and leave information for them on their windshields because I couldn't handle people's reactions when I had to actually talk to them. If I got a late start, people would have already discovered their car and would be pissed off. So my shifts started just as the bears' shifts ended.

Soon, however, Steve and Kate were back to burning the candle at both ends—doing daytime work and then going out at night to do bear management because bears were causing damage and people expected them to do "something" to control "their" bears. And there were a lot of bears. Looking back, Steve Thompson admitted that "[p]utting less emphasis on managing bears backfired on us a little bit because we accumulated a lot of conditioned and habituated bears."

Kate remembers her big "lesson-learned" when she changed her hours. When she worked in the early morning hours and through the day, Kate regularly saw one or two bears and assumed they were the ones doing most of the damage. Then, in the mid-1990s, when she started working late in the night, she realized it was multiple bears that changed guard all night long that were doing the damage:

> It turned out there were twenty-five to thirty habituated bears. The problem was so much worse than we had thought. Poor Steve, he would spend all day in the office writing grants to get funding for bear boxes and bear-proof trash cans and then go out at night and deal with bears that were being destructive. That guy was blond when I started working for him and gray by the time I left. I, however, was in my midtwenties and thought chasing bears was the funnest thing I'd ever done in my life.

Finally, in 1998, there were record numbers of incidents, car break-ins, and property damage in Yosemite, including more than fifteen hundred (1,584) reported incidents and $650,000 in property damage, with 90 percent of the damage from bears breaking into vehicles. The experts noticed. In February 1998, in a letter to Steve Thompson, bear expert Steve Herrero wrote:

The number of bear incidents that occurred during 1997 place *Yosemite in a class by itself in terms of bear problems* [emphasis added]. No other jurisdiction that I know of has anything comparable. The extent of problems is clearly not meeting your goal of protecting wildlife (bears), nor is it keeping bears in a natural state. The elevated risk of serious injury to a person means that with this number of incidents someone will eventually be seriously injured. It is time you be given the budget to do the job.

# IV

## Meanwhile, in the Backcountry

# 18

# HISTORIC BACKCOUNTRY USE AND INCIDENTS

The front country is only half the story, much less on a geographic scale, but it is the area of the parks most people visit. The front country is where the roads, hotels, campgrounds, visitor centers, and shorter trails are found. The larger portion of the parks is much less accessible, requiring at least a long day-hike, if not a several-day hike, to access. It is referred to as the backcountry, much of which is congressionally designated wilderness in these parks. The backcountry spans from the low-elevation oak woodlands to the midlevel coniferous forests to the high mountain meadows that are surrounded by steep rocky expanses and glacially carved lakes. It is truly a backpacker's paradise, luring in thousands of hikers every year. The lower and middle elevations of the backcountry are also a bear's paradise with plentiful natural foods, but the same is not true of the 65 percent of the backcountry in the Sierra parks (75 percent of Sequoia-Kings and 53 percent of Yosemite) that lies above eight thousand feet. There, the natural vegetation is too sparse to sustain bears. That gap, however, was filled with the arrival of large numbers of people with their food. Historic records, including those from Grinnel and Storer in 1924, show that bears rarely visited places over eight thousand feet. Bears didn't move into those higher elevations until human food became available there, and when it did, they came *en masse*.

The earliest known history of human use in the backcountry actually dates back thousands of years, to when Native Americans from both the east and west sides of the Sierra traveled to the high passes to trade. Their use however, was relatively minimal and didn't provide much of a food lure to black bears. Then, about 150 years ago, the backcountry was used to graze thousands of domestic sheep. During that period, grizzly bears came up to the high meadows to prey on sheep. They were often killed as a result. The shepherds created backcountry dumps for their waste, but since there weren't many shepherds, they didn't provide much of a food lure to black bears. After the parks were established, sheep and cattle grazing ended, but travel into the backcountry by stock increased. Some people spent the whole summer there. Since it is brutally hot in California's Central Valley in July and August, families would take their stock and head up into the mountains for the summer. Other groups of people came for shorter stays of one to several weeks to hike and relax. Starting in 1901, the largest of these groups at the time were stock-supported Sierra Club groups of up to several hundred people. There were also park work crews using the backcountry. Like the shepherds, all of these user groups dug backcountry dumps. Although there weren't a lot of these groups, the groups were large and carried a lot of food, so after several decades of use, the campsites became increasingly formalized and the dumps provided an increasingly predictable food source to bears.

Retired Yosemite ranger and wilderness manager Ronald Mackie describes the campsites from a park perspective:

> In the 1930s, the primary backcountry users were local ranching families and stock parties. They would stay in the backcountry campsites for ten to fourteen days. They came with their own horses and mules or would be brought in by concessions pack stations that would put them up near a meadow. The food was all Dinty Moore beef stew and Spam and stuff that would keep. There wasn't much freeze-dried food at the time, except I think we had Lipton soup. One of the primary jobs of the trail crew and the wilderness rangers at the time was to dig garbage dumps and privy holes at these primary campsites in the backcountry. We dug garbage pits for the backcountry users until about 1965. People threw everything in the pits.

Leroy Maloy, longtime packer, describes the camps from a user's perspective:

> I started packing in 1948 with my dad. We would start packing June fifteenth and quit the middle of November. We took a minimum of forty-two head of stock. It would be my dad, five packers, a cook, and

a flunkie. The shortest trip would be two weeks. The longest would be a month. We would resupply every two weeks. You would go in and never come out. It was beautiful. We had complete kitchens with the canvas back chairs and roll-up tables. The cook and us packers would serve, and usually it would be fourteen to seventeen people. The dunnage guy would have five mules just for dunnage, and he would go to each of their places and rake out a spot, roll out their beds, and blow up their mattresses. Every other day we would have a layover so the party could fish and the stock could rest and we would shoe the horses.

Most of the time, bears stayed out of the stock camps; most bears are afraid of mules and weren't yet habituated to humans. But as garbage started accumulating in pits, bears started coming in after the groups left to forage on the leftovers. This was just as true at stock-supported family camps as it was at Sierra Club camps. In Yosemite, there was also a network of rustic backcountry accommodations called the "High Sierra Camps," that were built and opened in 1916, closed in 1917, and then reopened for good in 1923. The trash from these camps also accumulated in designated pits. According to Ron Mackie, although you wouldn't see as many bears a night at the backcountry pits as you would at the front country pits, you would still see up to three bears a night at the High Sierra Camp pits.

In the early days, the worst backcountry problems occurred where human use overlapped with good bear habitat, especially where coniferous areas were interspersed with lush meadows. During this period, when humans and bears had conflicts, there was little sympathy for "marauding" bears, as is illustrated by this memory from old-timer Earl McKee:

I used to pack for old Ben Loverin. He would remind you of Grumpy of the Seven Dwarfs. He had an old woolly beard and lived on venison year-round. He used dynamite for everything and had dynamite boxes for chairs. Loverin could build trail, man, was he good, but he hated bear. One bit 'im one time back there when the bear was trying to get his meat. They had this guy by the name of Frank Randy who worked on Ben's crew. He was from the Ozarks, and he fit right in because he never took a bath. Their clothes would almost rot off—they were mountain guys. Anyway, a bear came into camp and got some of Ben's deer meat. He was mad and took a few ribs and tied them around about a quarter of a stick of dynamite and ran his detonator—a thousand feet of detonator—down the mountain to his camp. He sat up all night until he heard the cans rattle, and then he cranked the detonator. Old Frank Randy said, "You ought to have seen the look on that bear's face." And of course he couldn't see his face because he didn't have one anymore.

It wasn't just the concessions packers that didn't tolerate bears; the NPS crews didn't tolerate them either. Bill DeCarteret provides some insight:

> In the late '50s and '60s, we would put all our food in one basic area and cover it up with canvas. We would always lay some pots and pans on it, and then one of us would sleep right close by. The idea was that if the bears pulled anything open, it rattled the pots and pans and scared the bear or woke up the packer to scare off the bear. Usually, bears were easy to scare off, you would just throw rocks or something at them and they would be gone. Sometimes, well, this is probably not something that you want to keep written down, but part of the reason there wasn't so much problem early on was that the trail crews basically weren't resupplied real often and they did eat venison during the summer and if an old sow gave them problems, they just put some dynamite caps in a piece of venison and did away with the bear and then the bear didn't teach eight or ten cubs how to do this. I'm sure it happened at least once a summer.

Guarding kept most bears from getting food, but it was an imperfect method. Again, Earl McKee has a story:

> One time packing out of Cedar Grove we had a party the first night and drank a bunch of whiskey and everybody went to bed really zonked out. I was sleeping next to the pack because there was some meat and I was going to keep the bear out of it. Well, I woke up the next morning and there were meat wrappers all around my bed. The bear had come in during the night and ate a bunch of our apples and all our meat, and I didn't wake up.

Until the 1960s, most backcountry users were on stock. There were hikers, but they usually had their gear packed in on horses and mules and used backcountry dumps just like everyone else. There were a few diehard individuals who carried everything into the backcountry themselves on wooden-framed packs, but they were few and far between. Self-supported backpacking didn't take off until the late 1960s and early 1970s, and when it did, it was for two main reasons. First, with the space pro-gram, the technology evolved to develop lightweight packs and freeze-dried foods. Second, going into nature became part of the youth move-ment.

Almost overnight, backcountry use changed from a few backpackers and a lot of stock parties to a lot of backpackers and a few stock parties. The new popularity of backpacking added to a lack of wilderness-use quotas caused the number of backpackers to peak in the mid-1970s. In Sequoia, use went from an earlier average of six thousand people a year in the early 1960s to forty-eight thousand in 1978. Lifetime packer Bill DeCarteret remembers the backpackers heading down the trail one right after another. In the 1980s, it tapered off, and now continues to average between fifteen thousand and twenty thousand people a year. In Yosemi-te, in the 1970s, high user numbers meant there would be as many as four hundred to five hundred people in some of the more popular backcountry camps *at one time.*

At first, backcountry use was intensive and impacting and there were no regulations, but by the late 1960s, there was a move to modernize it and reduce impacts. It became no longer accepted practice to burn and bury trash in the backcountry. Backpackers started packing out their trash, and the parks started sending crews into the backcountry to dig up and eliminate the old dumps. Ken Hulick remembers being part of the NPS effort:

> In 1962, at Scaffold Meadow, part of my job was to haul trash out of the backcountry. They had probably been dumping trash into those lateral moraines for a hundred years. I ended up digging down into those things and pulling up cans and some glass and then flying it out by helicopter or packing it out by mule. But even as we cleaned them up, some pack trains were still burying their trash. It was a tough transition.

The NPS wasn't alone in hauling out the trash. Local packers also donated stock support to carry out hundreds of bags of trash.

Meanwhile, more and more bears had gotten food and trash from more and more users. As these bears became increasingly food-conditioned, they increasingly used areas of the backcountry where natural food was scarce and backpackers were plentiful. When the dumps were eliminated from the backcountry, the bears turned directly to the backcountry users for food, just as they had turned to front country users when the dumps were eliminated there. Stock parties used lash ropes to hang their panniers from trees where they were protected by mules left in a picket line, but backpackers had no real way to protect their food from bears, and the bears were having a field day. Once a rarity, by the late 1960s, (reported) backcountry incidents numbered in the hundreds, including a handful of injuries, every year. Since backpackers had the least protection for their food, they received the bulk of the incidents. These incidents weren't occurring all over, but mostly in places where high human use intersected with good bear habitat. Incidents in remote areas were generally still a rare occurrence. In some remote areas, it was still possible to protect unattended food in something as flimsy as a cardboard box—even for days at a time. In these remote places, backpackers only hung their food when they camped in areas with a known bear problem.

By the 1970s, that had changed. Backpacking was so prevalent that bears could live in areas of the backcountry that only had limited natural foods by supplementing them with fatty foods from backpackers. Bears were even reported on the top of Mount Whitney. Backcountry bear incidents went from being a rare and local occurrence to being wide-spread and common. Additionally, the increased emphasis on food storage in the front country spurred some front country bears to move into the backcountry where it was easier to get human food, thus making a bad backcountry situation worse.

At this point, everyone was losing patience, and some people even began to solve the problem in their own way, regardless of the legality. Retired naturalist and historian Bill Tweed remembers hiking in the back-country in the southern Sierra and finding "a dead bear with a bullet hole in its skull just laying by the trailside."

Regardless of all this frustration, the impetus for change didn't come from a desire to deal with the human-bear problem, it came from the need to deal with the growing sewage problem, another side effect of allowing too much unregulated, concentrating camping. Jan van Wagtendonk, Yo-semite's first wilderness manager explains:

> I got here in 1972, and they decided my first task was to go to all the High Sierra Camps to look at the sewage problems and find a solution. So in 1973, I went everyplace, and it was indeed a circus up there. It was pure chaos in Little Yosemite Valley [LYV], and there was toilet paper everywhere. It was the dawn of ecology and I was a scientist

with a PhD, so they tasked me with writing the first wilderness management plan. It set use limits on each area that we started to enforce in 1974. The park then went after food availability by installing cables and other devices. By the way, here we are thirty-four years later, still having sewage problems.

# 19

# BEGINNING OF THE COUNTERBALANCE

The need to store food properly was imperative, but how was it to be done? In the mid-1970s, solutions among backcountry user groups varied, partly due to their varying needs and partly due to their varying levels of tolerance for, and experience with, bears. On one end of the spectrum were the NPS trail crews who lived in the backcountry all summer. As retired Sequoia trails supervisor Steve Moffit explains, these crews had a lot of motivation to not lose their food:

> Trail crews are careful for three reasons. One, they know there are ramifications to a bear getting their food. If they screwed up and a bear got something, even a bottle of soap, the bears would become relentless and come in 24/7. Two, they would be looked upon as stupid. Three, the biggest reason is that the crew wants the food even more than the bear does. The crew knows they are only going to get a resupply every so often.

Since trail crews were motivated, experienced, and physically fit, they developed and perfected methods to protect their food. According to Moffit, guarding was one major method:

> Somebody always slept in the middle of the kitchen. We would pile up shovels and tools and tarp the food, and put the pots and pans over that. Bears didn't get our food with a few minor exceptions but the whole thing was still a pain in the rear. In big camps with bear problems, we always had to leave someone in the camp during the day unless mules were there to keep the bears away.

John "Jaybo" Sturdevant, longtime Sequoia trail worker, adds, "Sometimes when we had a really persistent problem bear that came in all night long, the person on bear watch would just sleep in their sneakers." As the bears became more sophisticated at obtaining food, the trail crews got more sophisticated at storing food, eventually using cables with pulley systems plus a human guard. Jaybo recalls life before and after the cables:

> Before the cables, we could only hang our fresh stuff and had to leave the cans out. One time when we were working at Hamilton, there were only three of us, so we couldn't leave anyone in the camp to guard the kitchen while we worked. One day, a bear came in, trashed our kitchen, and poked a hole in every one of our beers. Once we got cables, it was so much better because we would finally store everything.

On the other end of the spectrum were the backpackers. They generally had fewer people in their groups, less experience, less local knowledge, and less energy than the trail crews. Although some backpackers would sleep with their food to guard it, or simply leave it out, the method of choice during the 1960s and early 1970s was the basic food hang. Laurel Boyers, retired Yosemite wilderness manager, explains:

> In the mid '70s, backpackers were hanging their food in the tree and tying it off. It was throw your line over the tree, tie off one food sack, and then reach up as high as you can to tie it off on the trunk. And the bears, in their wonderful way, being smarter than we are, figured it out right away. Since part of our time was spent patrolling in the field, we actually saw bears walk into camps, find food hanging from a tree, and follow the line. You could watch their eyes follow the line to where it was tied off. They would immediately go to where it was tied off, and being good climbers, they had no problem getting it. So that didn't work well for long. We really underestimated the bears.

Luckily, in addition to packers, trail crews, and backpackers, rangers were also in the backcountry. Like trail crews, some rangers lived in the backcountry all summer, but unlike trail crews, part of their job was to protect the resources while making sure visitors could safely recreate. George Durkee, one of Yosemite's first rangers to be specifically assigned to the backcountry, first came to the park as a visitor:

My first trip in Yosemite was in 1967. We did the classic climb Half Dome and camp in Little Yosemite Valley thing, and I think they recommended hanging your food, but we were absolutely clueless. We must have hung the food, but just off the branch where it was absolutely no challenge to a bear. So in the night, I hear this rustling and ripping of canvas and I finally sat up and said, "All right, bear, I've had enough," and chased it off.

George started working as a backcountry ranger in Little Yosemite Valley (LYV) in 1973. When he first got to LYV, there was no protection from bears except an old steel outhouse the park put in for the rangers to store their food. George estimates there were probably eight bears routinely in LYV that summer, and LYV is less than one square mile. This was the year before limits were set on numbers of hikers, so they were getting up to five hundred hikers a night. George recalls:

The baby boomers were all getting out and hiking and having a great time. They were climbing Half Dome. They were hiking the Muir Trail. They were doing all kinds of fun stuff. But the Muir Trail hikers would get to LYV, hang their food off a tree limb, and lose all their food. Four weeks worth of food would be lost at once. I would guess that 60 percent of campers lost their food. And the bears, of course, were impossible to scare off. The park was recommending that you bang pots and pans together, and that hadn't worked in years. But it looks good on paper. I guess you've got to do something.

George continues:

My second year, Mead Hargis was assigned to LYV and Tina [Vojta] was there too. Mead is one of those incredible dynamic needs-a-project kind of guys. He is an incredibly hard worker who is skilled and good with his hands, which I am not. I have a lot of brilliant ideas. So we were a good combination. Mead and I had a routine. We would go around and talk to every single camper about bears and say you've gotta hang your food. There were no regulations, but in those days, you made your own regulations. We would tell them that it's got to be ten feet away from the tree trunk. Sometimes we would try to confuse bears with a fake line to the tree trunk and a real line to a tree farther away. But you know, it just didn't work. Bears are incredibly bright.

At the time, an old telephone line went up to Vogelsang High Sierra Camp. It was just a single strand, bare metal phone line, and the telephone company still had rolls of wire they stashed up there to repair the line. Since Durkee and Hargis thought the problem was with the branches, they grabbed a roll and strung the line between two trees. This allowed people to use the line for hanging, thus eliminating the need to throw a line over a branch, but there was still the problem of tying the whole thing off to the trunk of a tree, and with everyone using the same wire, everything got tangled together. George describes the mess:

> At first, the problem was that all the bags got tangled up. You'd have bags tied up that are probably still up there. Then bears figured out they just had to yank on the line forever until the cord finally cut through. So we decided we needed thicker rope. In those days, Ross Rice, procurer of anything, was our supervisor, and Ross got into the act and got us materials. So we got cable, but the cable would sag in the center and then everything would migrate to the center and get all tangled up. So we got tools and tightened it until the trees started bending and would twang. We thought that was pretty good, but the weak point was obviously where the whole thing was tied off.

So for a while they experimented with other ideas. George remembers experimenting with an electric fence:

> It may have been Ross's idea. We put an electric fence in the middle of the campground, and it was like six by six, and you could just see the bears going around and around the fence at night. We put one around the ranger station too, and that one worked pretty well because we maintained it and even hauled water up from the creek so the grounding would be better. But I remember one night, a bear just kamikazeed the fence. He just ran into it, grabbed a pack, and ran off back into the woods. That is another thing about this whole bear thing. The bears would never carry anything more than three hundred feet, but people didn't know the routine and some would say, "The hell with it, I'm never going to camp again in my life," and they would just leave it. And we ended up with quite a collection of ripped up packs, some valuable stuff, and a ton of garbage.

That experiment is a perfect illustration of why electric fences work in some wetter regions of the country so much better than in the dry Sierra.

So Durkee and Hargis went back to cables, but now added a pulley system similar to what the trail crews used for their own food. With so many people using these systems, there were many challenges and again, the system had its own evolution. Durkee explains:

> After using the cheap little phone lines and cheap little pulleys, Ross Rice stepped in and said, "No, we've got to use big honking pulleys and better cable." And unless they had constant attention, the cables would cut through the pulleys or the little pins would give way and then the whole cable would come down. In any event, they would eventually fail—catastrophically, as they say—which would cheer the bears to no end because suddenly there is this huge pile of food and nobody to chase them off. So we took quarter- and half-inch eyebolts and screwed them into the trees and added them to the system so if the pulley failed, the eyebolt would hold the cable. But then with all the weight, the eyebolts were cutting through too. In the meantime, the bears would still wank on the cable until all the stuff migrated to where they could reach it. We put swedges on the cables to limit how far the food bags could slide, but the bears still got them.

George continues:

> And there was another problem with the weight of the cables; it would take three people to pull it up. Then every night, a camper would come in late. You'd tell them they had to hang their food, and with 300 pounds of food already up there, you'd have to wake up three or four people just to help this poor guy do it. Then they'd lower the 300 pounds of food to attach the new guy's food and suddenly they'd get yanked up into the tree by the cable. There were simply weaknesses in everything we did, and since the pulleys weren't working, we said, "OK, no moving parts. We can't spend our lives maintaining cables." And there could very well have been the same experiments going on in Yellowstone or the Great Smokies, but we had absolutely no communication with them. I think we heard that someone in the Great Smokies was experimenting with poles or something, but we had no idea what that meant.

At that point, they started to experiment with counterbalancing two food bags over a cable or branch to eliminate the tie-off rope. They considered how high the food sacks had to be and how far from the trunk, and then they worked on ways to get them high enough up and far enough out. The basic method was to throw one bag over and use the rope to tie on a second bag. A stick would then be used to push the second bag up and use it to counterbalance the first bag. To get the whole thing high enough, the rangers even put out Lodgepole stumps out to give backpackers a few more feet. George remembers:

> I fashioned a stick with a hooked wire on the end with tape while Mead was gone for a few days. The idea was to reach up high and grab the stuff sack and pull it down. Then Mead came back and did a better hook, but then people started stealing the sticks and burning them. So we got metal sticks and metal wire to hook the bag and push it up or pull it down. So bears started getting less food, but less was relative; they still got about 30 percent. And you know, all of this was just staying one half step ahead of the bears. This was our existence. You know, we didn't have a television up there, so we would just watch people hang their food. Then we would spend the rest of our time doing all sorts of search and rescue and even making arrests for people stealing stuff.

Once hanging food with a counterbalance was perfected to the extent possible, the challenge was getting people to do it and to do it correctly. Apparently, the counterbalance was much more difficult than it appeared because when Jeff Keay and Brad Cella went into the backcountry to check how well visitors were storing their food in 1980, they found that while 92 percent of visitors believed they had it right, only 3 percent actually did. In fact, in Bob Roney's movie about bears, there is a scene with two hikers doing a perfect counterbalance. The truth is; they had to fake the scene for the movie. Since Bob was the only one who could do the perfect throw, he had to splice his throw in to look like the hiker did it.

That comes as no surprise to Mark Fincher, current wilderness specialist, and former wilderness ranger, at Yosemite. He remembers spending an enormous percentage of his time on bear education and then much of the rest of his time checking and fixing food hangs and staying up all night chasing bears from crowded campsites.

Laurel Boyers even remembers the challenge of educating her own staff:

> I remember one time when we were training all our new wilderness permit staff. We were in Yosemite Valley and we used this giant oak

to demonstrate, and I had the person in charge of the Valley permit operation demonstrate a good counterbalance. First, he threw the line up and had a couple of misfires with the rock. He didn't have the line tied off properly so the rock came off the line. Then he finally got the rock tied on and did the standard thing where you throw the line over the branch and it swings back and almost hits you in the head. Finally, he got the line up there and grabbed the line and pulled it to test the strength of the branch and the whole branch almost broke and creamed him. It was a good lesson on how complicated it was.

Laurel also remembers educating the public:

The counterbalance was certainly successful for a while. Then bears figured out that if they held onto a tree with one arm and leaned really far out, they could snag the food. So our management response was to get more specific about how we told people to counterbalance. We put food hangs in the parking lots, but in retrospect, I can see how difficult it was for people to really do it properly. And of course, at first the regulation was written wrong. It said the bag had to be four feet from the trunk instead of six. But I remember trying to show people the dimensions graphically because they didn't really understand how far out they had to counterbalance. We even paid someone a decent amount of money to make a drawing of a proper hang for us, but he made it with this giant person in the picture, so then we had to put a big disclaimer on it, saying, "Not to scale." That confused people even more because, of course they didn't read it, they just looked at the picture and saw a giant person with a food sack a couple of feet over his head.

Steve Thompson, NPS, explained:

The greatest shortcoming of this method was the complexity of doing it right. The instructions were ridiculously complex: find a branch at least twelve feet off the ground that is at least four inches in diameter where it joins the tree and no more than two inches in diameter where the food is to be hung. Divide your food into bags of approximately the same weight. Tie a line to a rock and throw the rock over the small-diameter portion of the limb, at least six feet from the trunk, and lower the rock. Tie one of the two food bags to the line as high as possible. Pull this bag all the way up to the limb, and then tie the second food bag to the other end of the line as high as possible. Leave a small loop of line attached to this or the first bag to enable retrieval. Shove the second bag at least twelve feet high, which should lower the first bag to approximately the same height. To retrieve your food, find a stick to snag the loop on one of the food bags and pull it down. This, of course, assumes that the two hanging lines have not become entangled. It was no wonder that proper use of this method was so low and so many people lost their food.

It is no surprise that people never got the hang of it. Even worse, there were several injuries when people would throw the rock over the branch and it would come back and hit them in the head. Jan van Wagtendonk still laughs guiltily at one memory:

> One time I was on a horse trip way up in the north part of the park and these two guys were sort of hobbling along the trail and once guy's whole mouth was mashed in and I asked what happened and he said he threw the rock over and the rock came back and hit him right in the mouth and broke some teeth.

# 20

# END OF THE COUNTERBALANCE

In the end, the counterbalance was short-lived. In addition to problems with user error and injuries, in the late 1980s, the bears figured it out. One method bears used was to send cubs out on the small limbs to get the food. A second method was to climb up and simply chew off the limb. A third method was to bounce on the limb or shake the limb until one of the bags came down. A fourth method was for a bear to jump from above and grab a sack on the way down. Bears that did this were referred to as "kamikaze bears." Retired newspaperman Gene Rose was one backpacker who actually witnessed it:

> I saw a young cub up at Vidette Meadow climb a tree, go out on a branch, flip off a food bag, and then fall twenty-five to thirty feet. You know, I think it would kill a human, and the bear just scampered off.

Even Jan Van Wagtendonk was eventually foiled by kamikaze bears in the backcountry:

> In Lyell Canyon, I hung my garbage on the last day of a trip and a bear went up the tree and dropped down on the bag and went *whomph* as it crashed to the ground and took off.

The problem with bears taking food hangs ranged from bears getting food rewards to people losing food and from trash being left in the backcountry to trees losing limbs or being girdled with ropes. When Bob

Meadows was a backcountry ranger and researcher in Sequoia-Kings, he saw a lot of this damage:

> I was always finding remnants. Ropes in trees and freeze-dried bags on the periphery of the camp. It was hard to quantify because unless hikers were willing to admit they had lost food, it never got reported firsthand.

Starting in about 1979, the parks tried installing cables to improve counterbalancing. The idea was that taut cables installed at appropriate heights near popular campgrounds would make hung food more secure from bears, while making hanging easier for visitors. Joe Abrel, one ranger involved with installing the cables, clarifies where they went up:

> Not in the real backcountry, but in places like Little Yosemite Valley. Of course, they didn't work.

The problems were the same as those experienced by Durkee and Hargis when they experimented with telephone cables. David Karplus, Kings Canyon trails foreman and longtime backcountry trail worker, elaborates:

> The main trail crew entertainment was watching backpackers try to throw rocks with ropes across the cables. They would be there for like twenty minutes tying a rope onto a pinecone or a stick, and would then tangle the whole thing when they tried to throw it. We could watch them endlessly and then finally, one of us would go over, tie one end of a rope to a stick and the other end to a rock, throw it over, and say, "Here's your rope." Then we would go back to our camp to applause from the rest of the crew. The cables would become collections of confetti from ropes that backpackers couldn't get back down. Every now and again we would climb up and pull the old ropes down. The cables didn't get loose—they just got clogged. Sometimes people would throw a rock over and the rope would wrap around and around and they wouldn't be able to get it off, so they'd just cut it and leave it there and start again.

In 1986, cables were deemed both unsightly and a maintenance problem and, to the relief of many, removal began. Jan van Wagtendonk was one. "I wasn't a fan of cables because they were like a magnet for [less experienced] people and there was so much resource impact to the trees."

After the cables, in the mid-1980s, the parks experimented with food-hanging poles, internally referred to as "Christmas trees." According to an article in the September/October 1982 issue of *Grist*, a publication put out jointly by the NPS and National Recreation and Parks Association (no longer in circulation), they were invented in Grand Teton National Park by Ranger Walter Dabney. George Durkee describes their use in Sequoia-Kings:

> They were big steel poles with hooks, stabilized with tiny little cement bases. They were chained to a small steel pole with a hook at the end. The idea was for campers to use the little pole with the hook to lift their food bags onto the hooks at the top of the big pole where the bears couldn't reach them. Well you know, food sacks are pretty heavy, so people would end up getting carried around by the weight while trying to get the food bags over the hooks. It was more entertainment for us, but it seemed to me that it wasn't working. The bears would shake the poles until one sack dropped to within their reach and the bases would crack because they were too small.

Mark Fincher of Yosemite explains that the bears would also get food bags off the poles by pushing on them until they got a harmonic going and the poles would sway back and forth enough for the bags to fly off. He also remembers how some bears would use the tiny metal sleeve that joined the two pole sections together as a step to climb the pole and get the bags. And then there were poles that just got old and rusty and would break when the bears pushed on them.

In 1987, most bear poles were taken down. They weren't keeping food from bears, there were problems with flying squirrels jumping onto them from nearby trees and nibbling into the bags, and many had been damaged by snow. The parks were desperate for a solution. In 1987 and 1988, Yosemite even tried putting a naturalist in the backcountry to educate the public about food storage and bears. Once it was clear that the only options available were simply delay tactics for bears, Laurel Boyers recalls how the parks started encouraging visitors to haze off the bears before they could obtain the food:

In 1987, we got to the point where we said, "Look, hanging is a delay tactic only. You are going to have to be aggressive." The old deal of banging pots and pans didn't work. Instead, you had to get up and throw rocks. We were lucky we never had problems with visitors hurting each other when they got up at night to throw rocks around, but we did have the very sad incident of a Boy Scout troop that stoned a [yearling] bear to death at Sunrise Creek in Yosemite. I remember seeing little piles of rocks all around. It was kind of a new backcountry characteristic of little rock piles where people slept. But even with rocks, the bears only went as far as you chased them. They stopped when you stopped and then they would wait until you got back into your sleeping bag to return to camp and find someone that was less trouble.

Trail crews, who had more time, energy, and determination than almost anyone else in the backcountry, tried more aggressive hazing methods. Due to their persistence, intensity, and intricate knowledge of the backcountry, these crews did have some success, but as David Karplus describes, the effort was extensive and the success was limited:

In 1986, I was on Fritz's crew, and we were camped in Kings Canyon at Sphinx, a heavily bear-infested area. When we got there, Fritz tried storing his food on top of a twelve-foot-high boulder with vertical sides and a flat top right behind camp. Of course the bear climbed the rock and got the food. So we left someone in camp every day and had people sleep in camp every night to keep the bears out of our stuff. But the bear would come into camp with her cub, we would chase her off, shouting and throwing rocks and she would run about fifty yards and then sit down and see if we were going to keep coming. We would keep coming and she would amble off about another fifty yards and sit down again. Then we would send like eight people out to get ahead of her and ambush her. One night, the crew chased her and her cub for almost a mile, and then treed them for a long time. The next time she came into camp, she came without her cub, and we treed her all night. After that, we saw her tearing into logs and thought, "Success." But the next day, I was in camp with a broken toe, and there she was. So I carefully watched the fire where we were making beef jerky in the coals while stirring dinner. I would stir the food and look up and watch for the bear, and stir the food and look up and watch for the bear, and stir the food and look up and—there is the bear eating the food from the fire. So by the end of it, the bear was more cautious and would leave rapidly when we chased her, but she was still getting our food. It was a big trauma for the bear and a lot of work for us.

That effort however, demonstrates a huge attitude shift among trail crew members toward bears. In the early days when bears raided camps, many trail crew leaders held an old-school mentality where they had less patience for the bears, and like some of the commercial packers, occasionally used their explosives to get rid of them. Jim Snyder is very clear on this point and describes the basic method that was referred to earlier:

> They used the DuPont sandwich. The DuPont sandwich is when you take two sticks of dynamite wrapped in bacon and you put that out with a cap in it and then you sit and wait for a bear to try and take a bite and blow its head off.

# 21

# SNEAKING LOCKERS INTO
# THE BACKCOUNTRY

Finally, someone had the idea of putting lockers in the backcountry. Yosemite tried it first. In 1978, Yosemite put eleven lockers into Little Yosemite Valley, which led to a big decrease in bear activity. George Durkee liked them:

> When we got the boxes into LYV, I said, "Aha, this is it." They were worried the lockers were interfering with wilderness, and I said, "What? You've got these truly ugly big silver poles versus a nicely painted brown box that you can stick behind a tree."

But LYV, even though in designated wilderness, isn't like the rest of the backcountry. It is a high-use area within a few miles of a trailhead. And when the lockers were installed there, they were installed reluctantly, with the intention of removing them when a good alternative was available. In more remote areas, Yosemite managers struggled with questions about cost, transport, and appropriateness. Managers struggled with the question of appropriateness because these were not only in the backcountry, they were in legally designated wilderness. According to the Wilderness Act of 1964, "legislated wilderness is an area where the earth and its community of life are untrammeled or unchanged by man. . . ."

The debate therefore was whether adding lockers was a negative impact (earth—meaning the land: trammeled by the addition of a structure, changed due to shift in human use patterns) or a positive impact (community of life—meaning bears: untrammeled and unchanged by no longer getting human food, no longer becoming food conditioned or habituated and not needing to be hazed or killed). The answers weren't clear, and no one wanted to make a decision. But in Sequoia-Kings, where the same questions were being debated, lockers suddenly appeared in 1987. How? Paul Fodor, a supervisory ranger in Sequoia at the time, explains:

> I didn't have a budget for boxes, so I didn't buy any boxes, I stole them. My partner and I found out where the front country districts stored their backup boxes, and we would go through the park and steal them. Then we would take them to the heliport at Ash Mountain and store them by the corrals camouflaged under tarps. I gave a list of locations where backcountry rangers told me they had problems to the helitack crew and the pilot. Then I told them that whenever they had a medivac from any of those locations, to sling a box on their way in and leave it there when they picked up the injured person. Most went in over a two-year period, but some never did get in since we didn't always have a medivac in the right location.

And then more lockers appeared. Historian Bill Tweed remembers:

> Serendipity intervened. It is almost completely forgotten now, but in the early '80s, Dorst Campground was being rebuilt, so it was closed during construction. Meanwhile, it had already been fully stocked with the original bear boxes and during construction, they were just sitting in piles. When the rangers said, "The backcountry is out of control, we need lockers," the chief ranger, who was Doug Morris, said, "Do it."

And according to Tweed, that is exactly what the rangers did:

> There was no environmental compliance and no analysis. They simply loaded up truckloads of lockers, drove them to Red Fir, and flew them into the backcountry, and to this day you will find boxes out there with big campground numbers still painted on them.

In the end, the lockers were scattered all over the Sequoia backcountry, and in a few places in the Kings Canyon backcountry. In Yosemite, the process remained more restrained. Yosemite wilderness managers decided it would be okay to put lockers in high-use areas with designated campgrounds and bathrooms, including all the High Sierra Camps, but kept them out of all undeveloped areas.

The effect, particularly in Sequoia-Kings, was striking. As Harold Werner explains, "Bears go the route of least resistance, so after we saturated the backcountry with lockers, the bear problem began to plummet." Jaybo adds, "It was amazing, the lockers went in and the bear problems in the popular camps were instantly gone. It blew all our minds."

In addition to limiting the bears' access to human food, the locker installations also fundamentally changed the way people camped in the backcountry—they clustered around the lockers. Jerry Torres observed the change:

> Before lockers, people were camped everywhere. Any place that looked like a nice camp spot became one. Once they started to locate those bear boxes, we saw a reduction in bear incidents and problems, but also in these satellite campsites.

The trail crews also started using lockers, or similar-type boxes, in the late 1980s. The concept of lockers, however, wasn't completely new to trail crews. For years, many crews used old powder boxes, once used to store explosives, to store limited amounts of food. With the larger boxes, however, the crews could secure their camps and no longer had to leave a lookout in camp during the day or in the kitchen at night.

Did lockers really eliminate the problem in the backcountry? Partly. Lockers kept many naïve bears from getting human food and becoming nuisances, but lockers did not cause already food-conditioned bears to change their ways. Instead, those bears just moved to even higher elevations where, especially in Sequoia, problems suddenly appeared at ten, eleven, and even twelve thousand feet.

# 22

# BACKCOUNTRY RESEARCH AND THE INVENTION OF THE CANISTER

Meanwhile, as Berkeley's research was beginning in the front country, research was also beginning in the backcountry, albeit unintentionally. Dave Graber recalls how it came about:

> Starting in 1976, a fellow by the name of Bruce Hastings, a student of Barrie Gilbert's from Utah State, was going to study hiker-grizzly interactions in Yellowstone. But in 1977, during their very first summer of research, a mother bear and her cubs popped out of nowhere and attacked professor Gilbert. It took half his face off and nearly killed him except that Bruce grabbed his radio and called for help. So after Dr. Gilbert was repaired with over a thousand stitches, he sent Bruce to do parallel work in Yosemite using black bears because he figured that was safer.

Bruce was interested in why black bears were so reluctant to injure people and wanted to learn to predict how bears would behave toward humans in various situations. To do this, he went into the backcountry and observed sequences of behavior between humans and bears and documented how each reacted to the other.

He found that in the bulk of situations, both humans and bears were most likely to respond to each other with neutral behavior and were least likely to respond with aggression. Of nine hundred and ninety-two observed interactions, Hastings only documented aggression 6 percent of the time. When the bear showed aggression, it was most often in June, with younger visitors, at closer distances, and during short interactions. He found that if you exhibited more aggressive behavior than the bear, the bear was likely to give up, as long as the bear hadn't yet gotten the food or didn't have a cub. Bears showed less fear of humans after obtaining food and starting to eat it, and humans were less aggressive toward bears after the bears started to eat. Bruce also observed that the bears rarely went after water bottles with caps off or backpacks with open zippers and flaps. He found that ranger patrols, advanced food storage techniques, and smaller groups were all correlated with reduced incidents.

Bruce also tried to understand the extent of the backcountry human-bear problem. At the time, there was no information on whether the number of reported human-bear interactions reflected the actual number of interactions. In 1979, he conducted a visitor survey and found that almost half of 1,647 parties had experienced bear activity in the last twenty-four hours: 41 percent directly interacted with the bears, and 12 percent of those sustained damage. He found that to get people to report incidents, reporting procedures had to be convenient. In the late 1970s, Jeff Keay and Jan van Wagtendonk also researched backcountry incident reporting and found that incidents also increased linearly with backpacker density, that only 8 to 11 percent of incidents were reported, and that reporting increased as the value of lost items increased.

Bruce also conducted some hazing experiments in the backcountry in 1978 and 1979, which he describes:

> We diluted ammonium hydroxide, put it in balloons, put balloons in stuff sacks and day packs, and put them all over the place at a campsite to see if we could get bears to leave the campsite alone. Sure enough, it didn't take long for them to quit using that campsite, but they just increased their activities at the other campsites. So it was interesting, but didn't really do any good in the bigger picture.

Bruce decided the best technique to get a bear out of a campsite was to run toward it while throwing objects at it, although bear aggression increased when humans got closer. He also found that yelling, clapping, and banging pots got bears to move, and that's when it became encouraged, as was referred to earlier. Unfortunately, although bears would move, it was soon clear they were just moving on to another group of people.

The research by Professor Barrie Gilbert and his student, Bruce Hastings, resulted in several management recommendations, including encouraging visitors to scare bears away aggressively *before* bears got food, reducing group sizes, increasing education, and leaving backpacks unzipped in camp to allow bears to investigate without damaging packs. But something even more revolutionary than these recommendations came out of their work because, just like everyone else, Bruce kept losing his food to bears and needing to hike out for more. The difference, in his case, was that Barrie took an interest.

Barrie got the idea for protecting Bruce's food after watching a video of African lions trying to break open ostrich eggs. As Barrie remembers:

> I thought about the size of the jaws, the strength of the teeth, and the muscles of the lions. If they couldn't get into an egg because the curved surface kept them from being able to get a purchase on it and use that strength, then there was something there that might be useful for black bears. So the obvious thing was to convert an egg-shaped object into a simple cylinder, and the closest and strongest item we had around were irrigation pipes. In 1978, I think we used six-inch or eight-inch PVC irrigation pipes. I got a couple of those and we cut them up.

Barrie then handed the pipes and the project off to Bruce, whose idea was to hold the whole thing together with a long threaded bolt that ran inside the length of the container. Caps were glued to the container on one end and held down with a wing nut and a washer on the other end. Although it wasn't easy for a human to open, Bruce first wanted to see if it could keep the bears out. If it could, he could perfect it later. Bruce's two assistants, Richard Strong and Jeff Picton, did most of the work to build the canisters. To test them, they drilled holes through the ends so that food could drip out and attract bears, and then put them out in the field. They had 98 percent success with the first trial run and decided to pursue the idea further.

From the one container that cracked, Bruce and Barrie learned how strong the containers had to be to resist a bear. From the amount of time the bear spent licking that crack, they learned how persistent bears can be for a tiny reward. They also quickly learned about the disadvantage of a cylindrical shape. That is, when bears bat them around, they roll downhill. Yosemite wildlife biologist Jeff Keay worked with Bruce on the field portion of the project. Looking back, Bruce remembers working hard and having a lot of fun:

> Jeff and I hit it off as friends right away. All the researchers and managers and biologists got along so well. It was a really wonderful time. I've never worked as hard as I did there. Jeff was one of two or three people who advised me to get a patent on it, and I did look into it, but they said it was going to cost a minimum of $1,200, and as a starving graduate student, I had about $12.

Bruce left Yosemite in 1980, and Jeff and his wildlife technician, the late Brad Cella, took over the project. They, too, worked hard and had a good time. Jeff recalls:

> Brad Cella, Doug Erskine, and I got really excited and went to Doug's garage and started fabricating all kinds of things with all different kinds of latches. The lids were sunk into the container and spring-loaded airline fasteners were added to close the container. Then we would take them to the zoo in Merced and Fresno and into the park and see if bears could get into them.

From those tests, they determined that eight inches was the perfect diameter: too large for a bear to get a tooth-hold, but small enough to fit into a pack. At this point, management started taking an interest. According to Dick Martin, a former Yosemite ranger:

> Brad Cella brought this long narrow container to a management team meeting in the ranger division, and there were about ten of us in the room. I remember sitting there and thinking, "Son of a bitch, why didn't we think of that fifty years ago? This is the answer."

The three biologists kept improving the model, but then Doug and Brad went to work in Alaska and Jeff went to the University of Idaho to begin a PhD. Meanwhile, in 1981, Sequoia-Kings biologists Harold Werner and Mike Coffey started to get involved with the container's design, construction, and field testing. When the Yosemite crew left, the Sequoia crew took over, and soon brought in Richard Garcia, a local machinist they found by flipping through the local phone book. Richard Garcia, owner of Garcia Machine Company, laughs about the beginning of his involvement:

In the spring of 1981, I had a couple of rangers show up at my door—fellows by the name of Mike Coffey and Harold Werner—and these guys were getting pretty fed up with having to destroy bears that were becoming nuisance bears in the backcountry. They had the concept that a container that would be light enough for a backpacker to put their food in, but strong enough that a bear couldn't get into it, might change the habits of bears in the backcountry. They had some ideas about what these containers should look like and even had sketches. They proposed a cylindrical container, approximately eight inches in diameter, made of PVC. They had the idea of gluing a cap to one end and holding a cap to the other end with some type of latching system. They thought the latch should have spring-loaded push buttons that came from the inside of the cylinder and engaged holes in the cap. That was their concept. They asked me to build some prototypes for them, which I did.

Harold and Mike then took the prototype containers to the Fresno Zoo, where the zookeepers tested them with grizzly bears. Harold would then bring back the pieces, and they would start all over again. After several failures, Richard investigated other types of plastics and decided to try eight-inch ABS. ABS was harder and stronger than PVC, though also more expensive. ABS was the plastic used for municipal sewer lines, a coincidence that, as Richard notes with a laugh, "they never advertised with the public." Richard built prototype containers with ABS using the same design he had used with PVC, except for the addition of a ring around the cylinder to reinforce the cap. The container was now stronger, but since the caps came down over the top of the cylinder, when a bear pressed on the side of the container, the bear could deform the shape enough to create a gap. Once the gap was large enough for a tooth or nail, the bear would rip the container open. Richard said, "You would swear someone had taken a screwdriver or something and wedged it in there and ripped it apart." So he switched to lids that fit inside the container, reinforced with metal ringers that acted as a bulkhead structure when a bear pressed on the side. Those containers were three and a half pounds.

As the idea of the container circulated through the bear management world, managers and biologists at other parks became interested. Terry Hostra at Redwood and John Dalle-Molle at Denali both became involved with the design, and in 1982, Denali even joined Sequoia in field-testing the containers, now commonly called canisters. With Denali, interest in the canister was a wilderness protection issue as much as a bear protection issue. In 1972, after a highway was built in Alaska between Anchorage and Fairbanks and a public shuttle system began transporting people into the park, visitation skyrocketed. Backcountry use went from a few hundred user-nights before the highway was built to more than ten thousand. Retired Denali Wilderness Manager Joe Van Horne explains how the increase in backcountry use relates to food storage:

> There are no trail systems and no designated camps up here; hiking is cross-country with an emphasis on dispersed use. Since most areas are above tree line, in the 1970s, people were just setting out their food a hundred yards from their tents in the open tundra. It was amazingly crazy since the issue here is primarily with grizzlies. In 1972, when visitation went through the roof, bears got pretty good at figuring out that humans were a good source of food, and some bears were relocated or destroyed. Around 1980, some people in management said, "We'll just put some cables and lockers in the backcountry and all will be good." John Dalle-Molle and I—and [John] was really the guiding light on this—said, "That is completely contradictory to the wilderness spirit of this place. That would form trails and concentrate use and cause impacts." We were in a tough spot with management wanting to deal with the problem by changing our whole wilderness philosophy. So John somehow got turned on to the fact that Harold was working on these [canisters]. Around 1982, we got about a dozen of the early models from Harold and [Richard] Garcia and started handing them out to backpackers. Then we'd send them feedback. For example, what grizzlies do is stand on them with their front feet and rock up and down. They could get the lids off, so we recommended that three latches would work better. In fact, we retrofitted all of ours until Garcia added a third latch in 1986. At that time, we had these two guys, Brad Schultz and Doug Waring, whose job was to catch bears that were raiding camps and experiment with hazing. They did most of the container tests.

While field tests were underway, zoo testing continued. In 1982, testing moved to the San Francisco Zoo, where Anthony Colonesse worked. He recalls the first tests:

> In 1982, I was the bear keeper at the San Francisco Zoo when some park people came down with a vendor, a fellow who had developed these bear-proof containers. That was the first time I had heard about

this idea, and I agreed to test them. So one morning, I fasted the bears, and when the zoo opened, the two fellows from the park and the manufacturer showed up with the containers. We put a can of tuna in each of two containers, poured some of the juice on the outside, and them put them in the grotto. Then I released three young Kodiak bears into the exhibit. They immediately found the containers, sniffed them, licked all the juice off the outside, and started batting them around with their paws and muzzles. The grotto had a fourteen-foot-deep moat, and eventually, the containers ended up in the moat. The bears followed them down and started attacking them more aggressively. They leaned on them, pinned them down with both paws, and whacked them as hard as they could. Then they started using both paws to pick them up and throw them down on the cement. What I found most surprising was when they started picking up the containers and continually throwing them against these two-inch iron pipes that are in the exhibit to drain water. The containers would bounce off the pipes and the bears would go to them and use their paws to shepherd them back, pick them up, and throw them at the pipe again. It may have been the resounding ring it made that stimulated them to do it, but after about twenty-five minutes of failing to open the containers, this behavior extinguished, and they left them to go and look at us. At that point, we terminated the trial. We examined the containers, and they were scarred up to a certain extent but they hadn't been breached in any way. So the rangers and the manufacturer were very pleased with the trial and were high-fiving and laughing.

Anthony continues:

That kind of annoyed me, so I suggested that we have the papa bear in the next exhibit try it. The papa bear was one of the largest Kodiak bears I've ever seen. After his death, we weighed him in at 1,640 pounds. They said, "Sure, bring it on." So we did the same thing with one container in his grotto. I let him out, and he investigated it for a couple of minutes. He licked it and sniffed it and then pinned it down and hit it a few times. Bears are left-handed, so he held it with his right paw and tried hitting it with his left paw, but he didn't get any results and it skidded away. So he found it and pinned it down with both his front paws and dropped his muzzle on it. I heard a loud crack, and suddenly, the park people and the manufacturer were no longer laughing. I got the container and it had a small hole in it, about three centimeters long and one centimeter wide, from which the bear had

extracted all the tuna. The next year, they came back with a revised
container with a recessed lid, and it stood up to all the bears. After that,
I understood that they did repeated trials at the Fresno Zoo, probably
trying to lighten them for backpackers. That was the last I heard of that
project.

Around this time, Harold finally received funding from both the NPS
regional office and the Sequoia Natural History Association for fabrication and testing of other designs with the intention of making them free to
the public. P.K. Machine in Emeryville, California, made rectangular and
cylindrical prototypes from PVC and various other materials, including
Lexan. They tried all sorts of permutations to make the container strong,
light, easy-to-use, and without any sharp edges. They wanted to develop a
container that an animal could not get a hold of with its mouth but that a
human could open with a coin or knife. Volunteers, including singer Toni
Tennille, tested these containers in Sequoia and Denali in 1984.

Many of these models were clever but flimsy by today's standards.
David Karplus recalls one particular day of testing:

> Nina Weisman was a trailhead ranger in 1986 when they were trying
> out all sorts of bear canisters. One day, Nina was about to go on
> backcountry patrol and she pulled out this bear canister that her super-
> visor had given her. I said, "There is no way in the world that thing is
> going to keep bears out of your food. A bear will swat it once and
> smash it against the rocks." And she was like, "No, no, no, a bear can't
> break it. It is bear-proof." And I said, "I can break it right now.
> Wouldn't you rather I broke it now than have a bear break it in the
> backcountry and get all your food?" And she said, "No, no, no, don't
> break it." And we went back and forth like this for a while until she
> finally said, "OK, OK, OK. You can try to break it, but don't try really
> hard." So I took it, and from about six inches up, I dropped it against a
> rock. It only had a fleece and few other things in it and weighed
> nothing, but it cracked right through the plexiglass.

At the end of the four years of canister testing (1982–1985) in Sequoia
and Denali, John Dalle-Molle and others wrote up the results. They found
that 91 percent of those asked to try the canisters agreed to try, but more
often in Denali (95.4 percent) than in Sequoia (59 percent), for a total of
1,618 parties testing them for 5,535 user-nights. Of those who used them,
over 90 percent said they would use them again. Most liked the cylindri-

cal shape, and the only model that consistently stood up to the zoo and field-tests was Richard Garcia's ABS model. Richard used this input to further refine his canister. Managers at Denali liked Richard's design so much that they quickly made its use mandatory. Joe Van Horn explains how it was done:

> At Denali, we just made them required in the Superintendent's Compendium. It was back when you could just do those things. It was a partial requirement in 1984 and an almost park-wide requirement by '87. We had almost four hundred canisters and didn't charge for their use. Up until '84, we had about twenty or more human-grizzly incidents a year. Once we had the canisters in circulation, we had maybe one a year. But the thing I want to stress is why we brought them to Denali. We looked at our wilderness situation and thought about what was unique that we were trying to protect, rather than looking at what other places were doing. We had a lot of pressure to change our whole backcountry system. I think that would have been a real tragedy. The canister helped us find a better solution and maintain the character of the wilderness. Looking back on my career, I think my involvement in that program was one of the best things I did.

Meanwhile, Harold and Mike continued to pursue a public design. Harold recalls:

> While [Richard] Garcia was making early canisters, we were still trying to make our own canister so we could keep it public. We solicited competitive bids and in 1986, Netra Plastics won the contract. We sent them our ideas to design a lighter but equally strong canister.

Netra's canister design had an octagonal shape with alternative curvy and flat sides, a domed top and bottom, and the use of a spongy gasket to put tension on the lid. To reduce the weight to three pounds and one ounce, it was going to be made of foamed polycarbonate and was going to be less expensive than Richard's model. Netra also created a set of tests including a compression test, puncture test, abrasion resistance test, and a drop test to evaluate the sturdiness of the canisters in relation to the Garcia canisters, since the latter were known to stand up to most bears.

But Netra never moved forward to create a prototype. The NPS requested the blueprints to get a prototype made, but in 1987, Netra decided to retain title on the design and pursue a patent, effectively shutting out the NPS. Netra obtained the patent in 1989 and was finally ready to begin production with an expected cost of twenty-five dollars each, but was then bought out by Hayward Industries, which gained ownership of the patent. Hayward Industries ultimately decided not to pursue production, but also didn't want to give the NPS the patent for free, since it originally cost $22,000. Instead, Hayward offered to sell the patent to the NPS for $10,000.

The NPS, however, didn't want to buy the patent outright until a prototype had been built and tested. Although the NPS had the right to require Hayward to grant a "responsible applicant" a license to use the patent and build a prototype, and the NPS regional office had the money to pay the applicant, it didn't happen. Mark McCall, the canister's designer, only believed one company could build an adequate prototype, but the NPS powers-that-be wouldn't allow Harold Werner to execute a sole-source (noncompetitive) contract with that company. So Harold returned the money to the regional office and a prototype was never built or tested. Harold recalls, "At that point, we walked away. We were so frustrated." Although the design is now in the public domain (Patent #4,801,039, *Animal Proof Container*), it has still never been built or tested.

Two other designs were also created around that time, with input from park biologists; one by Jack Shea, the director of recreational services at Berkshire Community College in Pittsfield, Massachusetts, and the other by an engineering professor at the University of Idaho. Since no one had the money to produce prototypes and test them, both designs sat in limbo. Meanwhile, since Netra did produce testing standards, Richard started using them to continually improve his product. One improvement came as a direct result of the impact test. If the containers were hit at a certain angle, the lid popped off, so he added a third latch in 1986. This third latch also took care of Denali's one major concern about grizzlies being able to push on the sides of the canisters and pop the lids off.

At first, selling canisters brought little profit to Richard, especially because he didn't mold the canisters; he made them individually. But interest in canisters increased steadily, and Richard got faster at making them. In 1987, Harold Werner conducted a market survey and found that there were seven hundred thousand potential users. According to Harold:

> In the meantime, Rich Garcia got more and more requests and started a
> business on the side. I put him in for a national award, but it never got

approved. If it weren't for him, there probably wouldn't be canisters. It wasn't until he started having success that other people got interested.

Many people have that same sentiment about Harold. Even after all the frustration, he just laughs and says, "I learned a lot about plastics." Joe Van Horne can't give Harold enough credit for his persistence in making bear-proof canisters happen. "Harold had a whole lot of bureaucracy and crap to deal with," Joe says, "and he stuck with it."

Joe and Harold both note that development of the canisters was very much a joint effort between Yosemite, Sequoia-Kings, Redwood, and Denali, and it all started with Barrie Gilbert daydreaming while he was watching television. Or did it?

Christina Vojta, who spent the summer in Little Yosemite Valley with Mead Hargis and George Durkee when they were figuring out the counterbalance, recalls:

> When I was up in LYV with Mead and George, we discussed the possibility of getting away from hanging by using metal canisters and hiding them in bushes overnight. When the weight problem reared its head, we abandoned the idea, but I personally used it several times during solo backpack trips on my days off. You know those matching sets of flour and sugar containers that people used to have in their kitchens? I'd use the sugar canister for short trips and the flour canister for longer trips. I put everything potentially smelly in them and tucked them under a bush at least one hundred feet from my tent each night. I never lost a thing.

Christina knows, however, the real reason bears didn't bother with her canisters was because they were getting so much food elsewhere.

As for Richard, he just kept improving his product. He explains:

> I used a lathe to cut the weight down to three pounds. Then I developed molds and built a prototype. Harold took them to the zoo, and they passed. In 1992, they were in stores like REI. Finally, in 1997, we came out with a completely molded model. It was made with better ABS plastic and only weighed two pounds and eleven ounces. We could probably make a smaller container for black bears, but we want all of our canisters to stand up to grizzly bears in Alaska. If any of your products start failing, the whole company's reputation goes down the

drain. Plus, if you start having failures, the bears become motivated to keep trying to get them open.

As bear-proof canisters were being perfected, stock users started to experiment with bear-proof panniers (bags slung over the animals to carry supplies). As with backpackers getting used to canisters, it took stock users some time to warm up to the idea of using bear-proof panniers. For stock users, the main sticking points were cost, habit, and concerns about comfort for the animals. Once pannier designs came in that cost less and fit the animals better, many packers become convinced to use them and even found they were more convenient than trying to hang or guard food. Bill DeCarteret, a lifelong packer who designed one of the more popular models, explains why he liked them:

> When you are sitting around the campfire and everything is all tied up in a tree and then somebody wants a cookie, you have to take everything down to get this cookie. With the box, you can just go over and get it.

Due to the need for employees stationed in the backcountry to store large quantities of food over long periods of time, other devices were also invented, such as retrofitted barrels, which are still used at some backcountry ranger stations. It should be no surprise that they have their own issues. Rob Pilewski, backcountry ranger in Sequoia-Kings, recalls:

> In 1996 at Crabtree, a group of people didn't close the barrel lid right, and the bear got food. A few days later, I heard shouts coming from the campground and went to investigate. There was a solo female backpacker upset because a bear trying to get into the barrel was rolling that barrel toward her. The bear then proceeded to steamroll this fifty-gallon barrel through her camp and to flatten her tent.

# V

# The "Final" Push

# 23

# FUNDING—TWO DIFFERENT STYLES

**M**eanwhile, in 1998, incidents were skyrocketing, even breaking new records in the Yosemite front country, with over fifteen hundred incidents recorded, over $650,000 in property damage, seven human injuries, and three bears killed. Yosemite biologist Steve Thompson finally had enough:

> Finally in 1998, I got desperate and was ready to commit career suicide. I had spent a lot of time and money putting the infrastructure in place, meaning the lockers and dumpsters, but we were still having record property damage because people were still leaving food in their cars and bears were breaking into them. So we had an aggressive sow with three cubs. The cubs were born that winter, but already weighed over one hundred pounds each. All three cubs were bluff-charging people. So we got approval to euthanize the whole family, which was a really tough thing for my staff and me to do. I said, as long as we have to do this, we are going to make a difference. There just happened to be a reporter in the park from the *Washington Post*, so I invited him to document us euthanizing the sow and cubs.

Kate McCurdy remembers what happened next:

> We would pick up the guy every day at seven in the morning and it took a couple of days for us to track the family down, but he stuck with us and wrote a really great article called "Three bears, too clever to live?" that appeared on the front page of the *Washington Post*, and the park got a ton of letters from people who were upset.

The article had some great quotes, like, "There is a reason bears performed at the circus." But the heart of the article came in the last two paragraphs:

> At first, [Miney's heart] beat strong and measured, but as the poison moved through Miney's system, the rhythm quickened, became irregular, faster, then slowed, grew faint and finally could not be felt. And the bear began to jerk and twitch. This took another few minutes. In a gesture old and unconscious, McCurdy held the bear's paw for a moment. She stood up, exhaled deeply, and said, "Okay, let's do the cubs." ... After two hours, all three were dead and loaded into the bed of one of the trucks. The biologists drove the bears to a hidden place and rolled them onto the ground, where they will become food for other bears, ravens, coyotes and grubs, problem animals no more.

At that point, Scott Gediman, Yosemite's public information officer, remembers the media snowballing:

> Bears certainly attract media attention. As the primary park spokesman, I've conducted literally hundreds, if not thousands, or interviews about bears. Going into 1998, we just got more and more media coverage. It went from local to national to international. At times, there were hundreds of stories at once. Things got really interesting.

So once again, there was enormous public pressure to change the way things were done. The problem was that the parks didn't have the funding to make the needed changes; that could only come from Congress. Luckily, in the midst of all the controversy, a visitor came to Yosemite during the summer of 1998 to vacation with his wife. His name was Philip Schiliro, and in 1998, he was the chief of staff to Congressman Henry Waxman. Phil Schiliro describes how he got involved:

> During the summer, my wife and I took a personal vacation to Yosemite. When I go on vacation in national parks, I like to stop in with the rangers and the superintendent and find out if there are any issues that would be helpful to know about. In Congress, we dealt with a lot of different kinds of issues in parks and sometimes you can get a feel of things talking with people in the parks directly rather than just reading briefing papers and going through formal channels. So we did that in Yosemite. We didn't have a scheduled meeting. We just stopped in,

and people were able to see us, and in the course of that, I heard a fair amount about the bear problem in Yosemite.

Steve Thompson, NPS, was blunt with Phil, and told him:

We are at our wit's end.

Phil Schiliro's interest was piqued:

So I asked if my wife and I could go out at night with a ranger to see the problem, and that was arranged. Again, it was very informal, but we were told to meet Kate McCurdy at about eleven o'clock. My wife, Jody, who is a documentary filmmaker, came as well. That night, Kate, her dog, Logan, Jody, and I went around monitoring to see if there were any bear break-ins. At some time that night, we did come across a bear, and Kate and Logan gave chase to get it away from the cars. I joined the chase too, not knowing quite what would happen if we caught the bear. So through the night, I got a sense of the challenge the rangers were faced with, trying to protect people's property and trying not to kill bears, in a place where people didn't always take the right precautions to keep bears out of their car. I think we only went out that one night, and the rest of the time was basically spent doing what you do on vacation like going on hikes.

According to Kate McCurdy, Phil and Jody were a great help:

They checked cars for food, talked to campers, and even chased a bear out of a trash can. They stayed until like two in the morning while they were on vacation. They said, "People need to see this. It is incredible what the bear problem is."

When Phil Schiliro went back to Washington, he thought about it some more:

I was so impressed with their dedication. Sometimes people just complain about a problem but Steve and Kate knew what they were dealing with and had some ideas for the solution, and so I called them.

Steve Thompson, NPS, remembered that call:

He said, "How much would it cost to make the problem better: to solve it?" I said half a million dollars because I had just written a project statement that laid out the detail and costs and knew what we needed.

Phil Schiliro took the proposal seriously:

I reviewed the proposal, and it looked like it made sense and would be very cost-effective. Whatever we spent would be more than saved in property damage and killing bears, so Congressman Waxman agreed to make the request. At the time, Congressman Obey was the ranking democratic on the appropriations committee, so I talked to Congressman Obey and his staff about why it was important, and they agreed and worked with the Republicans on the committee. I think Congressman Regula was the relevant Republican subcommittee chair who agreed we could put the $500,000 into the appropriations bill. We didn't do it with any fanfare, but it made its way into the bill with the language that it should be used for the human-bear management program. There was a conference agreement on the bill, and once that passed, Yosemite had the money. That is exactly what happened. That's as exciting as it gets. Some people think there are always massive lobbies and convoluted processes in Washington. This time, the process was relatively simple.

Steve Thompson, NPS, confirmed it:

We had the funding in the park by 1999.

But funding was only half of the deal. When Phil called from Washington, he was calling for two reasons. One was that he wanted a proposal with a price tag to fix the problem. The second was that his wife wanted to make a documentary about the bear problem. So soon after, Jody Schiliro came with a film crew from National Geographic television. Then the television show *Dateline* somehow got involved at the last minute and wanted footage of a bear breaking into a car.

Kate McCurdy remembers that night well:

The *Dateline* crew wanted to bait a car and then wait for a bear to show up, but the park service wouldn't let them do it. Instead, they sent Steve, park videographer Kristin Ramsey, and me to get footage. I had worked there for years and had never actually seen a bear break into a car, mostly because I would always chase them away, and we were pissed and didn't want to do it. So we went out and when we pulled into Camp 4, there was a bear breaking into a car right in front of us. Although when we pulled up, the bear that broke the window ran off, another bear came along and went right into the car. So we hopped out, Kristin got the footage, we chased the bear away, and were in bed by ten o'clock. That is the footage of the bear with the loaf of bread in its mouth in the silver car that everyone uses.

Although Phil and Jody Schiliro's trip led to a funding appropriation for the bear program and an important and widely seen documentary, Philip Schiliro sums up his and his wife's role quite modestly:

It was one of our more productive vacations.

Kate McCurdy has no doubt about the importance of Phil and Jody's contributions:

Keeping the media spotlight on the problem plus having the money come finally allowed Yosemite to get its act together.

Sequoia and Kings Canyon were also having record incidents, but didn't have the bad fortune to have incident levels as high as Yosemite did in 1998 or the good fortune to have Phil Schiliro vacationing there that year. But even without a congressional earmark, there was still a need to bear-proof the parks, educate the public, and update the bear management program. Jill Oertley, the wildlife biologist for Sequoia-Kings, moved to Arizona in 1999 for a job with the U.S. Forest Service. So the parks had to find someone new who would join a tradition of biologists who wholeheartedly dedicated themselves to running the program. From June of 2000 through 2008, it was my turn to be that person. (Like those before me, my contribution came in the form of blood, sweat, tears, and lots of extra hours. I also spent a lot of time leveraging funds and bringing in grant money.)

The latter was hugely necessary because internal funding for bear management at Sequoia-Kings continued to be sparse and unpredictable. It appeared late in the spring after other projects fell apart and dollars could be redirected, making it incredibly difficult to plan and hire. Sequoia-Kings therefore continued to rely heavily on grants, fund-raisers, and organizations like the Student Conservation Association, which annually supported the program by covering housing, stipend, and insurance costs for one or two interns. Eventually, internal lobbying and efforts by people in leadership like John Austin to promote the program finally succeeded in getting park management to redirect $60,000 to the bear management program's base allocation. It was a far cry from Yosemite's half million, but greatly expanded the parks' ability to plan, hire, and implement a safe and effective program while making headway on bear-proofing.

So, in their own ways, both the Yosemite and Sequoia-Kings bear management programs found funding and personnel to move forward in completing the last big push to bear-proof the parks while continuing to update the bear management programs.

# 24

# MODERN COMMITTEES, RESEARCH, AND PLANS

As this final bear-proofing phase began, both Yosemite and Sequoia-Kings created or updated committees tasked with overseeing both the overall bear management programs and decisions about individually identified bears. Prior to the parks convening these committees, individual rangers often made decisions about bears without input from others. The committees included individuals from all major park divisions—from education, maintenance, interpretation, and law enforcement—to ensure a more holistic approach. Yosemite biologist Ryan Leahy notes: "It was finally clear to everyone that bear management needed to be more than just two wildlife technicians running around chasing bears."

In Sequoia-Kings, a Bear Advisory Team was established in 1998 to oversee the program as a whole; prior to that, a Bear Management Committee was established to oversee decisions about individual bears. In Yosemite, the Bear Council was established in 1998 to oversee both of those tasks. The committees were comprised of members from all divisions and park partners. Now more common, the idea of interdivisional work groups was still relatively innovative in 1998. Steve Thompson, NPS, was thrilled with the collaboration, saying, "Much of the value of the council is in its diversity. All divisions now recognize their role and take ownership of the human-bear management program."

In Yosemite, another role of the Bear Council was to distribute funds across divisions. Steve noted, "We could've kept all the money in wildlife and simply expanded the program, but we knew the problem crossed

all park divisions and partners, and would require the involvement of all
of us to work toward solutions."

Concurrent to the establishment of these committees, biologists increased partnership efforts with local businesses, adjacent land management agencies, and other national parks. Bill Stiver, a biologist from the
Great Smoky Mountains National Park, visited in 2002 to collaborate. In
the early days, when committee meetings convened, they were often quite
intense, especially when determining the fate of a particular bear. Luckily, as Jeffrey Trust, a longtime ranger-naturalist and the chair of Yosemite's Bear Council describes, they have lightened up considerably:

> At first, Bear Council meetings were pretty contentious. Annual bud-
> get and priority-setting meetings would last three days and there was
> arguing and yelling and crying. One time, someone stormed out of a
> meeting and slammed the door. Once we figured out what we were
> doing and how to be effective, things normalized. Eventually, instead
> of developing a program, we were just tinkering with it. Now the
> annual meetings go quickly and we generally get along.

In Yosemite, one of the more interesting tasks of the newly formed
Bear Council was to select and oversee a new round of research on bears.
Kate McCurdy remembers it starting:

> Until late in my stint in Yosemite there was no new research. Most
> management was based on gestalt, feelings about what was right and
> wrong. With all the money that came in, some of it had to be ear
> tagged for research.

So Yosemite invited the Hornocker Wildlife Institute (later known as
the Wildlife Conservation Society or WCS) to come and evaluate the
state of the bear program. Specifically, the WCS was tasked with finding
out how effective Yosemite had been at returning the bear population to a
naturally occurring one within Yosemite Valley and finding more effective ways to reduce human-bear conflict. Sean Matthews and Schuyler
Greenleaf considered the questions from a biological perspective, and
Brenda Lackey considered them from a social science perspective. Malia
Leithead was on the project as a field technician. Sean also worked as the
project director. He thought they made a good team who worked well
with the park's staff. Although the project was a lot of work, Sean re-

members the great times in the field much more than the long meetings and drudgery of office time:

> I miss the bears; they were always entertaining. We really got to know their personalities, and although we tried to remain objective, we still had favorites. At one point, we even did some twenty-four-hour monitoring, and although we'd get pretty tired in the middle of the night, it was great to track bears under a full moon near Yosemite Falls.

Sean's research focused on the bears' use of Yosemite Valley in relation to human use. He used radio collars to track bears' movements and activity patterns along with data on human-bear incidents to compare the habits of bears during the study (2001–2002) with those Graber documented in the 1970s. Sean found bears were involved in fewer incidents than during the 1970s, and when he trapped them, found they were smaller, meaning they were back to a more normal physical condition. That said, he also found plenty of food-conditioned and habituated bears in the valley that were exploiting human developments and shifting their activity patterns from day to night when foraging on human food. However, those bears only used the valley part of the time; they also foraged in the backcountry and in other undeveloped areas of the park. With his tracking data, Sean was also able to describe which parts of the developments were most vulnerable to bears. For example, large campgrounds with more edge tended to have more incidents, a finding that fits with observations of bears using the edges as safe zones from which to sneak in.

Schuyler's research focused on diet. She used scat analysis to compare the portion of bear diets composed of human food in 2001–2002 to the portion Dave Graber found in bear diets using the same methods in 1974–1978. She found that the average percentage of anthropogenic food in fecal volume had dropped from 21 to 6 percent. While bears consumed only one-third of the human food and trash that they consumed during Graber's research, it still constituted a significant portion of their diets. Schuyler also found that the bears' use of non-native apples from historic orchards remained a high proportion of their diet.

Meanwhile, Sean, Schuyler, and Malia found that once visitors were bombarded with signs and education and even roving rangers, 95 percent of them stored their food properly, but that the remaining 5 percent who didn't perpetuated the problem. To improve, the parks needed to know how to motivate this small remaining subset of visitors. Brenda Lackey's research filled that gap. Brenda evaluated the content, dissemination, and effectiveness of the park's messages to look for ways to reach that last 5 percent. She considered signage, personal contacts, and mailings. She found Yosemite had plenty of signs, but they were poorly written, inconsistent (there were over one hundred and fifty different versions), dull, old, and only contained food storage and safety information. She found people were more attracted to signs that looked new and contained information about bear biology and behavior. She also found that the appropriate messages weren't always being given at the appropriate time. For example, there is no reason to explain to visitors how a locker works when they are home, but it is helpful to know how to prepack and how much space they will have in a locker.

At the end of the study, the WCS group made recommendations on how the park could increase its effectiveness. They recommended the park continue its proactive work while updating signs, making food storage more convenient, considering edge when designing campgrounds, considering destroying bears that break into vehicles, and increasing the enforcement of regulations. Sean Matthews explains why making these changes is harder than it sounds:

> In Yosemite, the problem and the solution aren't just one step apart, you have to get through a maze of administration. The big concern for the park is that it doesn't want to discourage people from visiting. That is one reason they hesitate to issue tickets with fines. It would be interesting to interview people who have been fined to see if it influences their likelihood of returning to the park.

In 2006, the Bear Council approved funding for two other projects: Kate McCurdy, a former Yosemite wildlife biologist left the NPS to pursue graduate work at Humboldt State University and studied human attitudes toward bear canisters. John "Jack" Hopkins, a former Yosemite bear technician, left the NPS to pursue graduate work at Montana State University to work on a project on the distribution, genetic structure, and behavior of Yosemite's food-conditioned bears. He later expanded his work to investigate the status of Yosemite's human-bear management program using stable isotopes. A description of both Kate's and Jack's results appear later in the narrative.

Meanwhile, in Sequoia-Kings, there was no money to attract research, but research still found its way to the park. First, Elena Rizzo conducted a social science project in 1998 that, although smaller than Lackey's later work in Yosemite, provided similar recommendations. Rizzo found that signs needed to be consistent and look new, and she stressed the importance of placement. She said they needed to be placed either in locations where people need the information, such as on bear lockers, or in locations where visitors give their undivided attention to signs, such as in bathroom stalls or above sinks. She said the level of detail should depend on the area, and that campground signs should include advice on what to do if one encounters a bear. Rizzo said the list of items to store should be explicit and include things that are commonly missed, including baby wipes, canned food, personal care items, toothpaste, soap, medication, saline, and formula. Additional signs could include information like the number of recent break-ins and pictures of ripped-up cars but should only be used if they are kept current. Rizzo also said the information should be available in several languages, and since over 90 percent of visitors plan their trips in advance, there should be information available to them through AAA, AARP, and on the Internet. Perhaps most importantly, she found that "the data confirm resource management assumptions that one-on-one contact is the most effective means of communication, leading to the highest compliance rates," as Brenda Lackey later confirmed.

It was also in Sequoia-Kings where I conducted my own research on bears. (For me, it was a PhD at UC Davis.) My dissertation on black bear ecology was divided into three studies. The first was an evaluation of the effectiveness of the hazing program. The second was an observational study on behavioral transmission from sows to cubs. The third was an examination of how bear movements vary in relation to natural-food variability. As with Kate McCurdy and Jack Hopkin's research, a description of these studies comes later in the narrative.

# 25

# BEING PROACTIVE—TAKE II

As research results came in, managers used them to update protocols and human-bear management plans. They rewrote the Yosemite Plan in 2002 and added SOPs for specific activities such as hazing. In Sequoia-Kings, Jill Oertley tried to update the human-bear management plan in the late 1990s, but management put it on hold because it included direction on food storage in wilderness and the wilderness plan was on the verge of an update. To date, the Wilderness Stewardship Plan is almost complete, so an update of the human-bear management plan will likely soon follow. In the meantime, it is kept current through the addition of guiding protocols. What was more important during the post-appropriation years was the commitment from the parks to take aggressive, decisive actions to increase bear-proofing and proactive management of bears in the parks.

And the parks did take action. To illustrate the flurry of activity during those years, I am using the introduction to the 2001 Annual Bear Management Report for Sequoia-Kings:

> One bear cub was sent to a rehabilitation center in Idaho.... Bear management personnel installed 378 food storage lockers in Cedar Grove, contacted over 45,500 visitors, presented over 50 training sessions to employees and neighbors, issued over 1,600 food-storage violation notices, collected 268 bags of trash, and assisted with wildlife emergencies, peregrine falcon monitoring, and bird banding. They also assisted on 20 river patrols, 2 carry-outs, 3 SARs, multiple disabled vehicle incidents, the President's visit, and dispatched for the Morgensen SAR. In 2001, we introduced two new web pages dedicated to bear

information, developed and hung new signs throughout the parks and on dumpsters, implemented the new SIBBG canister testing policy. "Slow Down for Wildlife" signs were installed as a result of an interdivisional effort, and the Dusy Basin food storage restriction was implemented. A new emphasis was placed on safety with reflective uniforms for bear volunteers and their vehicles, twenty-two tailgate safety sessions, and increased training. . . .

Meanwhile, the parks finally found a locker design that really worked and obtained funds to install hundreds of them. It came about serendipitously because an employee of a metal fabrication company just happened to be camping in Kings Canyon when bears were active and lockers were inadequate. Steve Thompson, sales manager of Bearsaver (no relation to former Yosemite biologist Steve Thompson), explains how that led to his involvement:

> As an adult, I spent a lot of time camping with my family and friends and for years our favorite place was Cedar Grove in Kings Canyon. During that time, I was doing marketing and sales for a large sheet metal fabrication facility, and we were making things for aerospace and passenger trains and business was down. It was so fricking boring that I wasn't happy with my job and couldn't relax. So there were like twenty of us that went there for like five years. The food storage was ridiculous. They had these tiny little boxes that we called "toe-smashers" because unless you put a rock under the front door, it would come down and smash your toe. We hated them. And bears would be all over the campground and would run by with a pack of hotdogs and everybody would put their flashlights on them and run after them and it was fun but there was some underlying thing that was bothering us. One year we were there and there weren't many bears and the ranger said they had to kill them because they had gotten into too many people's food and my daughter started to cry. So I started to think, "Why don't we just make a box that is big enough to hold all the food?" It turns out that size is about thirty cubic feet.

Steve continues:

> So I went to see the biologist and said I know less than nothing about bears but I know there is a problem and we can help solve it. So I go back home and get my company to build this contraption and then run all the way back up to Sequoia, which isn't much fun because it is a

six-and-a-half-hour drive. I'm there for four minutes when Rachel [Mazur] says, "It's not going to work." So I take it all the way back, tweak it, and bring it back to the park two weeks later. Rachel says, "It's better, but it's still not going to work." So I said, "OK, teach me about bears so I can understand." And Rachel and Kate [McCurdy] came up with all kinds of criteria for us to use, based on the bears' anatomy. And then we started talking to more people and found that they were starved for a good solution. It required a lot of trial and error, but luckily, our company was flexible. We did have one competitor that was very nice, but they were inflexible about changing their product, and the customers weren't happy. Since we didn't have the money to do warranty work, we wanted a great product up front. That process took about eighteen months. Then we sold a bunch to Lassen National Park and Sequoia and Yosemite and Yellowstone and then customers started asking us about trash cans. So we evolved into waste and recycling. Then we even got into the residential market. Business is good. You would think there would be some saturation after all these years, but there are always new communities that are pushing into bear-occupied habitat.

The new locker design became available right as the parks had cumulatively received over a million dollars in grants and donated funds to buy and install them. Lockers were installed throughout Kings Canyon, in several campgrounds in Sequoia and Yosemite, and in random important places like the Curry Village tent cabins and many trailheads. Putting lockers at trailheads finally allowed backpackers to remove food from their cars while they were gone overnight.

In addition to providing a locker that worked, Bearsaver made headway on the installation process. Before that, parks either contracted or internally hired work crews to do the installations. It was time consuming and expensive. Steve Thompson of Bearsaver came up with a better way that was then used widely in Sequoia-Kings:

> I noticed that where concrete slabs were used, they were cracked down the middle and there were rodent holes under most of them, so the lockers get tweaked and the doors don't open right. In other cases, lockers were mounted on four concrete piers and those don't weigh enough to work well. Bears can tip them over. So we developed a pole-mount that the locker attaches to with U-bolts and then the four corners don't have to be mounted. I've seen bears push them around in a circle,

but not push them over. These poles are cheaper, easier, and cleaner than the slabs. We have put in about fifteen thousand boxes with that method.

There was also progress on making garbage less available to bears, but it wasn't due to huge advances in technology or brilliant administrative decisions as much as to heroic, yet unsustainable efforts, from the field staff of all divisions. The efforts were heroic because field employees spent untold hours fixing and cleaning dumpsters, designing fluorescent signs in multiple languages to put on them, and hauling truckloads of trash late into the night. The efforts were unsustainable because there was still too much trash, too much packaging, not enough pick-ups scheduled, and broken dumpsters. There were also heaps of cans and bottles set aside for recycling, all with just enough beer or soda residue to reward a curious bear.

Unfortunately, fixes like increasing capacity by replacing trash cans with dumpsters, adding more or larger dumpsters, enforcing use limits, changing garbage pick-up schedules, and increasing garbage pick-ups were, and continue to be, political and financial decisions that continue to increase in scale as visitors continue to bring more and more trash. The litter is so bad in Yosemite that every September, a volunteer clean-up event called "Facelift," started by an environmentally dedicated local climber named Ken Yager, keeps over fifteen hundred people busy every day for an entire week just picking up trash.

The importance of picking up trash to keeping wildlife wild cannot be overstated. An excellent example of a park grasping this reality occurred in the Great Smoky Mountains National Park (the Smokies), where problems with bears, particularly in picnic areas, rival those in the Sierran parks. In the 1960s, the Smokies had only a few hundred bears after years of heavy poaching, and no real management strategy beyond killing the bears and tossing them into the Gatlinburg dump. Then in the 1970s, the park staff retrofitted their picnic area trash cans with the mailbox top lids and started relocating bears they caught during the day. After poaching declined radically in the region, the bear population began to increase to what it is now, about fifteen hundred, and the visitor numbers increased to about nine million visitors each year. Nine million visitors produce an astounding amount of garbage, and a lot of it was being left in places like

Chimney's Picnic Area. According to Kim Delozier, who retired in 2010 as the park's longtime wildlife biologist:

> It got so bad that in the '80s, people were setting up lawn chairs and driving around in the back of pick-up trucks all around Chimney's Picnic Area to watch bears. It was an absolute guarantee you would see a bear, and it was an absolutely chaotic situation.

The situation got progressively worse until 1989 when there was an incident that changed the course of things. Kim explains:

> That year, I had only one person helping me, and we had to capture bears in ninety-eight instances. I was just sick of bears, sick of them. Then this lady came from Ohio who was attacked by a bear in Chimney's Picnic Area. The bear broke her scapula and put her in the hospital for ten days, but she lived. So I started to survey the picnic area during the day for bears. If a bear was there, we would catch it and move it. We did this every few weeks and let people watch us. Everyone was happy and thought this was the greatest thing until I went to the picnic area at night and found twelve different bears there at once—twelve. We hadn't fixed anything by moving those day-active bears. And it looked like a garbage dump. Garbage cans were overflowing, there was trash everywhere, and grills were torn up. People were using the round grills on the ground as trash cans. It turned out the maintenance guy was coming in every morning at seven o'clock and cleaning everything up, so by the time anyone showed up during the day, it was all clean and no one knew there was a problem. But there was a problem, and it was with our communication.

Kim started thinking about the situation and charted how the bears' behavior progressed from night-active to day-active. All the bears followed the same progression; they went from being sneaky at night in the least risky situation to being bold during the day in the riskiest situation. Exceptions included some yearlings, injured bears, and bears that came from outside the park. Kim realized he had only been catching bears that were already boldly entering risky situations during the day. The more critical time was at night, when wild bears were naively entering empty picnic areas to forage and just starting the progression toward being a food-conditioned bear. The nighttime availability of garbage had to end.

So the Smokies added extra garbage cans, put in elevated grills, and every night at dark, Kim took volunteers to Chimney's Picnic Area to clean everything up, a task eventually taken over by maintenance. Then, they would catch and mark the naïve bears, fit them with radio-collars, and release them into the same area. They found the naïve bears would remain in the area and forage on natural food and only came back into the campground if there was a natural food shortage. Kim concludes, "So our switch from working with the daytime bears that were the existing problem to working with the nighttime bears that were a developing problem was really a switch from a reactive to a proactive approach to managing the bears." The lesson is that making garbage unavailable to bears is essential for successful wildlife management; the presence of garbage in unattended areas is, simply put, a training ground for nuisance bears and other wildlife.

Meanwhile in the Sierran parks, additional headway on reducing trash was made due to coincidental facility removals. In 1997, a flood washed away several campgrounds in Yosemite, and while some will soon be rebuilt, they have been closed since the flood. Also in 1997, Sequoia began the removal of hundreds of buildings from the Giant Forest, including cabins and a restaurant. In the works for decades, the removal wasn't politically viable until the sewage system needed replacement and it couldn't be done without damaging the delicate roots of the sequoia trees for which the park was created to protect. The facilities were replaced with a new development called Wuksachi plus a few new parking lots and trails in the Giant Forest. Although the new developments are more condensed and considerably more bear-proof, they created other, albeit smaller and more controlled, problems. Jill Oertley describes the irony:

> Unfortunately, like the Giant Forest facilities, Wuksachi and the new parking lots were all built within good bear habitat. We had problems right away. Harold and I tried to get people excited about parking their cars outside the park and getting bussed in. We wanted a big parking garage that could be closed up like a big box. And we were dead serious.

In Yosemite in recent years, some tent cabins in Curry Village have been closed or relocated due to rockfall danger. In one respect, the closures are advantageous to the bear situation because the cabins were those at the edges of the development, adjacent to the talus (rock debris). When the WCS did their twenty-four-hour bear monitoring, they found bears commonly used this talus area as a movement corridor sometimes to access cabins at the edges of the developed area. Unfortunately, replacement cabins were built at the edge of the Curry Orchard, where bears congregate in late summer.

## MODERN EDUCATION AND LAW ENFORCEMENT

With functional food-storage facilities that could accommodate all visitors finally in place, efforts to educate the public about how to store food properly finally made sense. Expanded education and enforcement initiatives included Yosemite's installation of a "Save-A-Bear" Hotline in 1999, bear quizzes for visitors entering campgrounds, new exhibits, employee training packets in both parks, articles on bears in the parks' newspapers, new signs, a new movie created by Steve Bumgardner called *Bears of Sequoia*, and my own new children's book, *If You Were a Bear*, published by the Sequoia Natural History Association. Ranger-naturalists gave thousands of bear talks and campground rangers instructed all overnight visitors in food storage and bear safety.

There was also a new emphasis, especially in Yosemite, to develop coherent messaging campaigns. According to Yosemite's Scott Gediman:

> We had a campaign called "Don't be Bear Careless," and later one called "Keep Yosemite Bears Wild." During those campaigns, you couldn't turn around without seeing the message on something. We were very vigorous at first to get the message established. It was very successful: even highlighted in *PR Week*, the industry's main publication.

Regionally, nonprofit groups such as the Bear League in Lake Tahoe appeared and worked tirelessly to educate communities about bears and proper food storage. On a national level, the U.S. Senate even declared May as "Be Bear Aware and Wildlife Stewardship Month" in 2008. The idea was to arm everyone with correct information while channeling their interest and enthusiasm into action and involvement. To do this with millions of visitors a year, many of whom need to hear the message several times in several ways before they take action was, and still is, a daunting and exhausting task, but it needs to happen. Caitlin Lee-Roney explains:

> Otherwise people forget their head when they see a bear because they are really excited. We need to take that excitement and teach them. There is a difference between understanding and "getting it."

Most importantly, there was a renewed emphasis on one-on-one contacts with the public. In Yosemite, when money came in 1999, field interpretive rangers were quickly hired, and in some cases, quickly thrust on the public. Jeffrey Trust, longtime Yosemite ranger-naturalist, remembers the steep learning curve from being on their own a little too quickly:

> All of a sudden, it was like, OK, we will have field naturalists and we will go out and educate people. On the first day, there hadn't been any training, and we had these employees that were brand new to Yosemite Valley that just jumped in and started talking to people. We called it "bear roving." Kate McCurdy gave us some supplies including pepper spray, and there was some confusion about whether the spray was for the people or the bears and at some point early on, two naturalists were at Curry pizza deck and there were raccoons who wouldn't go away. They decided to spray the raccoons, which caused a big cloud of pepper spray to drift over all the people on the pizza deck and then the naturalists didn't get to have pepper spray anymore. It was a wake-up call that we needed some training. We formalized the training the next year.

The bear techs and biologists had a learning curve too. Caitlin Lee-Roney recalls:

> When I was seventeen and started volunteering in Yosemite in 1999, we would follow campground bears for hours and when one would get on food, we would just yell at it and run at it to scare it away. It was nothing like the hazing we do now. I also remember we weren't very good with telemetry. We would just use it to find out what direction the bear went, but it took me a few years to realize we could use it to walk right up to a bear and scare it off.

Bear techs also adopted the use of new technologies like night vision goggles that made their jobs safer and more effective.

    With functional food storage facilities in place, together with an extensive educational program, law enforcement could finally be more proactive in issuing citations for improper food storage. In Yosemite, rangers got the authority to impound vehicles that contained food, and in 1999, they even got a fenced compound that held about ten cars. Interestingly, a bear quickly figured out how to enter, and the fence had to be retrofitted. In some campgrounds, visitors had to initial a form stating they received the information so protection rangers could later issue citations for food left out. Although the park superintendents generally prefer their rangers to use education over enforcement, the issuance of only one or two citations often motivated entire campgrounds of visitors to quickly store their food. And that often included the 5 percent that WCS encouraged the rangers to target.

# 26

# BEING REACTIVE—TAKE II

**A**lthough the implementation of more effective proactive work didn't end the need for reactive work, it gave park staff the space to rethink the way they did business. As former NPS biologist Steve Thompson noted:

> By the late 1990s, the situation had totally changed. Food storage lockers had been installed throughout the park and thorough public education programs were in place, but there were still problem bears around and the public had become less tolerant of the destruction of bears. But we had to do something. The bears wouldn't run from us. They were so habituated that they wouldn't even leave the campground.

Ryan Leahy remembers tracking a bear in Sequoia that had just gotten a significant food reward. He found her in a campsite where she ripped into a tent and grabbed a backpack:

> I was like, OK, I really need to haze this bear super hard and I was really gung-ho. So I started chasing her, and we both took off down a nearby trail. She was like twenty yards ahead of me, and we were flying, and I came over this lip full speed and there was the bear, just standing there. So I had no choice but to basically drop-kick the bear. She dropped the backpack and, thank God, didn't eat me. It was the scariest thing ever, and I definitely started slowing down my chasing after that.

So with bears becoming so habituated to humans, especially uniformed employees, Steve Thompson, NPS, said, "Retrying hazing and aversive conditioning was the next logical step." It started with simple things like water guns with ammonia and pepper spray. Sometime in the 1990s, the same pepper spray that was (mis)used in Yosemite was also stocked at Sequoia-Kings. (The pepper spray was designed to deter human attackers and was not very appropriate for bears, but bear techs did use it on many occasions before I replaced it, in 2000, with actual bear spray.)

Bear spray is a relatively new product. It's development started after Bill Pounds had a close encounter with a grizzly bear in 1977 and became interested in finding a safe, yet effective way to deter bears. At first, Bill thought about carrying a shotgun, but his wife didn't want one around their small children. According to an article in the September 13, 1999, issue of *High Country News*, Bill then remembered being in a small village in Mexico as a child when a group of kids tried to talk him into eating a small green pepper. As reported in the article, Bill said, "I got suspicious, so I just scratched the skin of the pepper with my teeth. That alone was enough to take my breath away." After he remembered that, he said, "I immediately tried to figure out how to get pepper into an aerosol can."

Meanwhile, in the early 1980s, Dr. Chuck Jonkel and his graduate student, Carrie Hunt, were already working on developing an aerosol-type bear deterrent at the University of Montana under a grant from the National Science Foundation. They conceptually knew what they wanted, but didn't quite have the right chemical or canister for delivery. Pounds teamed up with Jonkel and Hunt, and they worked together until they had a product that, as bear safety expert Chuck Bartlebaugh put it, "could emit a rapidly expanding cloud of spray that allowed for quick delivery of the capsaicin so it quickly entered a bear's eyes, nose, mouth, throat, and lungs and immediately block their functions in various ways." More importantly, it could stop a charging grizzly bear. Tom Smith, Steve Herrero, and others have even since shown that bear spray is more effective than firearms in stopping a grizzly attack, the firearms being found to sometimes escalate the conflict.

In 1986, Bill Pounds released Counter Assault bear spray onto the mass market. Soon other brands appeared, although unfortunately, several were nothing more than pepper spray with a bear-spray label. Since

1993, the Environmental Protection Agency (EPA) has required all bear sprays to be registered and carry an EPA approval number, but it is still critical to check the label for the active ingredients to be sure the product contains capsaicin or related capsaicinoids.

Although Pounds, Jonkel, and Hunt developed bear spray to be used as a defensive tool against charging grizzlies, the bear techs in Sequoia-Kings used it as a tool to haze black bears. Probably since most of these bears were already food-conditioned and habituated, the pepper spray had limited effectiveness in diverting them from their goals, but it did slow them down. They also experimented with plastic capsules filled with pepper residue that could be shot out of a paintball gun. They were easier to aim than the commonly used slingshots, but were expensive and left broken plastic shards on the ground.

Soon, however, newer, safer types of pyrotechnics (hazing deployed with an explosive charge) became available. In 1999, Steve Searles came to Yosemite to teach a formal course in their use. Searles, a wildlife specialist from Mammoth, California, is a colorful character who works out of a dumpster. He developed the "SCAT kits," which are the hazing kits Yosemite adopted. They included all the elements needed for hazing with pyrotechnics. Searles is known for his passion and enthusiasm, and Kate McCurdy credits him with teaching her crew "how to really make some noise around bears."

When Yosemite bear techs started carrying around a shotgun painted bright orange for safety and using the less-than-lethal rounds, some of the bears that were previously very difficult to get out of developed areas would quickly run away. Sherri Lisius recalls:

> Before we used the more aggressive hazing, there were dozens of times I got close enough to a bear to hit it in the face with bear spray. After we started using the less-than-lethal rounds, I never again got close enough to a bear to spray it in the face. There was a huge difference in how far the bears stayed from us.

After some initial success in getting bears to move, the biologists were excited by hazing's potential effectiveness.

Meanwhile, programs in and out of parks across the country started promoting hazing as a potentially effective tool. But was its effectiveness long term or did hazing simply get bears to temporarily leave or stop an unwanted behavior? I tested this question by reinstituting a hazing/aversive conditioning program at Sequoia-Kings in 2002, but with a formal study design so I could document the results. I modeled the program after the one at Yosemite but, for clarity and to avoid fire hazards, I limited the methods to chasing, using low-impact projectiles (i.e., throwing rocks and using slingshots), bear spray (the capsaicin kind), and high-impact projectiles (i.e., rubber slugs).

I found that hazing was effective at getting most bears to leave an area temporarily, which is important when bears get too close to humans or food needs to be put away. Hazing was also effective in getting some naïve bears to abandon nuisance behaviors. Hazing, however, was not effective in getting food-conditioned bears to abandon nuisance behaviors over the long-term. Hazing was also less effective with adolescent bears, particularly males, who sometimes progressed from naïve to severely food-conditioned so quickly that, in some cases, those bears wouldn't even leave an area when hazed with rubber slugs. One example from Sequoia would be bear H03, a young male, who was habituated to humans, but not food-conditioned until the Fourth of July weekend when he was fed by visitors and then got meat off a grill. Even with persistent aggressive hazing, he continually approached people and at the end of July, after H03 tried to enter an occupied vehicle, he was destroyed.

These results fit with what Kim Delozier and others found in the Great Smokies. When they used hazing on the extremely food-conditioned and habituated day-active bears, they got little response. They simply couldn't make the experience bad enough for bears to want to leave. When instead they targeted the more naïve night-active bears with their hazing, they were more successful.

The same was true of Jon Beckmann, Carl Lackey, and Joel Berger's study on the potential utility of using "hard releases" as a hazing method. A hard release was one in which a release would occur in the vicinity of where a bear was trapped and would be accompanied by either barking dogs, rubber slugs, or slingshots as the bear ran off. The idea behind this type of hard release was that the experience would be so negative that the bears would leave the area for good. They found it only had short-term success. Eventually, the bears, even when released with rubber buckshot and dogs chasing them, came back.

Downsides to hazing include cost, noise, and safety—both for humans and the bears. Although it is pretty easy to obtain refurbished shotguns and donated rubber slugs, it takes a lot of employee time for training and safe implementation. Many hazing tools, especially shotguns and barking dogs that are used late at night, are annoying to the visitors who have clean camps and are trying to sleep. Safety concerns include the danger of hurting animals, humans, and even property. There are documented cases of bears being wounded and killed with pyrotechnic hazing tools by trained personnel. The same is true for humans. In 2004, a Boston policeman fired less-than-lethal pepper pellets into a rowdy crowd after the Red Sox beat the Yankees in the American League championship series. One pellet hit twenty-one-year-old Emerson college student Victoria Snelgrove in the eye and killed her. Bear spray also has safety concerns, and allowing employees or visitors to carry it shouldn't be taken lightly. (At Sequoia-Kings, one bear tech inappropriately unloaded an entire can of bear spray on a bear at the edge of a campground. The wind carried the spray back through the campground, leading to general panic and the deployment of three ambulances.) Even simple chasing can lead to sprained ankles or sending a bear into traffic.

In both Yosemite and Sequoia-Kings, hazing is no longer thought to be a panacea, but rather a tool that has utility in appropriate situations. Only the safest tools are used and they are only used by highly trained staff. That means pyrotechnics with the potential to start fires are off-limits as is bear spray in Yosemite, where the potential for misuse is high. In Sequoia-Kings, current Wildlife Biologist Danny Gammons says, "aversive conditioning is well beyond our capacity. We just haze bears away from immediate conflict situations." In Yosemite where there is much more funding and a larger staff, biologists use both hazing and aversive conditioning, but only in appropriate situations. Ryan Leahy explains, "In Yosemite, we now focus our efforts on education and on young and naïve bears, even at the cost of letting the food-conditioned bears run their course through the evening."

Yosemite bear techs can now even focus their efforts on hazing particular bears because of alarms designed by Stewart Breck and others to notify rangers when bears enter developed areas. Stewart, an expert on human/carnivore conflict, came to Yosemite to develop alarms after acquiring funding from his agency, the National Wildlife Research Center. His idea was to combine the monitoring capabilities of data loggers to detect when collared bears entered monitored areas with the message transmission capabilities of the rangers' two-way radios to let field personnel know. In 2003, he tested six of these remote alarms in Yosemite's campgrounds and parking lots, and they worked. The boxes are now an integral part of Yosemite's program. In 2012, the Yosemite Conservancy provided funding to replace them and expand the program to include twelve systems.

In both parks, the entire process of trapping, drugging, and marking bears continued to improve. For one, better and less expensive technology became available. Starting in 2010, biologists could put radio transmitters on bears' ear tags at minimal cost. Concurrently, each park developed a dedicated core group of biologists, technicians, and rangers who became highly skilled in these techniques. With the advance of social media, it happened just in time. Caitlin Lee-Roney remembers the nontraditional way she once caught a cub that may not have gone over well in the media (or with the park safety committee):

> It was taking forever to catch it, and finally, the cub walked over to me, so I just grabbed it with my hands and Ryan [Leahy] ran over and drugged it. I could hear Tori [Seher] in the distance celebrating. It didn't put anyone, including the bear, at risk, but I'm glad no one saw. These days, our captures could show up on YouTube.

Meanwhile, although Sequoia-Kings had abandoned long-distance relocation long ago, Yosemite was still using it to a limited extent in lieu of killing bears, especially young bears or females with cubs. While Yosemite considered any relocation in which target bears did not return a management success, in reality, no one knew where the bears went after transport. As part of Jack Hopkins's research, he used data from radio-collared bears and management records to quantify the fate of relocated bears. He found that 75 percent of food-conditioned bears, including juveniles, were either legally hunted outside the park or euthanized upon their return. Conversely, bears not known to be food-conditioned did not return to developed areas after transport. However, their fate wasn't known, so although the park was no longer managing them, it couldn't be termed a success. As a result, Hopkins and coauthor Kalinowski suggested that Yosemite finally stop relocating food-conditioned bears and, instead, euthanize them. As for bears that are not food conditioned, they recommend that if the park relocates them, that biologists closely monitor their fate closely to inform later management efforts. Hopkins asks:

Why put thousands of dollars into managing problem bears that cause thousands of dollars of property damage each year? There is no convincing data from Yosemite, or elsewhere for that matter, suggesting that reactive management methods, such as hazing or relocation, are effective at modifying the nuisance behavior of problem black bears over the long term. If problem bears are going to be killed eventually anyway, it makes more sense to do so early so they don't reproduce. Instead, it'd be better to focus money and effort on keeping bears from becoming a problem in the first place. I think this strategy would lead to less bears being killed over the long run.

The park wildlife managers, armed with the same information, had the same thought, and finally—mostly—stopped the practice.

# 27

# MODERN DECISIONS ON DESTRUCTION

**F**inally, as in the past, there was the killing. As in the recent past, when a bear was considered for destruction, committees met to review the bear's history and determine if it met the criteria outlined in the human-bear management plans; specifically, if the bear was either damaging property where food was properly stored or demonstrating the potential to cause human injury in unprovoked situations.

But now, there was a critical difference; many of the same long-term, severely food-conditioned bears that in the past would have been spared were now being slated for destruction. Why? The parks were finally bear-proof, full proactive programs were in place, and research results were in. These three factors affected both the behavior of individual nuisance bears and the extent of their impact on the greater bear population, as well as the committees' understanding of how these outcomes could be affected by range of management actions available to the parks.

First, there was a change in behaviors of individual bears. In the recent past, when bears presented a safety risk by approaching humans for food, rangers hazed them away. The bears learned to stay farther from people, but simply foraged elsewhere for easily accessible human food. If the situation worsened, the parks relocated the bears, and when the bears didn't return (often because they had been shot or hit by cars), the parks considered it a success. After human food became less available to bears across the parks, many of those same bears became more persistent—even after being hazed—at finding human food. As a result, the chance of human injury and property damage increased. Since hazing is of limited value with severely food-conditioned or habituated bears, and relocation doesn't work, killing became a more defensible option.

Second, there was a change both in the actual impact nuisance bears had on the greater population of bears and in the parks' understanding of the dynamic. Before bear-proofing was completed, when one food-conditioned bear was killed, another bear would show up and take its place. This phenomenon was documented between 1975 and 1979, when Yosemite bears were intensively relocated and destroyed but the problems never let up. In 1979, when Brad Cella and Jeff Keay trapped the bears, they found the bears were all first-time offenders that were filling recently vacated "problem bear niches." Often, the new situation would be less manageable because the field staff would not know the new bear's behavior patterns, habits, and predictabilities. In many instances, field rangers purposely voted to keep known bears alive because they felt they were safer and easier to manage than an unknown bear. When bear-proofing was largely completed and visitors were largely complying with food-storage rules, the phenomenon of new bears continually filling vacated niches within developed areas became less of a concern. As Jeffrey Trust notes, "the conveyor belt that was continually replacing old [nuisance] bears with new ones is finally broken."

Another piece of the puzzle of how one nuisance bear affects the greater population of bears lies within the sow-cub connection. In the past, it was clear that nuisance sows often had nuisance cubs, but it wasn't clear if the cubs' behaviors came from genetically heritable dispositions or from observations of their mothers' behaviors. It also wasn't clear if all cubs of nuisance sows became nuisances or only some of them. Since no one knew how and when the behaviors were transmitted, no one knew if they could be prevented.

Many people have observed nuisance sows with nuisance cubs, even in the earliest years of the parks. In the Yosemite Superintendent's Report from 1930, a visitor reported seeing five bears begging along with road where there used to be just one. He said they "ambled onto the highway standing erect and failed to move until I had given each one a generous supply of chocolate, peppermints, and chewing gum." The report then says the rangers concluded that four of the "stick-up" bruins were the sons of the well-known bandit bear, Jesse James. Although the genders may well have been confused, the analysis of the origin of the behavior is likely correct.

Some people have even observed the phenomenon over multiple generations. Steve Thompson, NPS, recalled:

Swatter was a bear that had three cubs and went between Little Yosemite Valley and the Valley campgrounds. She was very aggressive and had injured people. We had a euthanasia memo on her, but the superintendent did not want to euthanize a sow and three cubs, and we thought it was too early in the year to euthanize the sow and leave the cubs on their own. So the superintendent wanted to try a long-distance relocation via helicopter to Slide Canyon, which is not very good bear habitat and meant we had to have a sow and three cubs down simultaneously to get them on the helicopter. So Kate and I went up there to catch them and as soon as we got her down, the cubs went up a tree. One by one we got the first two cubs, and I had to keep resedating them while we tried to catch the third cub. We were wondering, "Gosh, how much longer can we safely do this?" and we finally decided, two out of three ain't bad and loaded them onto a litter. Then the helicopter was coming and the third cub was going up a tree and I remember Kate had a jabstick and she lunged, jumping across a log and falling on the ground, but she got the cub, ran to the helispot, and stuffed it into the litter. We covered it up just as the helicopter took off. From there, all four of them were taken to Slide Canyon and all four of them were back in LYV in two weeks.

Steve continues:

So then, back up in LYV, Swatter got food from a tourist who was out-of-bounds camping with the food next to him. When the guy sat up, she swatted him across the face down to the fat layer. I mean, he was ripped. It was the final straw, so Kate McCurdy and I and a team of other people went up there in the middle of the night and set a snare. Then, we heard pans banging and people yelling and knew she was in the campground. She had put her three cubs up a tree in the middle of the campground and was tearing around in a cloud of swirling dust. She was swatting at people and people were sticking their heads out of their tents and then retreating just in time to avoid being swatted and screaming and shining their flashlights in every direction. It was like a scene out of Dante's Inferno. Then she was just twenty feet away from me, and she just stopped and stared. I knew the bear was going to come for me so I just took aim and I darted her right in the chest. She ran a short way and then went down. Then we euthanized her and dug a big hole and buried her. And by now, the cubs we had nicknamed, Eenie, Meenie, and Miney, were old enough to be on their own, so we left them there. We never saw Meenie again, but Eenie and Miney and their cubs became bad problems. Miney was the one that was the subject of the 1998 *Washington Post* article.

These observations clearly showed a connection between nuisance behaviors in sows and cubs, but there was still no resolution about how and when the nuisance behavior was transmitted. To get some resolution, I started a study with Tori Seher, a biologist at Yosemite, for a chapter of my dissertation. In both parks, we ear-tagged the cubs of tagged nuisance sows. In Sequoia, I also located wild family groupings and ear-tagged both the sows and cubs. We then observed where the sows raised their cubs and how the cubs behaved the following year when they were independent yearlings. The results were striking. Almost all cubs raised by wild sows became wild yearlings. Of the cubs raised by nuisance sows, those raised in developed areas became nuisance yearlings and those raised in wild areas became wild yearlings. In other words, the cubs' foraging behavior as yearlings depended almost entirely upon where they were raised and therefore what they had observed. Although there may be some heritable behavioral dispositions that give some cubs more or less of a tendency to try new things, the mode of transmission was clearly some form of observational learning.

At the same time Tori and I conducted our observational study, Stewart Breck, Carl Lackey, and others used banked blood to determine relatedness among bears and compared it with documented behaviors of those same bears. They concluded that strict genetic inheritance did not explain how cubs acquired nuisance behaviors, but since they didn't have observational data on how the cubs were raised, they were limited in what they could say about the role of learning. In a third study conducted between 2004 and 2007, Jack Hopkins paired observations of behaviors of known bears with an analysis of their diets using stable isotopes (explained later) to determine if they were foraging on human food. He then used genetic data to predict the relationship between each pair of bears in his sample. Using this third approach, he again found similar results. The management implication is that when food-conditioned sows have cubs, their cubs must be kept out of developed areas if they are to remain wild.

Outside of the sow-cub relationship, observations of other groupings of bears working together indicate they are likely learning from each other. Dave Graber once observed two unrelated yearlings cooperating to obtain a food sack. He also observed family groups regularly associating and adults taking temporary care of each other's cubs. Several bear techs observed unrelated bears work together to roll a food-storage locker in Dorst Campground in Sequoia. John Sturdevant witnessed what he believes to have been bears using each other as foils. After the trail crew would return from chasing one bear off, they would come back to find two others raiding their camp. Jeffrey Trust once saw a male bear take food from a locker and bring it to a female bear.

Dr. Barrie Gilbert puts social learning into the context of the greater population:

> In the beginning it is a learned phenomenon in one bear that is then socially transmitted to others. Mothers figure it out and then youngsters learn it by observational learning of their mother. Then it becomes a cultural trait, and I used the term, behavioral epidemic. And if managers don't get on top of some of these things, then the epidemic spreads among the animals while we are sitting around and waiting for an administrative decision. And then you have a complete change and people ask, should we move them, should we shoot them, or should we just, you know, try to do aversive conditioning; all of which are relatively ineffective compared to preventing it in the first place.

Steve Thompson, NPS, thought this sounded about right for Yosemite:

> It seems like a culture because car break-ins used to be common in El Portal. After some bears were killed, car break-ins became almost nonexistent there.

The question is how does one stop a cub from developing nuisance behaviors? Hazing is one potential option. In my research, hazing didn't get sows to stop entering developed areas, but it did stop some sows from bringing their cubs into developed areas, and therefore from passing on the behaviors. A potential future option may be to sterilize nuisance sows. Marc Kenyon, the human-wildlife conflict specialist for the California Department of Fish and Wildlife, doesn't think the potential for sterilization is as farfetched as it once was and is even looking into it for a group that approached him from Lake Tahoe. Of course, another option is to euthanize the sow, and in some situations, that may be the most appropriate course of action, but unless it is done during the alternate years when she has no cubs, it begs the question of what to do with the cubs.

Coincidentally, as my colleagues and I were studying the mechanism of behavioral transmission, rehabilitation of abandoned cubs emerged as a viable option. The idea is to send the cubs to spend their first summer in a rehabilitation center and then be brought back in the winter to den and (hopefully) spend their lives as wild bears. In 2001 in Kings Canyon, visitors found a six-pound cub on the trail in front of the General Grant Tree at about the same time that, in Yosemite, rangers had to euthanize Eenie, one of Swatter's three cubs, who now had two spring cubs of her own. Kate McCurdy remembers that it was John Beecham who first suggested sending the Yosemite cubs to Sally Maughan, a bear rehabilitator in Idaho:

> At the time, it was a pretty renegade idea. It hadn't been done at Yosemite, but the park let us try, so we euthanized the sow and transferred the cubs to California Fish and Game, a legal requirement before they were sent out of state. And when we got to their office, California Fish and Game made us sign an affidavit that the cubs had not been habituated or food conditioned and were less than six months old, which we did. And then one of the cubs took a big poop and it had plastic in it and they almost didn't let them go to rehab, but we talked them into it because the cub could have eaten a plastic bag and not gotten human food. So the cubs went to Idaho where they were thrown in with a bunch of other cubs including the one from Kings Canyon.

Sally Maughan, the rehabilitator, remembers those cubs well:

> The little female cub from [Kings Canyon] had the cutest white spot on her nose—the first time we ever saw that in a bear cub. She came in with two males from Yosemite. We fed them and once winter came, started them in hibernation here at [the Idaho Black Bear Rehabilitation]. Then in January 2002, John Beecham transported all three back to the parks for denning. At the time, the Yosemite males weighed 170 and 148 pounds and the [Kings Canyon] cub weighed 110 pounds.

Kate McCurdy received the Yosemite cubs:

> When winter came, they shipped the cubs back to Yosemite and with all kinds of media attention [including Fran Mainella, the Director of

the National Park Service, and Congressman George Radanovich]. We took them to a backcountry den we had excavated, radio-collared the cubs, put them in, covered up the den, and never saw them again. We got their signals once in a while, or got sightings reports, but they stayed skittish of people until their break-away collars broke off. It was a huge expenditure of our time for two bears the park won't miss, but it was a feel-good project the public loved and a way to deal with the problem sow.

While the Yosemite cubs were denned with helicopters and fanfare, the single Kings Canyon cub was tucked into her den by a group of interested people who assembled on their day off to volunteer. Both reintroductions succeeded in that none of the cubs exhibited nuisance behavior as independent yearlings. Since then, the parks have used rehabilitation six additional times. Rehabilitation has many downsides; it is heavy-handed, time-consuming, expensive, and only benefits individual bears, but it is an appealing option and gives managers a way to deal with severely food-conditioned sows with cubs in tow.

Getting back to how committees made decisions about the fates of nuisance bears, and the ways they have changed in the recent past, it is also important to point out the ways they haven't changed. For one, the national parks have a mission to preserve and protect "the natural and cultural scenery and the wildlife therein...." That means keeping bears alive as well as keeping them wild. Killing a bear means failing at the mission. Most visitors understand the parks' challenges and support occasional killing as long as there is a strong proactive program in place. Other visitors wish the parks had killed all the nuisance bears in the 1970s as was done elsewhere. Still others are staunchly opposed to the killing of any bear in a national park—even bears that injure people or are leading to multiple generations of nuisance bears.

In fact, until recently, there was an extraordinary tolerance for nuisance behaviors. Filmmaker and former ranger Steve Bumgardner remembers a bear that broke into his car as "[t]hat same bear that broke a window in everybody's car." Bear expert Steve Herrero explains:

Bears are creatures that evoke our sympathy and our attention. People are reluctant to pull the trigger even on bears that are incorrigible. Parks have tended to go soft on such bears because they don't want to take on an aggressive public let alone an aggressive bear. I think we

tolerated it because there wasn't an easy solution outside of removing
the bears causing the problems en masse.

There are also aesthetic, recreational, and political values to keeping
bears alive. For many visitors, seeing a bear is the highlight of their trip.
When they spend time watching bears, they become connected and increasingly committed to protecting them. Visitors who see bears in the
wild become more serious about food storage because they want to keep
the bears wild. Visitors who see bears in developed areas like campgrounds become more serious about food storage because they don't want
a bear in their car. Biologist Ryan Leahy is very familiar with the educational value of having bears around:

> If you are in Yosemite and you see a bear and there are bear prints all
> over your car, you are probably going to make sure that everybody in
> your site and all around know and get their food stored properly.

The fact is that in the present, the basic conditions have changed, to
the great benefit of all involved. The parks are now largely bear-proof,
most visitors store their food properly—at least when prodded by the
parks' intensive education campaigns, and the parks know how to be
most effective with their management. The number of new bears becoming food-conditioned or habituated has decreased drastically as have the
numbers of incidents and cost of damage.

But, in addition to proactive management and working with newly
food-conditioned bears, the parks are also still faced with managing the
remaining nuisance bears that developed their behaviors in the past. Increasingly, these bears are being euthanized. As sad as it is, these decisions are not only supported, but encouraged by several researchers, including Jack Hopkins and Sean Matthews, who argue that more harm
than good was likely resulting from keeping problem bears alive.

Jack Hopkins explains how euthanizing a few individuals can reduce
incidents and property damage:

> In 2006 [in Yosemite], there were about four hundred reported inci-
> dents and over $86,000 in property damage. Although that sounds
> pretty bad, it might sound even worse to hear that three females and
> their six offspring caused most of these incidents. A few targeted
> management actions could have reduced incidents and damage greatly

in the park. Yosemite is a very political park though, and some high-level managers [were] adamant about not killing bears. But keeping those problem bears alive has led to more incidents and damage because their offspring became problems as well. Ironically, more bears have likely been killed recently as a result of not killing these bears earlier.

Until there are better options for dealing with some of the worst nuisance bears, killing a few of them now is the only known way to prevent killing more of them in the future. Well-intentioned suggestions to send nuisance bears to zoos forget that zoos (regardless of whether the use of zoos is a good idea) don't have enough room to take all these bears, and pleas to rehabilitate the bears' behavior with hazing ignore the evidence that rehabilitating adults doesn't work. It isn't fun to be the superintendent of a high-profile park when an article about rangers killing a sow and her cubs hits the *Washington Post*, and it is even worse to be the ranger or bear tech tasked with doing the killing. Oftentimes, the individual tasked with killing a bear is the same person who has spent the most time trying to save its life.

The upside to these difficult decisions is that they are allowing managers to focus limited time and resources on proactive work and management of naïve bears. Danny Gammons, who now runs the Sequoia-Kings bear program, says:

> There was a conscious decision in 2010 to remove four severely food-conditioned bears over a four-month period. So now, we are working with a relatively naïve front country bear population. Even if they are food-stressed, they will be more leery of coming into developed areas.

Caitlin Lee-Roney, who now runs the Yosemite bear program, explains:

> Part of why we are seeing lower incident numbers is we are catching up with a lot of bears these days that had been around for ten or fifteen years and causing the same problems. Some of these bears have caused thousands of incidents and have been trapped multiple times. I think getting rid of those bears has helped. We now have a lot more time to focus on new bears that are just starting to learn the behaviors. This isn't true of all long-term problem bears. Some are still around, and many people are attached to them. They are individually known and

commonly photographed. Since people form bonds with these bears; it is very hard to have to kill them. People get mad at us when we euthanize bears, even people I have known for years and have grown up with. Some people have left their bear management jobs because they can't handle that aspect of it.

As long as the so-called conveyor belt stays broken, meaning the parks maintain bear-proof food storage and strong proactive programs, the killing of these few bears will lead to the deaths of less bears in the long-term. But, if the parks, and the communities around them, stop maintaining bear-proof facilities and allow their proactive programs to fall apart, the conveyor belt will start back up again, and these bears will have died in vain.

# 28

# HIDDEN DEATH TRAP

**R**egardless of whether one agrees with the justification for these killings, everyone agrees these killings are tragic, largely because they are so preventable. The order of tragedy, however, should be put in perspective. While black bears are protected within national parks, each year, between one thousand and two thousand bears are legally hunted outside the parks in California. Further, within the parks, management killing is not even close to being the highest source of human-caused mortality. In the Sierran parks, that cause is collisions with vehicles, motorcycles, and even bicycles, along park roads. Some recover, some die instantly, and many suffer significantly and die later as a result of their injuries. If rangers find badly injured bears, they generally euthanize the bears to end their suffering. When sows are hit and killed, dependent cubs usually die. In 2001 in Sequoia, Belle, one of the few bears known to become food-conditioned and then revert to natural behaviors, was hit and killed. When rangers found her, her dead cub lay nearby, apparently killed by another bear as it tried to nurse on its dead mother.

Ryan Leahy notes that in recent years, the parks are becoming increasingly aware of how significant this source of injury and mortality is:

> We've had as many as twenty-seven bears reported to be hit in one summer in Yosemite, which is easily 5 to 10 percent of the population. There have been as many as seventeen hit in one summer along the one main road in Sequoia. Since 1921, there have been about eighteen to twenty bears reported hit each year with a large number of them being killed. The numbers are astounding.

There are places where the problem is worse. According to Carl Lackey, wildlife biologist for the Nevada Department of Wildlife, in 2007, after a sixteen-month drought, there were sixty-three documented mortalities of bears hit by cars around Lake Tahoe.

Occasionally, there is a happy ending, as with a bear in Sequoia that came to be known as the "Concussion Kid." At the time, Nina Weisman was the local bear technician. She remembers:

> In the summer of 1995, when I was working bear management, I had a volunteer, Kim Sager, who was driving down the Generals Highway with Greg Stock when a bear came careening off the top of a cliff, ran into the road, and ran right into the side of a car. So they pulled over and the people who had hit the bear pulled over and they were hysterical and the bear was laying on the side of the road. The bear wasn't breathing until Greg opened its airway. Then it got up and stumbled around while Kim and Greg did crowd control and called me on the radio. I was in Lodgepole with a bear tranquilized in a trap and rushed over with several rangers. We found the bear stumbling around, and the couple who hit the bear hysterically crying and asking to put it in their trunk so they could take it to the vet. At that point, a van pulled up and a man said he was a dog and cat vet. He checked out the bear and said it was likely just a concussion and said the bear would be fine if we kept it quiet overnight and gave it a dose of dexamethazone to reduce brain swelling. So I asked one of the rangers to go back to Lodgepole to release the other bear and bring the trap here to let this bear rest in overnight. We couldn't get permission to use the dexamethazone we had for humans, so we just gave it an IV full of fluids and bought some dexamethazone from the vet the next morning. A few days later, we released it near where it was hit and it was fine. We saw it a couple of times later that summer.

More often, there is not a happy ending. In Yosemite, a naturalist named Moose took notice. In April 2003, Moose Mutlow was commuting from his home in Yosemite West to his job in the Valley. As he describes it:

> I was late for work and doing forty-two miles per hour on Chapel Straight while distracted by a snow cone and drove right into a speed trap set by ranger Eddie Visnovske. Eddie gave me a ticket and said one of the reasons for the enforcement was to protect wildlife. I got

intrigued and subsequently started to record every dead animal I saw as I drove back and forth to work over an eighteen-month period. I recorded the species, perseverance, location, appearance, and time, which created the acronym "SPLAT." And I really got into it and charted out the data to look for patterns. It was sobering to see how many animals were killed, knowing I wasn't even including those that could run or crawl away from the collision site. Then I combined my data with data Tori Seher had on where bears had been hit and found they were often hit near watercourses. I also did a side study on how to best use the horn to scare off animals, but it turned out the only thing that matters is that you drive slow enough to be able to quickly stop. Finally, I gave a parody science talk on the whole thing and called it, "SPLAT Goes the Weasel."

Moose continues:

I ended up giving the talk several times and was even interviewed on NPR's *All Things Considered* in 2008 for a series on national parks. Then somewhere along the way, I started thinking about a concept called "Red-Bear, Dead-Bear," which I thought could be a way to get people to slow down. So Tori and I wanted to use stencils to spray-paint outlines of dead bears on the highway where bears had been hit, but dropped it when we were told it wouldn't meet highway code. So then Tori made these little stenciled pictures of bears to hang on the dumpsters near where bears were hit, and I remember us ripping up and down the highway to test if we could see them while driving at different speeds. It turned out they were too small. At that point, I didn't have the bandwidth to take it further, but then Adrienne Freeman took it on as her master's project.

So Adrienne Freeman analyzed the data on where bears were hit, created a map of her results, and took it to interested people to increase their awareness and understanding of the problem. She then came up with a plan to implement the Red-Bear, Dead-Bear concept. Starting in 2005, at every place a bear was hit, the park placed a large yellow sign with a red profile of a bear that said, "Speeding Kills Bears." She also hung informational posters in visitor centers explaining the program, and the local concessionaire picked up on the idea and started selling merchandise with the logo in park stores. Although some signs were stolen, the program was a big success and continues to this day. Looking back,

Moose recalls being surprised the program had "as much legs as it did." It even spread beyond bears. One member of the staff became impassioned with butterflies and would put up a butterfly crossing sign in El Portal during migration. Moose thinks part of the reason for the success was that they used humor to talk about a really sad thing. In Sequoia-Kings, large yellow and black "Slow Down for Wildlife" signs were placed along park roads to increase awareness.

These were important steps, but still reactive ways to deal with the problem. In 2011, Katie Rodriquez, a Yosemite bear technician and graduate student at San Jose State, decided to investigate the underlying problem for her master's thesis to empower the parks to be more proactive. To do this, Katie took the existing data detailing the collisions and combined it with new field data she collected on habitat and road conditions to look for patterns and hotspots. Katie refers to the existing data as a "gold mine" because it didn't just give locations, but also the date and location of each accident; and the age, gender and disposition of the bear. From over two hundred and fifty collisions, and data on over ninety bears, she determined the collisions were correlated with slope, proximity to meadows, the curve of the road, the amount of roadside vegetation, and whether the local topography obligated bears to cross in a particular spot. "The worst place in the park for collisions is White Wolf, and not surprisingly," explains Katie, "it exhibits all of those characteristics." Katie also found most bears were hit between July and September, between six and ten o'clock at night, and mostly on Sundays as visitors rush home after a long weekend.

What can be done? Katie explains there are two approaches: "[O]ne is to change driver behavior and the other is to change bear behavior." Changing driver behavior means getting them to slow down in critical spots so they have more visibility and more time to react. Strategically placed signage and radar-feedback signs plus lower speed limits in more targeted areas could protect bears. Changing bear behavior means getting bears to cross at strategic locations such as where there is high visibility for motorists or where there are drainage culverts bears can use as underpasses. In addition to protecting Yosemite bears, these efforts would improve driver safety, and protect a myriad of other park species including federally threatened (proposed) fishers and state endangered great gray owls, both of which are often hit and killed by motorists. The parks are currently experimenting with all of these methods.

The problem of how to reduce wildlife-vehicle collisions is getting increasing attention nationally because populations of many urban wildlife species are increasing as is the existence of faster and wider roads. Usually, the animals that get the most attention are the ones involved in potentially fatal accidents with humans such as deer-vehicle accidents, or worse, moose-vehicle incidents. There is also a lot of attention on extremely rare animals whose entire populations are at risk when one is hit, such as the Florida panther. In Banff National Park in Canada, the issue of wildlife-vehicle collisions has reached epic proportions because both the Trans-Canada Highway and the Canadian Pacific Railroad run right through the park. In the mid-1980s, the highway was expanded from two to four lanes, and enormous multimillion-dollar over- and underpasses were built. Although targeted at elk, they benefit many of the park's species, including both black and grizzly bears.

# 29

# BACK IN THE BACKCOUNTRY

As the front county completed its major bear-proofing, finally even putting in bear-proof containers for recycling, the backcountry followed. By 1999, reliable canister designs were widely available for sale and rent, largely due to help from the parks' cooperating associations, the Sequoia Natural History Association, the Yosemite Association, and the Yosemite Fund (the latter two have since merged to become the Yosemite Conservancy). Retired wilderness manager Laurel Boyers recalls the last steps to finally being able to rent canisters at the Tuolumne permit station in Yosemite:

> It was about the size of a walk-in closet. So to think about being able to provide literally hundreds of canisters a day was out of the question. We thought about bringing in a cargo container, a truck, or shed; but then we'd wonder how we would wash them. Eventually, we got a grant from the Yosemite Fund to build the new building at Tuolumne and include a bear canister room. So it became more and more of a reality that we could get people on canisters and wean them off the counterbalance.

The challenge of getting people to use canisters no longer had to do with reliability or availability, it had more to do with getting people to use them and to use them properly. Some people loved them, but others thought they were heavy and bulky, too expensive, too small, or just preferred to hang their food. Some people insisted on using their own methods to deter bears. Rick Sanger, Sequoia-Kings backcountry ranger, remembers "Bucket Man":

> Dave Gordon and I called him "Bucket Man" because he had two five-gallon buckets he'd taped together and wear around his neck, and he was going out and putting food caches in the Rae Lakes and Charlotte Lakes areas. He would dig a hole and bury these caches and sure enough, a couple of weeks later we would find these totally trashed-out areas where bears had found them.

In 2002, a hiking-club leader taught her group of beginning backpackers to pile up their food, pour kerosene around it, and then sleep surrounding the food. Thankfully, a ranger found the group and put an end to that method. However, enough improper storage still took place that bears continued to be rewarded, incidents continued to be rampant, and in some cases, people were getting injured.

Most of the injuries happened when backpackers either tried to guard their food by sleeping with it, or when they tried to scare a bear off a food hang. In one incident, a bear reached for food next to a sleeping man's head, the man sat up, and the bear lacerated the man's ears and head. In another, a bear charged and lacerated a man's groin after the man tried to chase the bear off his food hang. Injuries occurred both to people who camped alone and in groups. In Kings Canyon, one terrified church group hiked out of the backcountry singing "Onward Christian Soldiers" the entire way to keep all bears at bay after a bear scratched their leader. The bear was trying to take food the man guarded.

The problem was that while some backcountry users embraced canisters or camped at lockers, others did not. Since voluntary use was limited, the parks toyed with the idea of implementing a requirement. Denali instituted a food storage requirement back in 1990 and immediately had 99 percent compliance. Denali, however, had a very different situation for several reasons. First, Denali has an order of magnitude fewer hikers than the Sierran parks, so they could offer free rentals. Second, most people fear grizzlies and are easily convinced of the need to carry a canister. Third, almost everyone gets backcountry permits at the same place so only one major canister rental location is needed. Finally, the decision to require canisters in Denali was only secondarily about reducing bear incidents, it was primarily about protecting the wilderness from concentrated use and trail formation.

In the Sierran parks, the primary goal was to reduce human-bear incidents and restore the bears' natural ecology. Park managers, however, were hesitant to implement a canister requirement until they were sure it was politically viable. So in the Sierra, the agency that made the first requirement wasn't the NPS, but was instead the USFS, specifically the Mount Whitney Ranger District of the Inyo National Forest, which lies adjacent to Sequoia-Kings on the east side of the Sierra.

Inyo National Forest started experiencing human-bear incidents in the backcountry in the 1980s. In the Mount Whitney area, the problem was particularly bad. Mount Whitney is part of the Sierra Crest and is the tallest mountain in the contiguous United States. The west side of Mount Whitney lies within Sequoia National Park; the east side lies within the Inyo National Forest. On the Inyo side, U.S. Forest Service rangers had, like the NPS rangers, already tried various bear-proofing techniques such as installing the tall metal poles with hooks (and uninstalling them in 1989), which all failed for one reason or another. One USFS ranger finally got fed up.

Calder Reid, Inyo National Forest Wilderness Manager, remembers him well:

> In 1996, a seasonal ranger named Jason Barbeau spent a lot of time in Onion Valley picking up trash. Frustrated by human-bear issues, he sent out a message forest-wide about the problem that was ill-received. Then, in 1997, Jason was in the backcountry when someone slept with their food at Big Pothole Lake. A bear came in and challenged the backpacker for his food and ended up swiping the fellow's behind. He went down to the hospital in Bishop and, as was legally required, reported the incident to [California] Fish and Game. So Fish and Game went to Big Pothole Lake, set up a tent with food in it as bait, and shot the first bear that came in. Jason heard the gunshot from his camp and later wrote to Forest Supervisor Dennis Martin requesting a canister requirement.

Meanwhile, Inyo wasn't just experiencing backcountry incidents, there were also incidents in the front country at the main trailhead to Mount Whitney. This trailhead is not found within the historic breeding range of black bears. Bears found there are rare transients, almost exclusively in the area to pursue human food. Evidence of their presence in the past includes historic pictures of a mess hall that a bear tore up in 1910 and of a decimated work camp from 1940. As with today, the bears came from the west side looking for human food. In the 1980s, Inyo installed small metal footlockers at the trailhead, but due to problems with maintenance and their small size, they were taken out in 1996 and people were again storing food in the trunks of their cars. Conflicts were skyrocketing. To further complicate the issue for the Inyo, when bears did show up, they arrived already food-conditioned and/or habituated.

Whereas the NPS is legislated to manage both the habitat and the wildlife, the USFS is legislated to primarily manage the habitat, while the state wildlife agencies primarily manage the wildlife. Since conflicts were a relatively new issue on the Inyo, neither the locally stationed employees from the USFS or any of the other responding agencies were properly trained, equipped, or ready to handle these human-bear situations.

Calder Reid describes what was happening:

> Here were these people coming from all over the world to climb Mount Whitney, the highest peak in the contiguous United States, and they would go up the peak and come down to find their window shattered or their door bent back at a forty-five-degree angle because a bear had been inside their car looking for food. Somebody would leave a little dog biscuit behind their seat and a bear would break in for that. Bears even broke into rental cars that were sprayed with freshening scents. Some of these cars were getting destroyed, and things weren't turning out well for the bears either—not just the bears that caused the problems, but for any area bears. In 2000, somebody thought they were being followed by a bear and called 9-1-1. The local sheriff's department drove up to Whitney Portal, pulled their cars up alongside the road, and got their rifles out and shot the bear. The bear had a cub. The fire crew had to come and pull the sow out of the creek while the cub sat in the tree screaming.

By 1998, Calder Reid had enough. She contacted Kate McCurdy at Yosemite to learn how to deal with bears. Calder then talked to Harold Werner at Sequoia-Kings and learned about canisters. And she became increasingly interested and involved.

Although Jason subsequently left the Inyo, the momentum grew. In 1999, Inyo designated the first bear-canister-required area in the Sierra Nevada. It went from Onion Valley to the top of Mount Whitney where the jurisdiction changed to that of Sequoia National Park. A lot of people liked it and a lot of others bucked the system by going over the pass and using lockers in Sequoia National Park.

But enough people complied that most food-conditioned bears on the east side now traveled back into the park where human food was more available, making park problems even worse. So in 2000, Sequoia followed Inyo's lead and implemented a canister restriction for the Rae Lakes area. It was expanded into the Dusy Basin area in 2001 and the Rock Creek area in 2005.

Concurrently, Yosemite began requiring canisters above the tree line in 1999 and added a few targeted high-use/high-problem areas, including Rancheria Falls and Sunrise Creek in 2001. A few years later, Yosemite wilderness managers Laurel Boyers and Mark Fincher went on a long backpacking trip through a non-canister-required area. They hung their food and crawled into a tent to sleep. It snowed all night, and they never heard the bear that came into their camp. In the morning, they found their food hang intact, but the tree stripped of its bark and surrounded by a pile of pine boughs. Astonished by the damage, they said, "This is nuts. Even when it works it doesn't work." In 2005, Yosemite expanded its requirement to include all areas within seven air miles of a road. After that change, wilderness manager Laurel Boyers took a two-week hike throughout Yosemite's backcountry and found every food-hang she came upon to be inadequate. Even so, she did see a wild bear and knew, with all the human food available, that it could soon be raiding campsites and marked it with a plastic tag in its ear. Since there was finally wide acceptance of canisters by the public, she decided, "This is going to be my legacy. I'm going to get the full closure done before I leave." In 2007, she rewrote the Yosemite requirement to be park-wide, and in 2008, it became regulation.

The necessity for canister requirements is backed up by peer-reviewed research. In 2003, I surveyed backpackers about their use of canisters in Sequoia-Kings. Of the 219 groups that traveled through areas where canister use was voluntary, 63 percent used canisters and 28 percent used lockers. It was a high percentage of voluntary compliance, including everyone who had lost food to a bear in the past, but not enough compliance to keep bears from getting food. Nine percent of people surveyed still persisted in hanging food either out of habit or because they found canisters to be too small or too heavy.

In Yosemite, Kate McCurdy conducted more detailed survey work in 2005 and 2006 after the park began requiring canisters within seven air miles of a road. She surveyed 1,079 individuals and found that 59 percent had been on a previous wilderness trip in Yosemite and of those, 18 percent had an experience where they lost food to a bear. The top reason people didn't carry canisters was not wanting the extra weight. Kate also found that most incidents were in areas along main trails, within a day's hike of a trailhead, in less-than-optimal bear habitat, associated with large groups, and in heavily traveled sites.

The Sierran National parks and Inyo National Forest instituted canister requirements primarily to protect bears and wilderness but also to benefit hikers; more canisters meant less nuisance bears in camp, fewer human injuries, and fewer hungry hikers who had lost their food. But whether the restrictions are inherently binding just by virtue of having a restriction or inherently liberating by providing hikers more freedom of movement—meaning allowing hikers to camp anywhere—seems to rest in the eye of the beholder. Laurel Boyers sees the latter:

> Canisters allow people to have freedom of movement. That is really a keystone of our management philosophy here. We have trailhead quotas rather than designated sites because we feel a huge component of wilderness is the minimum regulatory or bureaucratic or government oversight of your actions once you clear the trailhead, so we wanted maximum freedom once you have gained access and entered the wilderness.

Ironically, in 1994 the U.S. Forest Service published a booklet called "Low Impact Food Hoists" that illustrated how to hang food in the backcountry. It said to hang it at least ten feet up and four feet out and to tie it off. Although, as with the previous publication on lockers, Sierran biologists were again listed in the acknowledgement, by 1994, no one in the Sierra would suggest using a tie-off food hang, particularly not just four feet out. That said, what is true in the Sierra isn't true everywhere. Yellowstone and other parks, including Banff in Canada, successfully use bear poles, and the Great Smokies still successfully uses food-storage cables with pulley systems. On the other hand, just a few years ago, a bear known as "Yellow Yellow" that lived in the Adirondack Park of New York State, where bears are generally less food conditioned than in the Sierra, was consistently able to open one type of canister that bears in the Sierra could not.

Meanwhile, Calder Reid kept talking to the Sierran parks. Once the key players in these land-management agencies were communicating, it became obvious to them that they would be more effective working together. As a result, Yosemite, Sequoia and Kings Canyon, and Inyo National Forest created a collaborative group called the Sierra Interagency Black Bear Group (SIBBG) on a snowy day in Sequoia in 2000 with the goal of sharing information, techniques, and ideas; to coordinate policies and information; and to eliminate political barriers to progress. The ultimate goal was to preserve a healthy black bear population free of human influences on a regional scale. In 2003, Stanislaus National Forest joined, and other agencies soon followed.

Together, the agencies addressed issues like how to coordinate policies, canister rentals, and education for hikers that start their trips in one jurisdiction, travel through a second jurisdiction, and end in a third. They created coordinated maps, a joint website, and fliers, and sought funding as a single entity. The SIBBG forced administrators to listen because they were a regional coalition with energy, enthusiasm, and ideas for solutions.

But the SIBBG spent most of its time on canisters, attempting to make canister restrictions geographically consistent so one agency wasn't just pushing nuisance bears into another agency's land. The SIBBG also focused on the increasing issue of making sure all canisters brought into the backcountry actually worked. As more canister manufacturers got involved, flimsy and ineffective models appeared just as quickly as ingenious and effective models appeared. When hikers carried ineffective models into the backcountry, bears that had been foiled by effective models once again received food rewards and renewed their interest in canisters—effectively taking the entire program a giant step backward.

To prevent the use of ineffective models in the Sierra, the SIBBG adopted "[u]niform testing standards and approval protocols for SIBBG approved bear-resistant food-storage containers." The parks and the Inyo National Forest then required all canisters used by visitors to be SIBBG-approved. The SIBBG wasn't the first to institute a protocol like this one. The Interagency Grizzly Bear Committee (IGBC) created and published structural standards for bear-resistant containers in 1989 and instituted a formal approval process. The difference, in addition to the targeted spe-

cies of bear, was that the IGBC was targeting panniers and trash containers and the SIBBG was targeting canisters. Dick Karsky, retired IGBC
lead on the project, recalls:

> In 1989, [IGBC] looked at a bunch of panniers and storage boxes and
> chose one they thought Bart the Bear, the star of the Grizzly Adams
> movie, might be able to get into. We took that box to Bart and baited it
> and let the bear bat it around and jump on it and so forth, but he didn't
> get in. Then we built an impact tester based on the strength of that box
> to test and approve other boxes. We have only had one instance where
> a bear got into an approved pannier, and as it turned out, the manufac-
> turer had changed some of the latches of the model we tested. We
> added live bears to the testing protocol in 2000.

In 2001, the first SIBBG testing protocol was ready. The SIBBG
obtained an impact machine from the IGBC and started approving canisters and panniers that passed visual inspections, impact tests, zoo tests,
and then field tests. Once containers made it through all the tests, the
parks approved them for use. Occasionally, approved containers would
later fail and the parks would then pull their approvals until the problem
could be remedied. Some manufacturers, certain their products worked,
chose to ignore the testing protocols. Rangers caught some users before
they took their unapproved canisters into the backcountry, but missed
others and heard about them only after they failed. Phil Gross, who was a
trailhead ranger in Kings Canyon at the time, remembers one fiasco:

> A party of five came to get a permit at Road's End, and I told them
> they had to have a bear canister and they told me they had made their
> own canister. I looked at the canister and it was basically two giant
> spaghetti pots, one flipped upside down onto the other, with hose
> clamps attached handles on the left right side of each pot, and it sealed
> relatively well. Since it wasn't approved, I told the gentleman who was
> getting the permit that he would have to get his own professionally
> made canisters that were approved by the park and he wouldn't be able
> to take the canister that he had made. This was frustrating to him,
> because he had such a clever idea and was determined to make it work.
> But I was persistent, and I told him, "It is a great idea, I love it, but you
> are going to have to take something that is already approved." Of
> course, being an experienced backpacker, he was also very persistent
> and determined to prove his canister was equally as effective as the

canisters that we were renting. So he took the spaghetti pot contraption, which already had all the food in it, and weighed like twenty pounds, lifted it above his head, and threw it down on the wooden decking in front of the ranger station. Unfortunately, the entire thing burst open. Spaghetti noodles and jelly beans went everywhere, and toilet paper rolls ran off the deck and into the creek. Obviously, he didn't test it at home. Of course there were people waiting in line to get their permit and they all laughed for quite a while. Everybody in his party didn't want to laugh, but did anyway. I think even he knew it was funny, even if embarrassing at the same time. So he rented five canisters, one for each person, and they took less food because half of it had fallen through the cracks on the porch of the ranger station.

More commonly, manufacturers worked with SIBBG to ensure they had a reliable product before releasing it onto the mass market. Most manufacturers submitted hard-sided containers for approval, but occasionally, a manufacturer would submit a soft-sided design. Soft-sided containers are an exciting idea in concept, but have many of the same issues as the hung bags of food from the past. For one, if they are tied to trees, they can cause damage to the tree when bears yank on them. If they aren't tied to trees, they can be carried off by bears and left in the wilderness as trash. Second, when bears chew and suck on soft-sided bags, the food inside becomes mutilated, and mixed with saliva and nonedible items (e.g., sunscreen), making the food dangerous to eat, likely to be dumped, and potentially contaminated with rabies. Third, hikers are likely to try to scare bears away from soft-sided food containers to prevent the bears from sucking on them, thus putting themselves at risk if the bears decide to defend "their" food.

Still, some soft-sided containers have been developed and tested. For example, one manufacturer designed a soft-sided bag that was to be left on the ground and electrified. While the SIBBG was discussing the bag, one member, Adam Rich, a biologist from the Stanislaus National Forest, placed it on the floor and turned it on. He paused momentarily and then grabbed it, received only a small jolt, and declared it a delay tactic only. If he could grab it with hardly any effect, so could a bear. Then another manufacturer submitted a soft-sided bag made of bulletproof material and intended to be tied to a tree. The idea was that bears couldn't bite through material and because it was tied to a tree, a bear couldn't carry it off. The parks approved it, but revoked the approval after bears ripped into three of the bags in the field. The manufacturer and the parks then got into a cycle of the manufacturer upgrading the bag, the parks approving it (or not), the product failing in the field, and then the parks rescinding approval. It eventually ended in a lawsuit. In the end, although the NPS prevailed, including standing up to an appeal, in 2007, the parks' administration decided to discontinue SIBBG's testing program.

As a substitute, the parks began relying on the IGBC for testing the sturdiness of new products. Once products passed, and were submitted to the parks for consideration, the parks then assessed whether the containers provided for things like human safety and wilderness protection before making a decision on whether to allow them. At first, that worked well. The IGBC protocol was, by this time, purposely very similar to that of the SIBBG. Testing included a visual inspection, standardized impact testing to easily eliminate substandard containers from consideration, and time with a captive bear. Then, in 2014, the IGBC revised its testing protocol to only include a one-hour test with a captive grizzly. Since the Sierran parks need black bears to test their containers because black bears have shorter and more strongly curved claws than grizzlies, but don't need containers to stand up to the strength of a large grizzly, they are currently considering other ways to test the structural soundness of new products. Possibilities include coordinating with IGBC to test containers on captive grizzly and captive black bears, or requiring all IGBC-certified products to be tested on captive black bears before being considered for allowance in the Sierran parks.

Today, there are several functional models of canisters available on the mass market, but there is room for new ideas and for considering old ideas with new improvements. Netra's patent, #4,801,039, *Animal Proof Container*, which has long since expired, is even available on the Internet if anyone wants to build a prototype and test it. As for Richard Garcia, he is ready for the competition, and at the time of this writing, had even passed on much of his business to his son:

> Me and my wife are getting to the point where we are encouraged to see some of the new people coming in. For a long time, we had that market to ourselves. Now, we know that when we fade into the sunset, the bears will still be protected.

Use of bear-resistant canisters is now fairly standard. Today, it is rare to see a food hang, whereas in the 1990s it was rare to see a canister. Prior to the 1990s, so many people hung food that bears were said to "enter wilderness campsites with their heads up, looking into the trees." The same is true of bear-resistant panniers. They are now used by most packers and finally by the trail crews in all three parks thanks to proactive government purchasing in Sequoia-Kings and a grant from the Yosemite Fund. Even rapid-response fire crews are using bear-resistant food containers.

# VI

## A Draw?

# 30

# THE ISSUES OF TODAY AND THE PROSPECTS FOR TOMORROW

So that brings us, roughly, to the present. "At this point," says Sherri Lisius, "most people are storing their food properly, the garbage is mostly taken care of, and once the rangers have patrolled in the evening to educate the public, there is well over 95 percent compliance on a regular basis." In 2013, Yosemite Valley didn't have a single car break-in. The current numbers of human-bear incidents are now so low that Danny Gammons, the current wildlife biologist at Sequoia-Kings remarked, "I have a hard time even imagining what it was like."

There are some great benefits to this level of success. In addition to all the obvious benefits of lower levels of human-bear conflicts, there is the added benefit of park biologists having time to focus on other wildlife initiatives. Examples include modifying culverts so wildlife can safely cross roads, conducting inventories for rare wildlife species like the Sierra Nevada red fox, restoring meadow habitat for the Yosemite toad, and collaborating with the California Department of Fish and Wildlife to increase numbers of endangered Sierra Nevada bighorn sheep into both Sequoia and Yosemite. There is also great benefit in being able to help others follow a more efficient path. Philip Koepp, retired ranger from Big Bend National Park, remembers Yosemite's advice to bear-proof the park as soon as the bears appeared:

Big Bend had no history of bear problems, but the bears were naturally coming back in the 1990s after being killed off in 1946. I was advised by Yosemite bear management to not go down the path they took but to work quickly to be proactive. As a result, I avoided a lot of problems.

Rocky Mountain National Park made a similar decision to be proactive. Mark Fincher recalls, incredulously:

I was sitting here one day and this guy comes in from Rocky Mountain National Park. He was a wilderness ranger and wanted to talk about bears and canisters and food storage. He wanted to know how we did it because their bears were just starting to get habituated and he wanted to get ahead of the curve by starting a canister program. So I spent like three hours with the guy. I found copies of all the closure notices, explained how we phased it in, and tried to come up with the long and complex history of our rental program. And he just soaked it all in. Then about a year later, I get an e-mail from him, and he said, "Mark, we did everything you suggested. We've got a full-scale rental program, canisters are mandatory, and we are no longer having any bear problems, everything is wonderful. Thank you for your help." And I was like, "Wow." The credit goes to that guy for jumping on it and to the Rocky Mountain bureaucracy for letting him move so fast.

Unfortunately, 95 percent is not 100 percent, and it takes 100 percent compliance to bring the incident rate to zero, and even that probably won't work due to bears' curiosity. Even back in 1977, Leopold and Allen knew that when they said, "A program that will really keep bears out in the woods making an honest living has to be specific, incisive, and rigorously enforced—meaning 100 percent, not 90 percent." And we simply are not, and may never be at, 100 percent.

Not that the parks aren't trying. There are new ideas of ways to store food while it isn't in use. Ideas like putting electric fencing around entire campgrounds as was done at Lake Louise in Canada where the ground is much wetter than in the Sierra. Ideas like keeping people away from bears with closures or facility removals while the bears use seasonally important foods. Ideas like keeping bears away from people by removing seasonal foods from developed areas and planting them elsewhere. Ideas like actually getting the process started to work with the State Historic Preservation Office to remove the apple trees from the Curry parking lot. There is also now a renewed emphasis on the importance of getting people to protect food while it is in use. Jeffrey Trust explains the change:

We used to just tell people to store their food, but we really needed to tell them to store their food when they aren't using it, and to keep it within arm's reach when they are using it. People used to be angry about it, but after all these years, [the public is] no longer surprised.

But the parks are also being realistic about the end of human-bear conflict. Jeffrey Trust said, "I used to think that one day bear incidents would be a distant memory, like the Firefall. Now I realize that is pretty unlikely." Recently retired researcher David Graber puts it all in perspective:

Bears are great folk. They are less neurotic than most of the people I know, and I don't think we are ever going to make most of the problems go away. I think we have to define what is manageable at some level and say we are going to live with this. We all know you can never let down on food control, you have to have eternal vigilance, but at the same time, you can't expect to have 100 percent success. That is absurd.

Steve Thompson, NPS, agreed:

People who say we are going to end human-bear conflict and work towards a day when we never have to kill bears are delusional. Even though it is gut-wrenching for us and also accompanied by hate mail, some bears cannot be salvaged. In Yosemite Valley, there is just too much interface between humans and black bears because the habitat is so good.

So incidents continue, albeit at a much lower rate. Exactly how much lower, of course, depends on the metric one uses to measure the scope of the problem. The traditional metric used is a simple comparison between incident numbers, total damage costs, or total bears killed between years. The problem is that reporting varies widely from year to year and cost estimates are highly variable. Schuyler Greenleaf, like Dave Graber before her, used a different metric. She analyzed bear scats to compare the percentage of human food in bears' diet across years as a proxy for the amount of human food available to bears. The problem with using bear scats is that you can only measure the nondigestible portion of food consumed, rather than all food consumed. Well aware of this problem and looking for a greater challenge, Schuyler looked for an alternative:

I started working with Charlie Robbins at Washington State University. We got talking about isotopes from food and how they pool in the body and are incorporated in the hair. Then we talked about trying to come up with an isotopic signature that would be different in natural vegetation versus human food. Our premise was that if bears were getting corn syrup or cane sugar from human food, a C4 signature would show up. If they were only feeding on naturally occurring foods, a C3 signature would show. So I compared isotopes in bears that spent time in developed areas with those that didn't, and it worked. The isotopes from the bears in developed areas, which were presumably getting more human food than the other bears, did have a C4 signature whereas the isotopes from the other bears had a C3 signature. So we found you really could use the isotopes to figure out what the bears were up to.

After this pilot test, Schuyler handed the isotopic reigns over to Jack Hopkins. To determine how many bears currently seek out human foods in the park, Jack set up "hair-snare" stations throughout Yosemite from 2005–2007. Each hair-snare was comprised of a single string of barbed wire wrapped around a group of trees to form a corral. In the middle, he poured rotten cattle blood to attract bears to the area. When a bear came in to investigate what it thought was a dead carcass, it had to pass under the wire, snagging its hair on the barbs. Every few weeks, Hopkins and his team would collect the hair.

A clever technique, Canadian researcher John Woods and several of his colleagues first used baited hair snares in the late 1990s to systematically sample grizzly and black bear DNA around the town of Golden, in British Columbia. Then, Kate Kendall, a research biologist with the USGS, modified the method by pairing baited stations with naturally occurring bear rub sites. Since some bears will not come to baited stations, Kendall found that also sampling at natural rub sites increased the proportion of the population one could sample. Today, the combination of hair-snare stations and natural rub sites as a means to collect DNA noninvasively from free-ranging wildlife is used throughout the world.

In Yosemite, Jack identified 195 different individual bears using genetic analysis. Of those, he knew from park data that fifteen bears were feeding on human food, but based on the isotopic analysis, was able to predict that an additional eighteen were food conditioned. Although the park was already actively managing many of the known food-conditioned bears, the others had gone undetected, and therefore, unmanaged. Some of the undetected bears were likely ones causing the incidents in the backcountry that the park was aware of, but didn't have time or resources to manage. To get a rough estimate of incidents and damage per bear, Jack divided the number of bears by the reported incident and damage statistics and found that between 2005 and 2007, each food-conditioned bear was involved in less incidents and causing less property damage than bears were between 2001 and 2003. Therefore Yosemite was making progress. Although the comparison using averages is an oversimplification—bears do widely varying amounts of damage—it does help one visualize the overall improvement.

Taking it a step further, Jack and his colleagues decided to use isotopic analysis to compare the average amount of human food bears obtained across four time scales. The time scales represented four periods of management: 1890–1922 represented the beginning of the dumps and bear pits, 1923–1971 represented the organization of formal bear shows through the closing of the dumps, 1972–1998 represented the major period of bear proofing, and 1999–2007 represented the final intensive period of bear proofing and outreach made possible by the $500,000 appropriation. For this analysis, Jack used the hair he collected as well as hair and bone from museum specimens to measure carbon and nitrogen content.

It turned out the proportion of human food in the average bear's diet doubled from the period 1890–1922 to the period 1923–1971, when bears went from occasionally foraging behind hotels to being intentionally fed. The proportion then leveled off between the end of that period and the next one (1972–1998) after both the bear pits and dumps were closed and early bear-proofing was initiated. Finally, the proportion declined drastically from the end of that period to the period 1999–2007, when Yosemite received the $500,000 appropriation and finally had the time, technology, funding, and the will to make food less available. In fact, the proportion of human food in bear diets decreased to the same level as it was in the early 1900s. What makes this achievement particularly notable is that while bears, on average, are consuming the same proportion of human food now as they did before the bear shows ever began, there are now millions of visitors in the park each year, whereas during the turn of the twentieth century, only thousands of people were visiting. In Sequoia-Kings, the improvement is also striking.

Looking into the future, if the parks hope to stay on this path, they need to focus on what they do best, which is proactive management, while maintaining the skills to professionally engage in reactive work. Importantly, everyone needs to stay motivated—and they need to stay motivated whether they see bears or not. Ryan Leahy worries not just about keeping visitors and local residents motivated to store food, but keeping seasonal employees motivated to motivate the visitors:

> Although educating people about food storage is the most important part of the job, it isn't the most fun. The most fun is chasing bears and getting a chance to handle them. That is what keeps the bear techs coming back.

Given that proactive work includes educating millions of visitors a year, motivation is critical. The same is true for educating the parks' own staffs. Although the emphasis tends to be on visitors, in the last decade, over 40 percent of the bears killed in these parks first got food from employees. Retired Sequoia-Kings biologist remembers a year when he "killed more bears due to employee carelessness than visitor carelessness. Pet food left out in housing was really a big problem." Although to be fair, hundreds of employees live and work in the parks and have endless opportunities to make mistakes. Ryan Leahy explains that food-storage problems among staff are some of the trickiest to manage. He says, "Some of the most frustrating problems are those in the housing areas because they are perpetuated by complacency, but then we get lashback from the community if we take any actions."

On this point, Moose Mutlow, the creator of SPLAT, weighs in:

> Employees can be terrible offenders. Although we write tickets freely to the public, we don't write them to employees who leave food out and windows open. A good example is with pumpkins. On Halloween, kids love pumpkins, and some residents put them out on their porches. But pumpkins are food for a bear: a lot of food. I can't believe some employees put bear techs and rangers, who are their coworkers and live in the neighborhood with them, in the position of having to enforce food-storage rules. Some employees want to debate about it, but it isn't a debate. We are lucky to live here and should be held to a higher standard than the public. Plus, it is the bear techs and rangers who have the crappy job of euthanizing the bears. It is a lot of trauma for them, but they carry out the responsibility with integrity and grace.

On the communications front, the agencies are embracing new ways to reach out to the public. Marc Kenyon, of the California Department of Fish and Wildlife, says his agency is increasingly opportunistic at getting out the food-storage message. Often, that means tying it onto developing stories about almost any urban wildlife issue because so many of those issues originate with an animal obtaining human food. It is also important to get the message out that seemingly minor infractions can have major unintended consequences. Former Yosemite wildlife technician Erica Helling still gets upset when talking about the summer the park killed two mountain lions. The lions were hanging around Curry Village, eating raccoons that were eating scraps of food left by humans. "In just a short time, the mountain lions became so habituated they would casually walk through crowds of people," she recalls, "and park management was too uncomfortable with their proximity to kids to keep them around."

Marc Kenyon also notes that social media has improved his agency's relationship with the public. Now, the agency's public relations people tweet updates of incidents as they occur to involve the public, rather than keeping incidents internal and allowing the media to critically dissect them later. The parks use social media to keep the public involved and interested in seasonal happenings and teach visitors how to prepare ahead for their visits. Rangers and other wildlife managers also engage the public on social media to do "damage control." In 2014, this was necessary when visitors to Lake Tahoe started taking "selfies" with habituated bears in the background. Each year, there are also visitors who post videos of bears from close range. Sequoia-Kings Superintendent Woody Smeck is dismayed by the number of people who post videos of bears coming into their camps and taking food:

> We had a family last summer literally film a bear dig into their ice chest, climb up on their picnic table, and consume their food. You can hear the laughter in the background and the "ooh" and the "ahh" and then you hear another visitor in the background saying, "You know you really should be shooing that bear off and discouraging that." You know, they were absolutely clueless as to the long-term effect of what was happening there on that bear.

Although a powerful tool, social media is limited in its use—it will never be a substitute for one-on-one contacts between real live park rangers and real live visitors.

Looking forward, the parks need to be flexible and ready to deal with new challenges ranging from technological to social to natural. If today, we remove food lures from cars by placing coolers in lockers, what do we do tomorrow if the car itself is fueled by French fry grease and is itself the lure? If today, our campground layouts provide the right balance between small camping sites and large group sites, what do we do if everyone starts camping in groups and there aren't enough lockers for their food? What do we do if there is pressure to try new hazing methods on bears such as Tasers? What do we do when bears start opening things we thought were bear-proof? Caitlin Lee-Roney provides an example:

> There are bears that can open door handles now. They don't break in. They just open the door gently and enter. We have a similar problem on buildings where we have the ADA-compliant lever-style door handles instead of the regular round ones.

What about naturally occurring, yet unpredictable events? Fires can quickly eliminate dead trees that formerly brought in important insects and wipe out huge acreages of live trees that formerly provided bears important mast like acorns. In other areas, an absence of fire can lead to reduced berry crops after they are shaded out by an overstory that hasn't been burned off. More worrisome, a long-term absence of fire can lead to such an enormous fuel buildup that when an area finally does burn, the fire can be catastrophic rather than beneficial, even leading to a compete conversion of the habitat type. Droughts can stunt the growth of nutritious roots and forbs in normally productive meadows. They can cause berries to dry on the vine and oaks to abort their acorns. When any of these conditions occur, bears that normally graze problem-free on naturally occurring foods quickly turn to humans as they look for an alternative. This is especially true in the Sierra, where the climate is already hot and dry. After a three-year drought, 2014 was one such year. Bears ranged widely looking for food. Some followed the slippery-slope from orchards and gardens to cat food to kitchens and were killed as a result. With the parks increasingly bear-proof, adjacent communities that aren't bear-proof are seeing increasing problems as bears go where it is easiest to obtain food.

Carl Lackey, with the Nevada Department of Wildlife, experienced a similar event in Nevada:

We know from research done by John Goodrich that there were bears in the mountains west and south of Reno in the late 1980s, but there were no garbage bears. In the late '80s, there was a drought that lasted several years, and we believe that when it ended, bears came into urban areas for food and then their cubs learned to be urban cubs. Combine that with a growing bear population, and more people in urban areas, and the problem progressed exponentially from there. Suddenly in about 1995, bears were a big issue. We now see bears coming back all over. They are now in their historic habitat in central Nevada from where they were extirpated in the '20s and '30s.

It would benefit everyone to bear-proof these communities as additional years of drought are certainly on the horizon. As dire as drought years seem, there is a bigger unknown with bigger potential consequences: climate change. Climate change will disrupt the distribution, timing, and availability of natural foods while exacerbating nature's unpredictable events like fires and drought. Bill Tweed, the naturalist and historian, provides a prediction:

My guess is that bears are better positioned than most to deal with climate change. They are flexible, intelligent scavengers, and will work with what's out there. So I tend to think their world will change, but they do fine with change. My guess would be that the more narrowly designed and obligate an animal's behavior is, the more trouble it is likely to be in and the more flexible and broad-scale an animal's behavior, the more likely it is to be able to adapt. So I tend to think the survivors will be bears and coyotes, and things like pikas will be in a lot of trouble.

The problem for bears, however, is that as they search far and wide to find alternative foods, they are more than likely going to get into conflict with humans.

This thought brings me to the third research question from my own dissertation, how does a shift in the availability of natural foods affect bears' foraging patterns? To research this, I studied how bears traveled in relation to the availability of their preferred foods in 2005 and 2006 in Sequoia National Park. To do this, I used GPS to track the movements of adult female bears, oak surveys to measure acorn availability each year, and seed data (conveniently collected by the USGS for other research in the same area) to measure pine seed availability each year. To confirm that acorns and pine seeds were the bears' preferred food during fall, as was suspected from years of observations, I compared the bears' use of acorns and pine seeds to their use of other available foods by overlaying their movements on Sequoia's vegetation map. I found that not only were pine seeds and acorns the bears' preferred foods, but that their relative abundance would cause the bears to stay put to feed on pine seeds, or range far out of the summer range to feed on acorns, the latter of which caused them to cross more roads and come into contact with more humans and human developments than they would by staying put. The implications for a time when climate change could cause a loss of one of these, or another important seasonal food source, is obvious.

Related to the possibility of bears coming into closer contact with humans is the issue of how to deal with habituation. Habituated bears are more likely to be along roads and get hit by cars and are more likely to be near people and obtain food or injure people than nonhabituated bears. For those reasons, most parks, including Glacier, Sequoia-Kings, and to some extent Yosemite, haze bears away from the roads. In these parks, there is just too much risk of bears being hit by cars or getting fed. This is especially true of the sow-cub groupings. In Sequoia-Kings, biologist Danny Gammons notes another reason some parks haze bears from roadsides, which is, the roads are too windy even to consider allowing bears to forage alongside while cars group into "bear jams" to watch. He says, "It is just too dangerous: a terrible safety hazard."

Why do other parks, like Banff and Yellowstone, do exactly the opposite and purposely allow bears to forage along roads? It turns out these are two of several areas where important seasonal foods for bears either only occur, or occur in a particular abundance, along roads or human developments. In recent decades this has become increasingly true, as fire suppression has reduced available berry patches and meadow habitat. So instead of chasing the bears off, they send out naturalists to supervise the bear jams and educate the people to stay at least one hundred yards from grizzlies so the bears can forage on important foods. There is also the secondary, but very important and valued, benefit of giving visitors the chance to observe bears. As a result, the bears in these parks have become increasingly habituated and increasingly use roadside habitats. In Yellowstone, biologist Kerry Gunther estimates that while ten years ago there were hundreds of bear jams, there are now thousands, and it is difficult for the staff to manage them. He worries about what will happen if the budget, and therefore his staff, is cut, especially if it happens during a natural food shortage. Steve Michel, a human-wildlife conflict specialist in Banff National Park, has similar fears. He says:

> We based our decision to manage roadside bear jams on the premise that we would have the staff to deal with it. I know if our Bear Guardians program was cut, we would be in no position to still be able to manage bear jams.

The hope is that a balance will be found that allows bears to use important foraging areas while keeping them safe. Steve Michel at Banff is clear that we simply don't have it figured out:

> A paradigm shift is happening in bear management. Habituation was once all bad and all evil. Now we understand the reality, which is that bears need some level of habituation to succeed in these landscapes. But I would say habituation is also the area that I think is going to continue to evolve. The spectrum of opinions is diverse, and I never try to fool myself into thinking that fifty years from now, bear managers are not going to look back and mock us in disbelief at what we didn't know.

Danny Gammons from Sequoia-Kings is interested in pursuing research on habituation, but for now, money is tight. Even the Yosemite funds for research have shrunk as inflation has reduced the value of the base increase. In 2014, however, Yosemite's bear team received a grant from the Yosemite Conservancy to buy fifteen GPS collars to improve management efficiency by knowing where bears are in real time. To date, these collars have allowed the biologists to make huge advances in their proactive work and are hugely popular with the media. Not being one to miss an opportunity, the bear team has also joined up with Nalani Ludington, a graduate student at Humboldt State University, to analyze the data collected and delve further into the secret lives of bears. A final consideration is that, even in areas that have perfect food storage and zero food-conditioned or habituated bears, there is the possibility of bears coming in from outside areas. Usually, the parks can't tell where a bear picked up its bad habits because, as Danny Gammons explains, "park bears are wearing giant ear tags when they show up on private property, but not vice-versa." The phenomenon of food-conditioned bears showing up seemingly out of nowhere isn't new. As Ryan Leahy notes, "Off and on, we have bears appear out of nowhere that immediately start ripping doors off houses." It is another reason the parks need to be prepared to respond rapidly to changing circumstances and need to work with neighbors and partner agencies to bear-proof and educate beyond their boundaries. Luckily, Marc Kenyon of California Fish and Wildlife calls the current relationship among state and federal biologists "a strong one." Related factors will be shifts in natural food availability, a further expansion of humans into natural areas, and a further expansion of bears into human-inhabited areas. Marc Kenyon notes this is happening all over. Black bears are expanding their range in a northern march up the coast, possibly filling the niche left vacant by grizzlies. Black bears are already in Monterey County where the habitat is lower quality than in the Sierra, and residents are not prepared.

For bear management programs to stay nimble and effective, they need to stay relevant to the leaders that fund them. Without funding, educational program disappear, signs start to fall apart, and lockers fall into disrepair. Without field rangers, there is no one-on-one education about food storage and less enforcement of food-storage regulations. There is no one to notice when dumpsters are overflowing or lockers are broken. There is no one to notice when campgrounds are full beyond the capacity the dumpsters, lockers, or even bathrooms can handle, and no one to divert campers elsewhere. In just a few years, the human-bear problems could slide back to an unmanageable situation. This possibility is especially true in Yosemite, where over two hundred new campsites will be built in the valley in the next ten years to replace some of those lost in the 1997 flood. The parks could then either accept a return to the chaos of the past or decide to kill bears that obtain unsecured food. The possibility of these scenarios is particularly critical to remember in years of funding cuts that threaten to slice budgets. Barrie Gilbert was serious when he said, "You'd think I would have nightmares about bear attacks after getting mauled, but I used to have nightmares about this problem cycling again and again and again."

Jack Hopkins's research results, park incident records, and anecdotal evidence already point to something of a backslide in the backcountry. These data have Ryan Leahy's attention:

> After backcountry incidents dropped way off, it seems that in recent years people are hanging their food again. Maybe people think that

bears aren't in the high country anymore because they think we took care of it. So now we are having high numbers of incidents again along the John Muir Trail at the really popular camping spots, especially those after the resupply stops where long distance backpackers stop to replenish their food supplies. But even where people do use canisters, some items get left out and other people don't close them correctly.

Add that to the fact that backcountry use is way up, especially along the John Muir Trail where use is up over 500 percent in less than ten years, likely due to a popular book about the trail, released as a film in 2014, and things could go downhill fast.

Meanwhile, there is a discussion going on in the parks as to if and when it is appropriate to remove backcountry lockers. As Mike Coffey said of these discussions in the past, "I know that the arguments are very heated on the installation of food storage lockers in the backcountry—but there is nothing wrong with heated discussion." Hopefully, the discussion will be informed and help the parks choose the best path. The idea is that in the backcountry, and particularly designated wilderness, there should be no human developments, but if there are, they should constitute the minimum tool necessary to get a job done, as is required by the Wilderness Act. Importantly, bears are part of the wilderness and "getting a job done" for bears means keeping them alive and wild. The points of discussion generally include the following pros and cons.

Arguments for keeping lockers in the backcountry/wilderness:

- They work.
- They provide a good backup system if canisters fail.
- They provide storage for overflow food or trash.
- They allow hikers who cannot carry a canister to backpack in certain areas.

Arguments for removing lockers from the backcountry/wilderness:

- They are a human development in backcountry/wilderness.
- They require occasional maintenance or replacement.
- They are often stuffed with trash that must be hauled out.
- Hikers should take responsibility for their own needs.

Pros or cons depending on one's perspective:

- Lockers could provide temporary storage for resupply drops for through-hikers, although this is currently not a permitted use in the parks.
- Lockers concentrate use, impacts, and human waste.

It is important to note that both canisters and lockers will occasionally fail. In Yosemite in 2013, a bear learned to roll canisters off a four hundred-foot cliff into Snow Creek where they broke and provided the bear with a reward. There were about twenty-five incidents involving multiple brands of canisters. After the Yosemite bear team darted and collared her so she could be tracked and hazed, she stopped the behavior. In Yosemite in 2014, a person left a locker unlatched in Little Yosemite Valley that held several campers' food. A bear got all of it.

Some would argue this discussion is occurring prematurely. Kate McCurdy's 2005–2006 research on canister use clearly showed that most people simply cannot fit all of their food, trash, and toiletries into a canister. It wasn't subtle. She found that a full 38 percent of users left some food-related items out on at least one night of their trip even though 75 percent planned their trips in advance, 85 percent packed the day before, and most were carrying dehydrated food. Importantly, she also found that 84 percent of incidents occurred when bears obtained overflow food from people who were carrying canisters. Until the issue of overflow food is resolved by a real solution that works for all visitors, it will not be helpful to remove the lockers. Until then, useful discussions would be ones considering things like whether the existing lockers could be redistributed more appropriately to target areas where high visitor use overlaps with high bear use.

Here, I end the story of the history of bears and their interactions with humans in the Sierra as I understand it. While some parts of the story are less apparent than others, several things are very clear. One, although no one has yet found a way to rewild individual bears, and hundreds of bears have tragically died along the way, the greater population is wilder than it has been in decades. Two, a lot of people, often without funding or support from leadership, worked tirelessly to rewild the bears. There were certainly missteps along the way, and things that could have been done better, but on the whole, the program moved forward to the point where a really good program is now in place. Three, although the hardest work is done, future success is only possible with continual commitment. Finally, it is clear that, as George Durkee likes to remind us by quoting Mel Manley, "One must never underestimate an animal that can ride a bicycle."

# EPILOGUE

At the end of most of the interviews I conducted, I would turn away from management and ask, "What is it like to watch a truly wild bear?" Here is one answer from retired Yosemite ranger-naturalist, Bob Roney:

I don't know why, but lately I've been seeing a lot of bears. I'll be walking through the forest and I'll hear a crackling noise and stop and look up the hill and there will be a mom and two cubs about fifty yards upwind and she is tearing apart a log and licking up ants. And you can see the pink tongue in the distance and the cubs are watching her and licking too. Then they get bored just like little kids and roll off and tumble and wrestle, and as mom goes from log to log the cubs some-times stay near and sometimes get a little farther away and then they come running up to her. They jump on her, and she pushes them away and finishes eating. After a little while, she stops and makes a noise and the cubs come from some distance. She rolls over on her back and the two cubs crawl on her and start nursing. There is no garbage. There is no car broken into. There are just these symbols of wilderness and what national parks are meant to be. To me, having an experience like that brings an indescribable joy.

# ACKNOWLEDGMENTS

When I first thought of researching this history, I was working in bear management, living in the Sierra Nevada, and single. I had all the time in the world. Then somewhere between coming up with the idea and actually starting it, I got married, moved to Nevada, and had twin babies. Bears were no longer my focus, and this project was in my past. Or so I thought. Too quickly, those babies grew into toddlers, and toddlers, like bears, are clever and persistent. To keep them safe, you have to stay a half step ahead of them. They reminded me of bears, and before I knew it, I started writing. Slowly, over hundreds of naptimes, during which I would extricate myself from blankets, stray legs, and piles of stuffed animals to write, a draft of this book came into existence.

While writing was a mostly solitary endeavor, researching it was not, and I am enormously grateful to the people who graciously shared their stories and ideas with me, and through me, with the reader. Those people are Joe Abrell, Theodore Bartlett, Harold Basey, Bruce and Barbara Black, Michael Botkin, Laurel Boyers, Stewart Breck, Steve Bumgardner, Mary Anne Carlton, Brad Cella, Les Chow, Mike Coffey, Anthony Colonesse, Lance Craighead, Lois Dalle-Molle, Bill DeCarteret, Kim Delozier, Tim Downey, George Durkee, Mark Fincher, Jack Fiscus, Paul Fodor, Jonathan Fusaro, Danny Gammons, Richard Garcia, Scott Gediman, Barrie Gilbert, David Graber, Schuyler Greenleaf, Philip Gross, Kerry Gunther, Billy Hancock, Bruce Hastings, Michael Hauptman, Erica Helling, Steve Herrero, Jack Hopkins, Ken Hulick, Diane Ingram, David Karplus, Dick Karsky, Jeff Keay, Kate Kendall, Marc Kenyon, Philip

Koepp, Jeannine Koshear, Carl Lackey, Ryan Leahy, Caitlin Lee-Roney, Sherri Lisius, Ron Mackie, Leroy Maloy, Dick Martin, Sean Matthews, Sally Maughan, Kate McCurdy, Earl McKee, Bob Meadows, Steve Michel, Steve Moffit, Jack Morehead, Ray Muray, Moose Mutlow, Linda Neal, Jill Oertley, Jack Phinney, Rob Pilewski, Pat Quinn, Marcia Rasmussen, Calder Reid, Wally Rice, Andy Ringgold, Katie Rodriguez, Bob Roney, Gene Rose, James Rouse, Tony Rowell, Dave Sampietro, Rick Sanger, Philip Schiliro, Dorothy Scott, Tori Seher, Dean Shenk, Rick Smith, Robert Smith, Jim Snyder, Bill Stiver, John Sturdevant, J. D. Swed, Steve Thompson (NPS), Steve Thompson (Bearsaver), Mike Tollefson, Jerry Torres, Jeffrey Trust, James Tucker, Bill Tweed, Joe Van Horn, Jan van Wagtendonk, Carrie Vernon, Vic Viera, Christina Vojta, Linda Wallace, Mary Kay Watry, Nina Weisman, Harold Werner, Dan Whitehair, and Robert Winter. I am also grateful to the larger group of fellow bear biologists and enthusiasts who provided the intangibles needed to develop this book: the discussions and debates, the passion, and the belief that a book like this was necessary. This list is too long to include here, grows by the year, and is loaded with some of the most enthusiastic, clever, and dedicated people I've met.

I also appreciate the many people who helped me access the tangibles: the data, documents, and photographs. Those people are Alicia Barber, Chuck Bartlebaugh, Steve Bumgardner, Linda Eade, Katie Ehler, Ward Eldridge, Danny Gammons, Ryan Leahy, Caitlin Lee-Roney, Brenna Lissoway, Rukmini Martin, Linda Mazzu, Sonny Montague, Kristin Ramsey, Jim Snyder, Jeffrey Trust, John Woods, Bill Wade, Peri Wolff, and Jackie Zak. After many years slipped past and I finally melded this gigantic accumulation of stories and ideas and information together and completed a rough draft, I sought reviews, advice, and edits from people with various skills and expertise. Their corrections, suggestions, and thoughtful comments greatly improved the book, and I can't thank them enough. Those people are Malinee Crapsey, Dave Graber, Jennifer Hardin, Caitlin Lee-Roney, Brian Lefler, Allan Mazur, Kate McCurdy, Rebecca Rising, John Sturdevant, Steve Thompson (NPS), Julie Mazur Tribe, Jeffrey Trust, and Harold Werner. Then I found David Legere, who believed in my book, agreed to be my editor, and helped me negotiate the last, but hugely important, part of the whole project: taking it from a draft to a final product. Of course, the journey was made easier with generous encouragement from Savannah and Danny Boiano, Melissa Granat, Krista Hart, Katie and David Karplus, Chris Lanier, and Jenny Mahon.

Finally, I am grateful to my family. My kids, Max and Wren, not only reminded me of bears, but also took three-hour naps, giving me time to write the book. They also provided endless comic relief. When Max entered his first bear den at age two, he described it as "yucky" and then coined the term "drop down" for dens in trees that dropped below ground level. When Wren, also at age two, was bluff charged by a female bear with cubs, her reaction was to announce, "I want a pink bear to keep in my drawer." My parents, Allan and Polly, have always been supportive of my love for wildlife and natural areas and have often helped during visits, as has my sister Julie, brother-in-law Matt, and niece Marlo. My husband, John, is my partner in all things and an incredible father to our cubs. He has helped me observe bears, catch bears, and even skin dead bears. For this project, he was my sounding board, editor, and cheerleader. I am so grateful I married my best friend and can't thank him enough for all his support.

In the end, even with all this help, there are sure to be errors and omissions. I apologize for them and will make appropriate edits in any future editions. In the meantime, I hope you enjoyed the story and learned something along the way. If nothing else, please store your food properly.

# REFERENCES

Albert, D. M., and R. T. Bowyer. 1991. Factors related to grizzly bear-human interactions in Denali National Park. *Wildlife Society Bulletin* 19:339–49.

Anonymous. 1973. Letter to Nathaniel Reed and others from a Sequoia seasonal.

AP. 1978. Some Yosemite bears are really bad news. *Observer-Reporter*. July 10.

Archer, M. 1990. Black bear management in Yosemite National Park: implications for ecosystem management. Undergraduate thesis, University of California, Santa Barbara, USA.

Armbruster, S. 1998. On the bear watch. *Fresno Bee*. Aug 10.

Associated Press. 2004. Offbeat: Bear drinks 36 cans of favorite beer. *USA Today*. August 18.

Ayers, L., Chow, L. S., and D. M. Graber. 1983. Black bear activity patterns and human induced modifications in Sequoia National Park. *Proceedings of the Fifth International Conference on Bear Research and Management* 6:151–54.

Bacon, J., Roche, J., Elliot, C., and N. Nicholas. 2006. VERP: Putting principles into practice in Yosemite National Park. *George Wright Forum* 23:73–83.

Barbeau, J. T. 1996 (October 10). Internal letter to Inyo Forest Supervisor Dennis Martin. Inyo National Forest, California, USA.

Barrett, S. A., and E. W. Gifford. 1933. *Miwok material culture*. Yosemite Association, Yosemite National Park, California, USA.

Bear necessities: love and learning. 2001. *Kaweah Commonwealth*. May 4.

Bear-proof food boxes get new latches. 1997. *Visalia Times-Delta*. September 22.

Beatty, M. E. 1938. New weight record for Sierra Nevada black bear. *Yosemite Nature Notes* 17:151–52.

Beatty, M. E. 1943. Bears of Yosemite. *Yosemite Nature Notes* 22:1–16.

Beckmann, J. P., and J. Berger. 2003. Rapid ecological and behavioral changes in carnivores: the responses of black bears (*Ursus americanus*) to altered food. *Journal of Zoology* 261:207–12.

Beckmann, J. P., Karasin, L., Costello, C., Matthews, S., and Z. Smith. 2008. Coexisting with black bears: perspectives from four case studies across North America. WCS Working Paper No. 33, Wildlife Conservation Society, New York. USA.

Beckmann, J. P., and C. W. Lackey. 2008. Carnivores, urban landscapes, and longitudinal studies: a case history of black bears. *Human-wildlife Conflicts* 2:168–74.

Beckmann, J. P., Lackey, C. W., and J. Berger. 2004. Evaluation of deterrent techniques and dogs to alter behavior of "nuisance" black bears. *Wildlife Society Bulletin* 32:1141–1146.

Belant, J. L., Simek, S. L., and B. C. West. 2011. Managing human-black bear conflicts. Human-wildlife Conflicts Monograph No. 1, Center for Human-Wildlife Conflict Resolution, Mississippi State University, Mississippi, USA.

Bergstresser, L. S., Burton, J. F., and J. R. Kendall. 2001. Dining at the bear pits: archaeological investigations at the Taft Toe Site (CA-MRP-70/H), Yosemite National Park, California. National Park Service Publications in Anthropology No. 22, Yosemite National Park, California, USA.

Biel, A. W. 2006. *Do Not Feed the Bears*. University of Kansas Press, Lawrence, USA.

Booth, W. 1997. Three bears too clever to live; at Yosemite, sharing humans tastes can be deadly. *Washington Post.* December 11.

Breck, S. W., Lance, N., Bourassa, J., Matthews, S., and V. Seher. 2007. An automated system for detecting and reporting trespassing bears in Yosemite National Park. *Ursus* 18:230–35.

Breck, S. W., Lance, N., and P. Callahan. 2006. A shocking device for protection of concentrated food sources from black bears. *Wildlife Society Bulletin* 34:23–26.

Breck, S. W., Lance, N., and V. Seher. 2009. Selective foraging for anthropogenic resources by black bears: minivans in Yosemite National Park. *Journal of Mammalogy* 90:1041–44.

Breck, S. W., Williams, C. L., Beckmann, J. P., Matthews, S. M., Lackey, C. W., and J. J. Beecham. 2008. Using genetic relatedness to investigate the development of conflict behavior in black bears. *Journal of Mammalogy* 89:428–34.

Brody, A. J., and M. R. Pelton. 1987. Seasonal changes in digestion in black bears. *Canadian Journal of Zoology* 66:1482–84.

Brook, C. E., Bernstein, D. P., and E. A. Hadly. 2013. Human food subsidies and common raven occurrence in Yosemite National Park, California. *Western Birds* 44:127–34.

Brown, G. 1993. *The Great Bear Almanac*. The Lyons Press. New York, New York, USA.

Brown, S., K., Hull, J. M., Updike, D. R., Fain, S. R., and H. B. Ernest. 2009. Black bear population genetics in California: signatures of population structure, competitive release, and historical translocation. *Journal of Mammalogy* 90:1066–74.

Brunet, A. 1995. *Survey of food storage needs in the Curry Village parking lot at Yosemite National Park*. Internal report, Yosemite National Park, California, USA.

Buettner, R., Bundy, S., Dinerstein, E., Duffield, J., Kaye, E., Loquvam, J, McElfish, D., Shimamoto, K., and J. R. Parmeter. 1974. Black bear population of the Yosemite Valley and human related behavior. Report to the National Park Service, National Science Foundation Student Originated Studies Program, University of California, Berkeley, USA.

Bumgardner, S. 2007. *Bears of Sequoia*. California, USA.

Burghduff, A. 1935. Black bears released in southern California. *California Fish and Game* 21:83–84.

Burton, J., Farrell, M., Bonstad, L., Bergstresser, L., Kehres, H., and M. Martz. 2003. Victory culture: archeological investigations at nine trash dumps at Yosemite National Park, California. National Park Service Publications in Anthropology No. 24, Yosemite National Park, California, USA.

Cahalane, V. H. 1939. The evolution of predator control policy in the national parks. *Journal of Wildlife Management* 3(3).

California Department of Fish and Game. 2002. *Outdoor California* 63.

Charle, S. 1997. To bears in Yosemite, cars are like cookie jars. *The New York Times.* November 30.

Chin, M. 1979. Radio-tracking fall movements of black bears in Sequoia and Kings Canyon National Parks. Internal Report, Sequoia and Kings Canyon National Parks, California, USA.

Claar, J., and D. Zimmer. 2008. Bear spray overview, background, IGBC partnership with Center for Wildlife Information and summary recommendations. Special Report to the Interagency Grizzly Bear Committee, Montana, USA.

Coffey, M. A. 1983. Preliminary report on bear-proof backpack food canister. Internal Report, Sequoia and Kings Canyon National Parks, California, USA.

Cooper, D. 1995. Parks' donors boost funding. *Visalia Times-Delta.* December 14.

Crapsey, M. 1991. Bear-watcher. *Sequoia Bark*. Fall edition.

Crapsey, M. 2000. The death of #583. *Sequoia Bark*. Fall edition.

Cushing, B. S. 1983. Responses of polar bears to human menstrual odors. *Proceedings of the Fifth International Conference on Bear Research and Management* 5:270–74.

Dalle-Molle, J. 1984. Field tests and user's opinions of bear resistant backpack food containers in Denali National Park, Alaska, 1982 and 1983. Internal Report, Denali National Park, Alaska, USA.

Dalle-Molle, J. L., Coffey, M. A., and H. W. Werner. 1985. Evaluation of bear-resistant food containers for backpackers. *Proceedings of the National Wilderness Research Conference* 1985:209–14.

Dilsaver, L. M., and W. C. Tweed. 1990. *The Challenge of the Big Trees*. Sequoia Natural History Association, Three Rivers, California, USA.

Dixon, J. S. 1940. Special report on bear situation at Giant Forest, Sequoia National Park California. Internal Report, Sequoia and Kings Canyon National Parks, California, USA.

Dixon, J. S. 1942. Special report on bear situation: Kings Canyon in May, 1942. Internal Report, Sequoia and Kings Canyon National Parks, California, USA.

Dixon, J. S. 1943. Report on numbers, distributions, and feeding of bears in Yosemite Valley. October 12, 1943. Internal Report, Yosemite National Park, California, USA.

During, M. M. 1979. Environmental measurements of black bear dens in Sequoia and Kings Canyon National Parks, CA. Graduate Student Report, California State University, Fresno, USA.

Elliot, J. 2002. Bear affair: Three Rivers man convicted in bear case. *Kaweah Commonwealth.* January 11.

Fradkin, P. 1971. Personnel shifted to change image of Yosemite Park. *L.A. Times*. August 4.

Garshelis, D. L., and E. C. Hellgren. 1994. Variation in reproductive biology of male black bears. *Journal of Mammalogy* 75:175–88.

Gniadek, S. J., and K. C. Kendall. 1998. A summary of bear management in Glacier National Park. 1960–1994. *Ursus* 10:155–59.

Godfrey, E. H. 1942. A cub bear sticks its neck "in" too far. *Yosemite Nature Notes* 21:51–52.

Goldsmith, A. 1979. *Movements of black bears in Sequoia and Kings Canyon National Parks*. Internal Report, Sequoia and Kings Canyon National Parks, California, USA.

Goldsmith, A., Walraven, M. E., Graber, D. M., and M. White. 1980. *Ecology of the black bear in Sequoia National Park*. Report to the National Park Service, California, USA.

Graber, D. M. 1979. Among the bears. *California Explorer* 2:7.

Graber, D. M. 1981. Ecology and management of black bears in Yosemite National Park. Dissertation, University of California, Berkeley, USA.

Graber, D. M. 1982. Ecology and management of black bears in Yosemite National Park. Cooperative Park Studies Unit Technical Report No. 5, University of California, Davis, USA.

Graber, D. M. 1985. Conflicts between wilderness users and black bears in the Sierra Nevada National Parks. *Proceedings of the National Wilderness Research Conference*.

Graber, D. M. 1989. Winter behavior of black bears in the Sierra Nevada, California. *Proceedings of the Eighth International Conference on Bear Research and Management* 8:269–72.

Graber, D. M., and M. White. 1983. Black bear food habits in Yosemite National Park. *Proceedings of the Fifth International Conference on Bear Research and Management* 5:1–10.

Greenleaf, S. 2005. Foraging behavior of black bears in a human-dominated environment. Yosemite Valley, Yosemite National Park, California, 2001–2003. Thesis, University of Idaho, Moscow, USA.

Greenleaf, S., Matthews, S. M., Wright, G. R., Beecham, J. J., and H. M. Leithead. 2009. Food habits of American black bears as a metric for direct management of human-bear conflict in Yosemite Valley, Yosemite National Park, California, *Ursus* 20:94–101.

Grinnel, J. 1929. The two races of black bears in California. *University of California Publications in Zoology* 32:395–408.

Grinnel, J., and T. Storer. 1924. *Animal life in the Yosemite*. University of California Press, Berkeley, USA.

Grossi, M. 1997. Human food cost Sierra bear her life. *Fresno Bee*. August 8.

Grossi, M. 2002. Keep out bears. *Fresno Bee*. May 11.

Gunther, K. A. 1994. Bear management in Yellowstone National Park, 1960-93. *Proceedings of the Ninth International Conference on Bear Research and Management* 9:549–60.

Guse, N. G. 1970. Large black bear from Yosemite. *California Fish and Game* 56:208–09.

Harms, D. R. 1977. Black bear management in Yosemite National Park. *Proceedings of the Annual Conference of the Western Association of State Game and Fish Commission* 57:159–81.

Harms, D. R. 1980. Black bear management in Yosemite National Park. *Proceedings of the Fourth International Conference on Bear Research and Management* 4:205–12.

Harwell, C. A. 1932. Hibernating bears. *Yosemite Nature Notes* 11:1–3

Harwell, C. A. 1937. Our changing bears. *Yosemite Nature Notes* 16:28–30.

Hastings, B. 1982. Human-bear interactions in the backcountry of Yosemite National Park. Thesis, Utah State University, Logan, USA.

Hastings, B. C., and B. K. Gilbert. 1981. Aversive conditioning of black bears in the backcountry of Yosemite National Park. Report to the National Park Service, Utah State University, Logan, USA.

Hastings, B. C., and B. K. Gilbert. 1981. Black bears-human interactions in Yosemite National Park: 1978-1980. Report to the National Park Service, Utah State University, Logan, USA.

Hastings, B. C., and B. K. Gilbert. 1987. Extent of human-bear interactions in the backcountry of Yosemite National Park. *California Fish and Game* 73:188–91.

Hastings, B. C., Gilbert, B. K., and D. L. Turner. 1981. Black bear behavior and human-bear relationships in Yosemite National Park, 1978–1979. Cooperative Park Studies Unit Technical Report No. 2, University of California, Davis, USA.

Hastings, B. C., Gilbert, B. K., and D. L. Turner. 1986. Black bear aggression in the backcountry of Yosemite National Park. *Proceedings of the Sixth International Conference for Bear Research and Management* 6:145–49.

Herrero, S. 2002. *Bear Attacks: Their Causes and Avoidance.* Revised Edition. Lyons-Globe Pequot Press, Guilford, Connecticut, USA.

Herrero, S., and A. Higgins. 1998. Field use of capsicum spray as a bear deterrent. *Ursus* 10:533–37.

Herrero, S., Higgins, A., Cardoza, J. E., Hajduk, L. I., and T. S. Smith. 2011. Fatal attacks by American black bear on people: 1900–2009. *Journal of Wildlife Management* 75:596–603.

Herrero, S., Smith, T., Dbruyn, T. D., Gunther, K. and C. A. Matt. 2005. From the field: brown bear habituation to people–safety, risks, and benefits. *Wildlife Society Bulletin* 33:363–73.

Hollis, R. 1999. Remember: wildlife roams the Sierra. *Visalia Times-Delta.* March 18.

Hopkins, J. B. III. 2013. Use of genetics to investigate socially learned foraging behavior in free-ranging black bears. *Journal of Mammalogy* 94:1214–22.

Hopkins, J. B. III., Herrero, S., Shideler, R. T., Gunther, K. A., Schwartz, C. C., and S. T. Kalinowski. 2010. A proposed lexicon of terms and concepts for human-bear management in North America. *Ursus* 21:154–68.

Hopkins, J. B. III., and S. T. Kalinowski. 2013. The fate of transported American black bears in Yosemite National Park. *Ursus* 24:120–26.

Hopkins, J. B. III., Koch, P. L., Ferguson, J. M., and S. T. Kalinowski. 2014. The changing anthropogenic diets of American black bears over the past century in Yosemite National Park. *Frontiers in Ecology and the Environment* 12:107–14.

Hopkins, J. B. III., Kock, P. L., Schwartz, C. C., Ferguson, J. M., Greenleaf, S. S., and S. T. Kalinowski. 2012. Stable isotopes to detect food-conditioned bears and to evaluate human-bear management. *Journal of Wildlife Management* 76:703–13.

Hull, K. L. 2009. *Pestilence and persistence: Yosemite indian demography and culture in colonial California.* University of California Press, Berkeley, USA.

Hunt, C. L. 2003. Partners-in-life: bear shepherding guidelines for safe and effective treatment of human-bear conflicts. The Wind River Bear Institute, Heber City, Utah, USA.

Ingram, D. 1989. Keep black bears wild. *Sequoia Sentinel.* October 18.

Ingram, D. K. 1995. Sequoia and Kings Canyon National Parks—black bear management techniques and program update. *Proceedings of the Fifth Western Black Bear Workshop* 5:99–104.

Jones, R. 1971. National Parks: A report on the range war at generation gap. *New York Times.* July 25.

Keay, J. A. 1990. Black bear population dynamics in Yosemite National Park. National Park Service Technical Report No. 39. University of California, Davis, USA.

Keay, J. A. 1990. Black bear population dynamics in Yosemite National Park. Dissertation, University of Idaho, Moscow, USA.

Keay, J. A. 1995. Accuracy of cementum age assignments for black bears. *California Fish and Game* 81:113–21.

Keay, J. A. 1995. Black bear reproductive rates in Yosemite National Park. *California Fish and Game* 81:122–31.

Keay, J. A., and J. W. Van Wagtendonk. 1983. Effect of Yosemite backcountry use levels on incidents with black bears. *Proceedings of the Fifth International Conference on Bear Research and Management* 5:307–11.

Keay, J. A., and M. G. Webb. 1989. Effectiveness of human-bear management at protecting visitors and property in Yosemite National Park. *Bear-people conflicts: Proceedings of a symposium on management strategies* 1987:145–54.

Keene, S. 1987. *Earthly treasures*. Harlequin Enterprises Limited, Ontario, Canada.

Kilham, B., and E. Gray. 2002. *Among the bears: raising orphan cubs in the wild*. Henry Halt and Company, New York, New York, USA.

Klein, W. E. 1981. An enlightening and sobering experience in California. Internal report, Region 1, California Department of Fish and Game, California, USA.

Lackey, B. K. 2002. Empirical and theoretical analysis of communication focused on human-bear conflicts in Yosemite National Park. Dissertation, University of Idaho, Moscow, USA.

Lackey, B. K. 2004. Assessment of communication focused on human-bear conflict at Yosemite National Park. *Journal of Interpretation Research* 8:25–40.

Lackey, B. K., and S. H. Ham. 2003. Contextual analysis of interpretation focused on human-black bear conflicts in Yosemite National Park. *Journal of Applied Environmental Education and Communication* 2:11–21.

Lackey, B., and S. Ham. 2003. Final Report: Human element assessment focused on human-bear conflict in Yosemite National Park. *Journal of Interpretation Research* 8:25–40.

La Vine, K. P. 1992. Bear management in the backcountry of Yosemite National Park. Undergraduate Senior Thesis, University of California, Santa Barbara, USA.

Leigh, J., and M. J. Chamberlain. 2008. Effects of aversive conditioning on behavior of nuisance Louisiana black bears. *Human-wildlife Conflicts* 2:175–84.

Leopold, A. S., and D. L. Allen. 1977. A review of National Park Service bear management problems. Memorandum to NPS Director Whalen, University of California, Berkeley, USA.

Leopold, A. S., Cain, S. A., Cottam, C. M., Gabrielson, I. N., and T. L. Kimball. 1963. *Wildlife management in the National Parks: the Leopold Report*. Advisory Board on Wildlife Management, Washington DC, USA.

Lippincott, W. S., Jr. 1981. Bear management in the National Park Service: a review. Internal Report, National Park Service Division of Natural Resources, Washington, DC, USA.

Madison, J. S. 2008. Yosemite National Park: the continuous evolution of human-black bear conflict management. *Human-Wildlife Conflicts* 2:160–67.

Masterson, L. 2006. *Living with Bears: A Practical Guide to Bear Country*. Pixyjack Press, Masonville, Colorado, USA.

Matthews, M. 1999. Bear spray manufacturer gets a hit of reality. *High Country News*. Sept. 13.

Matthews, S. M., Beecham, J. J., Quigley, H. B., Greenleaf, S. S., and H. M. Leithead. 2006. Activity patterns of American black bears in Yosemite National Park. *Ursus* 17:30–40.

Matthews, S. M., Lackey, B. K., Greenleaf, S. S., Leithead, H. M., Beecham, J. J., Ham, S. H., and H. B. Quigley. 2003. Final Report: Human-bear interaction assessment in Yosemite National Park. Hornocker Wildlife Institute/Wildlife Conservation Society, Bozeman, Montana, USA.

Mazur, R. 2007. Human-black bear conflict: an analysis of origins and solutions. Dissertation, University of California, Davis, USA.

Mazur, R. 2008. Backpacker use of bear-resistant canisters and lockers at Sequoia and Kings Canyon National Parks. *Ursus* 19:53–58.

Mazur, R. 2008. *If You Were a Bear*. Sequoia Natural History Association, Three Rivers, California, USA.

Mazur, R. 2010. Does aversive conditioning reduce human-bear conflict? *Journal of Wildlife Management* 74:48–54.

Mazur, R., Klimley, A. P., and K. Folger. 2013. Implications of the variable availability of seasonal foods on the home ranges of black bears, *Ursus americanus*, in the Sierra Nevada of California. *Animal Biotelemetry* 1:16.

Mazur, R., and V. Seher. 2008. Socially learned foraging behavior in wild black bears, *Ursus americanus*. *Animal Behaviour* 75:1503–08.

McArthur, K. L. 1981. Factors contributing to effectiveness of black bear transplants. *Journal of Wildlife Management* 45:102–10.

McCall, M., and J. W. Vinson. 1989. US Patent 4,801,039: *Animal proof container*. Netra Plastics, Mountain View, California, USA.

McCurdy, K. 2006. Beliefs, attitudes, and behaviors about bear resistant food canister use among wilderness users in Yosemite National Park. Thesis, Humboldt State University, Arcata, California, USA.

McCurdy, K., and S. R. Martin. 2007. An assessment of bear resistant canister use in Yosemite National Park. Report to the National Park Service, Humboldt State University. Arcata, California, USA.

McMillin, J. M., Seal, U. S., Rogers, L., and A. W. Erickson. 1976. Annual testosterone rhythm in the black bear (*Ursus americanus*). *Biology of Reproduction* 15:163–67.

Miller, C., editor. 2010. *Cities and nature in the American west*. University of Nevada Press, Reno, USA.

Muir, J. 1898. Among the animals of the Yosemite. *Atlantic Monthly* LXXXII:617–31.

National Park Service. [1940]. *Sequoia National Park Annual Report*. Sequoia National Park, Three Rivers, California, USA.

National Park Service. [1895–1896, 1902–1924, 1929, 1937, 1972–1977]. *Yosemite National Park Superintendent's Monthly and Annual Reports*. Yosemite National Park, California, USA.

National Park Service. 1939. Wildlife conditions in national parks. *Conservation Bulletin* No. 3.

National Park Service. [1959–2009]. *Bear Management Annual Reports for Sequoia and Kings Canyon National Parks*. Sequoia and Kings Canyon National Parks, California, USA.

National Park Service. 1972. *Bear Management Plan for Sequoia and Kings Canyon National Parks*. Sequoia and Kings Canyon National Parks, California, USA.

National Park Service. 1975. *Yosemite National Park Human-bear Management Plan*. Yosemite National Park, California, USA.

National Park Service. [1979, 1992–2013]. *Bear Management Annual Reports for Yosemite National Park*. Yosemite National Park, California, USA.

National Park Service. 1980. *Bear Management Plan for Sequoia and Kings Canyon National Parks*. Sequoia and Kings Canyon National Parks, California, USA.

National Park Service. 1982. *Human-bear Management Plan for Yosemite National Park*. Yosemite National Park, California, USA.

National Park Service. 1986. *Bear Management Plan for Sequoia and Kings Canyon National Parks*. Sequoia and Kings Canyon National Parks, California, USA.

National Park Service. [1987–2010]. *Bear Tech Annual Reports for Sequoia and Kings Canyon National Parks*. Sequoia and Kings Canyon National Parks, California, USA.

National Park Service. 1989. *Wildlife Management Plan for Sequoia and Kings Canyon National Parks*. Sequoia and Kings Canyon National Parks, California, USA.

National Park Service. 1992. *Bear Management Plan for Sequoia and Kings Canyon National Parks*. Sequoia and Kings Canyon National Parks, California, USA.

National Park Service. 2002. *Human-bear Management Plan for Yosemite National Park*. Yosemite National Park, California, USA.

National Technical Systems. 1986. Report of compression, puncture, abrasion resistance, and drop tests on canisters. Report No. 677-5440. Testing Division, Fullerton, California, USA.

News of the Neighborhood: Three Rivers Man to establish skull as that of grizzly bear. 1930. *Visalia Times-Delta*. February 14.

Novick, H. J., and G. R. Stewart. 1982. Home range and habitat preferences of black bears in the San Bernardino Mountains of southern California. *California Fish and Game* 67:21–35.

Núñez, J. J., Fritz, C. L., Knust, B., Buttke, D., Enge, B., Novak, M. G., et al. 2012. Hantavirus infections among overnight visitors to Yosemite National Park, California, USA, 2012. *Emerging Infectious Diseases* 20(3).

Oertley, J. 1995. Bear this in mind. *Kaweah Commonwealth*. June 9.

Olsen, J. 1969. *Night of the Grizzlies*. Signet, New York, New York, USA.

Parker, H. C. 1950. *The bear problem in Yosemite National Park*. Internal report, Yosemite National Park, California, USA.

Payson, A. L. 1991. A survey of backpackers: their response to black bears. Thesis, University of California, Davis, USA.

Reigelhuth, D. 1979. *A synopsis of the black bear in Yosemite National Park*. Internal report, Yosemite National Park, California, USA.

Rizzo, E. M. 1998. New perspectives in bear management: a human management approach. Final Report to Sequoia and Kings Canyon National Parks, California State University, Fresno, USA.

Rogers, L. L. 1987. Navigation by adult black bears. *Journal of Mammalogy* 68:185–88.

Rogers, L. L., and S. C. Durst. 1987. Evidence that black bears reduce peripheral blood flow during hibernation. *Journal of Mammalogy* 68:876–78.

Rogers, L. L., Wilker, G. A., and S. S. Scott. 1991. Reaction of black bears to human menstrual odors. *Journal of Wildlife Management* 55:632–34.

Rowell, G. 1974. The Yosemite solution to *Ursus americanus*. *Sierra Club Bulletin* 59:27–31.

Runte, A. 1993. *Yosemite: The Embattled Wilderness*. University of Nebraska Press, Lincoln, USA.

Russell, C. P. 1923. Zoo bears prefer captivity. *Yosemite Nature Notes* 2:2–3.

Russell, C. P. 1924. Liberated zoo bear again appears. *Yosemite Nature Notes* 3:3.

Russell, C. P. 1925. Some animal friends you make in Yosemite. *Yosemite Nature Notes* 9:36–37.

Schnoes, R., and E. Starkey. 1978. Bear management in the national park system. Report to the National Park Service, Oregon Cooperative Park Studies Unit, Oregon State University, Corvallis, USA.

Schullery, P. 1992. *The Bears of Yellowstone*. High Plains Publishing Company, Worland, Wyoming, USA.

Secrest, William B. 2008. *Day of the Grizzly: the Exciting Story of Man Against the Mighty California Grizzly Bears*. Quill Driver Books/Word Dancer Press, Sanger, California, USA.

Sellars, R. W. 1997. *Preserving Nature in the National Parks: A History*. Yale University Press, New Haven, Connecticut, USA.

Sinclair, L. 1995. *Animal resistant garbage containers*. San Dimas Technology and Development Center SDTDC-9523-1205, U.S. Forest Service, San Dimas, California, USA.

Sinclair, L. 1997. *Bear-proof food lockers, Second Edition*. San Dimas Technology and Development Center SDTDC-9723-1811, U.S. Forest Service, San Dimas, California, USA.

Smith, J. K. 1983. BIMS—The bear reporting network for the National Park Service. *Proceedings of the Fifth International Conference on Bear Research and Management* 5:297–301.

Smith, T., Herrero, S., and T. D. Debruyn. 2005. Alaskan brown bears, humans, and habituation. *Ursus* 16:1–10.

Smith, T. S., Herrero, S., Debruyn, T. D., and J. M. Wilder. 2006. The efficacy of bear deterrent spray in Alaska. *Journal of Wildlife Management* 72:640–45.

Smith, T. S., Herrero, S., Layton, C. S., and K. R. Johnson. 2012. Efficacy of firearms for bear deterrence in Alaska. *Journal of Wildlife Management* 76:1021–27.

Snyder, S. 2003. *The California Grizzly: Bear in Mind*. Heyday Books, Berkeley, California, USA.

Steinhart, P. 1978. Getting to know the bruin better. *National Wildlife*. 16:20–26.

Stenhouse, G. 1983. Bear Detection and Deterrent Study, Cape Churchill, Manitoba, 1982. Wildlife Service File Report No. 31, Northwest Territories, Canada.

Storer, T. I., and L. P. Tevis, Jr. 1955. *California Grizzly*. University of California Press, Berkeley, USA.

Storer, T. I., Vansell, G. H., and B. D. Moses. 1938. Protection of mountain apiaries from bears by use of electric fence. *Journal of Wildlife Management* 2: 172–78.

Sullivan, M. 2001. Letter to the Editor. Bear with Us. *Kaweah Commonwealth*. October 12.

Sumner, L. E. Jr. 1936. Special report on a wildlife study of the high sierra in Sequoia and Kings Canyon National Parks and adjacent territories. Internal Report. National Park Service Western Regional Office, California, USA.

Sumner, L. E. Jr. 1939. Special report on electric fence investigations for wildlife control. Internal report, National Park Service Western Regional Office, California, USA.

Tate, J., and M. R. Pelton. 1983. Human-bear interactions in the Great Smokey Mountains National Park. *Proceedings of the Fifth International Conference on Bear Research and Management* 5:312–21.

Thompson, S. 1998. *An outline of black bear management and biology in Yosemite National Park*. Unpublished report, Yosemite National Park, California, USA.

Thompson, S. C., and K. E. McCurdy. 1995. Black bear management in Yosemite National Park: more a people management problem. *Proceedings on the Fifth Western Black Bear Workshop* 5:105–15.

Ursack Inc. v. Sierra Interagency Black Bear Group, 639 F.3d 949 (9th Cir. 2011).

Vachowski, B. 1994. *Low impact food hoists*. Missoula Technology and Development Center MTDC-9523-2809, U.S. Forest Service, Missoula, Montana, USA.

van Wagtendonk, J. W. 1981. The effect of use limits on backcountry visitation trends in Yosemite National Park. *Leisure Science* 4:311–23.

van Wagtendonk, J. W. 2003. The wilderness simulation model: A historical perspective. *International Journal of Wilderness* 9:9–13.

van Wagtendonk, J. W., and P. R. Coho. 1986. Trailhead quotas, rationing use to keep wilderness wild. *Journal of Forestry* 84:22–24.

Vinson, J., and M. McCall. 1986. Report of test findings and design recommendations: bear-proof food canisters. Report to the National Park Service, Netra Plastics, Mountain View, California, USA.

Walraven, M. E. 1978. A simulation model for management of black bear problems in Sequoia National Park. *Cal-Neva Wildlife* 1978:52–64.

Walraven, M. E., and M. White. 1975. Population ecology of the black bear in Sequoia and Kings Canyon National Parks. Progress Report to the National Park Service, University of California, Berkeley, USA.

Welush, L. 1998. NAU student bearish on bad-habit bears. *Flagstaff Daily Sun*. November 27.

Werner, H. W. 1987. Market survey for backpacking food-storage containers. Internal Report, Sequoia and Kings Canyon National Parks, California, USA.

Werner, H. 1990. Food volume monitoring study, Lodgepole Campground. Internal Report. Sequoia and Kings Canyon National Parks, California, USA.

White, P. J. 1929. Billy, the bear, sets a record. *Yosemite Nature Notes* 8:96–97.

Woods, J. G., Lewis, D., McLellan, B. N., Proctor, M., and C. Strobeck. 1999. Genetic tagging of free-ranging black and brown bears. *Wildlife Society Bulletin* 27:616–27.

Wooldridge, D. R. 1984. The "Ferret" 12 gauge soft-slug as a black bear deterrent. *Proceedings of the 1984 International Predator Symposium*, University of Montana, Missoula, USA.

Wright, G. M. 1929. Notes of a mid-winter wanderer in Yosemite Valley. *Yosemite Nature Notes* 8:4.

Wright, G. M., Dixon, J. S., and B. H. Thompson. 1933. *Fauna of the National Parks of the United States: A Preliminary Survey*. National Park Service, Washington, DC, USA.

Wright, P. A., Obbard, M. E., Battersby, B. J., Felskie, A. K., LeBlanc, P. J., and J. S. Ballantyne. 1999. Lactation during hibernation in wild black bears: effects on plasma amino acids and nitrogen metabolites. *Physiological and Biochemical Ecology* 72:597–604.

Zardus, M. J., and D. J. Parsons. 1980. Black bear management in Sequoia and Kings Canyon National Parks. Reprinted from Bears: Their Biology and Management. *Proceedings of the Fourth International Conference on Bear Research and Management* 4:195–200.

# INDEX

# ABOUT THE AUTHOR

**Rachel Mazur,** an expert in bear biology and management, ran the bear management program in Sequoia and Kings Canyon National Parks for nine years. Rachel also worked in many other national parks including Denali, Redwood, Yosemite, and North Cascades. She earned her PhD from UC Davis studying black bear ecology and also holds an MS in forest biology from the SUNY College of Forestry and an MPA in public administration from Syracuse University. Besides publishing several scientific and popular articles on bears, she is the author of a best-selling children's book called *If You Were a Bear,* from which all proceeds go to environmental education. Rachel currently lives in El Portal, California, with her husband, John, and her two cubs, Max and Wren.

## DATE DUE

| | | | |
|---|---|---|---|
| | | | |
| | | DEC 9 2017 | |
| | | | |
| | | | |
| | | | |
| | | | |
| | | | |
| | | | |
| | | | |
| | | | |
| | | | |
| | | | |
| | | | |
| | | | |
| | | | |
| | | | PRINTED IN U.S.A. |